Humoring the Body

HUMORING THE BODY

*Emotions and
the Shakespearean Stage*

GAIL KERN PASTER

*The University of Chicago Press
Chicago and London*

The University of Chicago Press, Chicago 60637
The University of Chicago Press, Ltd., London
© 2004 by The University of Chicago
All rights reserved. Published 2004.
Paperback edition 2014
Printed in the United States of America

21 20 19 18 17 16 15 14   2 3 4 5 6

ISBN-13: 978-0-226-64847-7 (cloth)
ISBN-13: 978-0-226-21382-8 (paperback)
ISBN-13: 978-0-226-64848-4 (e-book)
DOI: 10.7208/chicago/9780226648484.001.0001

Library of Congress Cataloging-in-Publication Data

Paster, Gail Kern.
    Humoring the body : emotions and the Shakespearean stage / Gail kern Paster.
        p. cm.
    Includes bibliographical references and index.
    ISBN 0-226-64847-8 (cloth : alk. paper)
        1. Shakespeare, William, 1564–1616—Knowledge—Psychology. 2. Drama—
    Psychological aspects. 3. Mind and body in literature. 4. Body, Human, in literature.
    5. Emotions in literature. I. Title
    PR3065.P38 2004
    822.3'3—dc22

                                                    2004003473

∞ This paper meets the requirements of ANSI/NISO Z39.48-1992 (Permanence of
Paper).

Dedicated with gratitude to
The Folger Shakespeare Memorial Library
and all the people therein

CONTENTS

ILLUSTRATIONS

ACKNOWLEDGMENTS

I hope I have not failed to acknowledge, in person, the many people and institutions that have humored me in the writing of this book, but it is a great pleasure to reiterate those thanks in writing here. Much of this book was completed during an Andrew W. Mellon Foundation Fellowship at the Folger Shakespeare Library. The Mellon Foundation is extraordinary for its imaginative and wise support of scholarship, and I feel privileged to be among the many scholars who have benefited hugely from Mellon generosity on more than one occasion (see below). I am grateful to George Washington University, my academic home for nearly three decades, for granting a year's sabbatical ahead of schedule and then for graciously forgiving that loan of time when I did not return at the end of that leave.

I want above all to give notice that the Folger Shakespeare Library and the people one finds there, both on the staff and among the scholars in the reading rooms, have been the primary source of intellectual and material sustenance for this project—just as for every other project I've attempted. Let me add my own gratitude to the thankful chorus of scholars that regularly sing the praises of the Folger Reading Room staff—Betsy Walsh, Luellen DeHaven, Rosalind Larry, Camille Seerattan, and Harold Batie—for their meticulous, unflagging, and knowledgeable support of research in early modern studies. As Head of Reference, Georgianna Ziegler provokes awe on a regular basis, using an inspired determination to find the unfindable with great cheerfulness and sweetness of nature. I am similarly grateful to John Bidwell, Astor Curator of Printed Books and Bindings at the

Pierpont Morgan Library, for his diligence in tracking down German calendar woodcuts of the four temperaments at a time when the Morgan was in the midst of construction and parts of its collection were very hard to access.

This book has benefited at two crucial stages from the gracious interest and support of Kathleen Lynch and the Program Committee of the Folger Institute. In the book's early stages, now almost ten years ago, I taught a Folger Institute seminar titled "Humoring the Body," which laid the groundwork for this book. A second Folger seminar, "Reading the Early Modern Passions," was underwritten by the Andrew W. Mellon Foundation as part of its interest in answering basic questions in the humanities. Not only did these seminars represent the best teaching experiences of a long academic career, but they also provided key intellectual discipline to a project that threatened at every step to outgrow its proper limits. Let me thank my brilliant colleagues in both seminars—Julie Robin Solomon, Carol Thomas Neely, Steven Mullaney, Zirka Filipczak, Catherine Lutz, William Ian Miller, and Gary Tomlinson—for giving me the benefit of their knowledge about the emotions and the history of consciousness across many disciplines. Many of the other wonderful participants on those two occasions have also proved crucial to this book's completion. Ian MacInnes and Doug Trevor are certainly in this company, and I want to single out especially Mary Floyd-Wilson and Katherine Rowe, extraordinary younger scholars whom I honor here for their energy, enthusiasm, learning, and talent for friendship.

Everyone who writes academic books knows the crucial role that the right audiences play in their development. Thanks for rounding up such audiences go to Coppélia Kahn, William Carroll, Ann Christensen, Frank Whigham, Eric Mallin, Peter Stallybrass, Carla Mazzio, David Hillman, David Cressy, John King, Michael Neill, and Peter Holland. Valerie Traub, Steven Mullaney, and Michael Schoenfeldt not only provided a great set of listeners at the University of Michigan but also have provided the intellectual stimulation of their own related work and much focused conversation. John Sutton's work is everywhere reflected in these pages, and I am grateful to him for initiating our very long-distance friendship and corroborating my hunches with his learning. I am much indebted to Bruce Smith, Jeffrey Jerome Cohen, Cynthia Marshall, Mary Thomas Crane, Tony Dawson, and Paul Yachnin for asking the right questions and for trying to repair my shortcomings in the area of theory. Robert Miola and Owen Williams proffered the great benefit of their classical learning just when I needed it most. Mary Fissell, Wendy Wall, Natasha Korda, Gil Harris, Garrett Sullivan, and Rick Rambuss shared odd and wonderful gleanings from their readings in the early modern archive—and generous helpings of particular wisdom besides. Finally, for her never-failing support, editorial brilliance, and years of deep and sustaining friendship, I want to thank Barbara Mowat—first and best of readers.

Portions of this book were published previously. Part of chapter 1 appeared in "The Body and Its Passions," *Shakespeare Studies* 29 (2001): 44–50. Part of chapter 2 appeared in "The Unbearable Coldness of Female Being," *English Literary Renaissance* 28 (1998): 416–40. Part of chapter 3 appeared in "Melancholy Cats, Lugged Bears, and Early Modern Cosmology," in *Reading the Early Modern Passions*, edited by Gail Kern Paster, Katherine Rowe, and Mary Floyd-Wilson (Philadelphia: University of Pennsylvania Press, 2004); © 2004 by the University of Pennsylvania Press, reprinted by permission of the University of Pennsylvania Press. Part of chapter 4 appeared in "The Humor of It: Bodies, Fluids, and Social Discipline in Shakespearean Comedy," in *A Companion to Shakespeare's Works, Volume 3: The Comedies*, edited by Richard Dutton and Jean E. Howard (Oxford: Blackwell, 2003); reprinted by permission of Blackwell Publishing.

Randolph Petilos has been a perfect and responsive editor. I am delighted to thank him for finding just the right readers for this book, at two stages, and to thank the readers themselves for performing such invaluable anonymous service. My former student Susan Comilang was enormously helpful in readying this book for the press, even though allowing her to see my many small errors of quotation and citation was a high-risk strategy indeed. Mary Tonkinson, Elizabeth Pohland, and Solvei Robertson, too, were more helpful than they knew in these latter stages and stand as great examples to me of editorial excellence.

Finally, there are the incalculable contributions of Howard Paster—whom I thank above all for his special brand of joie de vivre.

A NOTE ON CITATIONS

In quoting from early modern sources, I have generally retained original spelling, except where I have used modernized editions. I have silently altered the long *s* and expanded abbreviations. Quotations from Shakespeare follow *The Riverside Shakespeare*, ed. G. Blakemore Evans et al. (Boston: Houghton Mifflin, 1997), though I have referred freely to other editions, which are noted in the bibliography.

INTRODUCTION

In Bishop Edward Reynolds's *Treatise of the Passions and Faculties of the Soule of Man* (1640), there is a surprisingly vivid comparison of the passions of Christ to those of ordinary men. Reynolds writes, "The *Passions* of sinfull men are many times like the tossings of the Sea, which bringeth up *mire and durt*; but the *Passions* of *Christ* were like the shaking of pure Water in a cleane Vessell, which though it be thereby *troubled*, yet is it not *fouled* at all."[1]

Seeking to refute Neostoicism's attack on the utility of the passions, Reynolds argues that Christ in his life on earth allowed himself to love, rejoice, weep, desire, mourn, and grieve like other men and that he used the passions as an occasion for the exercise of his perfect reason. Christ's passions "never proceeded beyond their due measure, nor transported the Mind to undecencie or excesse; but had both their rising and originall from Reason, and also their measure, bounds, continuance limited by Reason" (49). Christ embodies temperance, then, not by avoiding emotions altogether but by keeping his emotions within the bounds of moderation. While this perfect temperance distinguishes Christ from ordinary men, it also serves Reynolds as a strong defense of human emotion. It is human sinfulness that makes immoderate passions an instrument of self-harm— an instrument of excess and indecency—not the passions themselves.

---

1. Edward Reynolds, *A Treatise of the Passions and Faculties of the Soule of Man*, ed. Margaret Lee Wiley (Gainesville, FL: Scholars' Facsimiles and Reprints, 1971), 49.

Whatever the passions may do to the minds and bodies of ordinary men, however vehemently reason and passion may fight for predominance within the souls of other men, in Christ the passions are not opposed to reason but apparently an instrument of it.[2] Even more crucially for Reynolds, the mere existence of passions in Christ points to their functionality, their role in the divine endowment of nature.

There is much in Reynolds's anti-Stoic defense of emotion to interest the student of the early modern passions. But it is Reynolds's picture of the passionate Christ as a glass vessel with its liquid contents shaken (but not stirred) that most catches my imagination, because it is a striking image that is nevertheless representative of its moment in time. For embedded in the terms of this double analogy are many of the early modern themes that occupy my attention in this book. Reynolds employs a commonplace set of comparisons—of passions to water, of the roiling ocean to the clear contents of a vessel, of sinlessness to cleanliness, of sinfulness to dirtiness, of Christ's passions to the passions of men, of Christ's perfect body to the imperfect bodies of men. Readers of early modern emblem literature were entirely familiar with comparisons of the ocean to the human passions, as when Henry Peacham in *Minerva Britanna* compares the constant man to a rock amid the waves (see fig. 1) or allegorizes the valiant mind as belonging to a man, like Aeneas, undaunted by the waves battering his vessel.[3] Du Bartas reverses the figure, comparing "the constant man" to the

> Sea, whose brest
> Lyes ever open unto every guest,
> Yet all the waters that she drinks, can not
> Make her to change her qualities a jot.[4]

Yet the overall effect of Reynolds's troping of the passions of Christ is not at all commonplace. Rather, the trope is a dense metaphorical layering of the key elements of early modern cosmological thought, and it ends with a surprising and vivid image—of Christ as a vessel of clear liquid. Beginning with the force

---

2. On Renaissance defenses of the passions generally, see Richard Strier, "Against the Rule of Reason: Praise of Passion from Petrarch to Luther to Shakespeare to Herbert," in *Reading the Early Modern Passions: Essays in the Cultural History of Emotion*, edited by Gail Kern Paster, Katherine Rowe, and Mary Floyd-Wilson (Philadelphia: University of Pennsylvania Press, 2004), 23–42.

3. The allegorization of Aeneas on a ship tossed by the waves occurs in the emblem "*His graviora*" in Henry Peacham, *Minerva Britanna* (London, 1612), 165.

4. See Guillaume de Salluste du Bartas, *The Divine Weeks and Works*, translated by Joshua Sylvester, ed. Susan Snyder (Oxford: Clarendon, 1979), 304.

AMID the waues, a mightie Rock doth ſtand,
  Whoſe ruggie brow, had bidden many a ſhower,
And bitter ſtorme; which neither ſea, nor land,
Nor *IOVES* ſharpe-lightening euer could deuoure :
  This ſame is *MANLIE CONSTANCIE* of mind,
  Not eaſly moou'd, with euery blaſt of wind.

Neere which you ſee, a goodly ſhip to drowne,
Herewith bright flaming in a pitteous fire :
This is *OPINION*, toſſed vp and downe,
Whoſe Pilot's *PRIDE*, & Steereſman *VAINE DESIRE*,
  Thoſe flames *HOT PASSIONS*, & the *WORLD* the ſea,
  God bleſſe the man, that's carried thus away.

Vide Lipſium de
Conſtantia.

Z 1. *Pręcocia*

Figure 1. Emblem of the constant mind, from Henry Peacham, *Minerva Britanna* (London, 1612). By permission of the Folger Shakespeare Library.

of analogical explanation itself, all of Reynolds's comparisons rely on the fundamental assumptions as well as on the rhetoric of early modern cosmological
models.[5] "To search for the law governing signs," Foucault has famously
remarked of this early modern reliance upon analogy, "is to discover the things
that are alike."[6] Reynolds knows the human body, conventionally, as an image of
the world—microcosm and macrocosm. The other elements in his analogy
draw upon features of the body as features of the world.[7] Analogy bore the
imprint of God, the visible workings of divine patterning. It organized the world
in a network of mutual functionality that enlivened all animate life in a hierarchical continuum of ensoulment (*empsychos*), ascending from vegetables to
imperfect animals such as sponges, to perfect animals such as birds and mam-
mals, and finally to the human being, uniquely endowed with an intellective
soul. In this analogical structure, ordinary microcosmic man's flesh is earth and
his passions are the seas, because the body itself—whether an ordinary body or
the body of Christ—is a vessel of liquids. Reynolds, again conventionally, understands the nature of the passions as liquid—contained or uncontained, clear or
muddy. The passions are like liquid states and forces of the natural world. But
the passions—thanks to their close functional relation to the four bodily humors
of blood, choler, black bile, and phlegm—had a more than analogical relation to
liquid states and forces of nature. In an important sense, the passions actually
were liquid forces of nature, because, in this cosmology, the stuff of the outside
world and the stuff of the body were composed of the same elemental materials.
This is a literal early modern understanding of the relation of body to world, as
old as Greek thought and derived ultimately from it.[8] Thus, in the Galenic
scheme of the six "nonnaturals," the passions were one of the six factors (along
with air, diet, repletion and evacuation, sleeping and waking, and exercise) that
together determined the immediate state of well-being in a given body.[9]

5. See Joseph A. Mazzeo, "Universal Analogy and the Culture of the Renaissance," *Journal of the History of Ideas* 15 (1954): 299–304.

6. Michel Foucault, *The Order of Things: An Archaeology of the Human Sciences* (New York: Pantheon Books, 1971), 29.

7. The classic treatment of the macrocosm analogy is Leonard Barkan, *Nature's Work of Art: The Human Body as Image of the World* (New Haven, CT: Yale University Press, 1975); on analogy, see Marie-Christine Pouchelle, *The Body and Surgery in the Middle Ages*, trans. Rosemary Morris (New Brunswick, NJ: Rutgers University Press, 1990), 190–97.

8. This is a founding assumption of Greek thought that extends into the early modern period; see Ruth Padel, *In and out of the Mind: Greek Images of the Tragic Self* (Princeton, NJ: Princeton University Press, 1992), 88.

9. On the six nonnaturals, see Nancy G. Siraisi, *Medieval and Renaissance Medicine: An Introduction to Knowledge and Practice* (Chicago: University of Chicago Press, 1990), 101; and Ian Maclean, *Logic, Signs, and Nature in the Renaissance: The Case of Learned Medicine* (Cambridge: Cambridge University Press, 2002), 251–53.

I have much more to say about the role of passions within the Galenic scheme of the nonnaturals in later chapters. For now, it is important only to note that this placement of the passions alongside air and diet as factors in bodily health clues us in to important historical differences in the understanding of the passions between then and now. As Charles Taylor has argued, post-Enlightenment habits of thought regarding mind-body relations are profoundly dualistic; even when countered by mechanistic or monistic models, the burden of proof falls to dualism's challengers.[10] Thus, for us, air and diet do not consort readily in conceptual categories also inhabited by the emotions. Air, diet, and the passions—though all may be considered determinative of health—do not work on the body in analogous ways because we tend not to imagine the emotions (as Bishop Reynolds clearly does) as part of the *fabric* of the body. In this way the early modern placement differs importantly from modern ontologies, which tend to distinguish sharply between psychology and physiology, between the mental and the physical. Taylor sums up the difference between the two ontologies in comparing early modern understandings of melancholy to our own:

> Melancholia is black bile. That's what it means. Today we might think of the relationship expressed in this term as a psycho-physical causal one. An excess of the substance, black bile, in our system tends to bring on melancholy. We acknowledge a host of such relationships, so that this one is easily understandable to us, even though our notions of organic chemistry are very different from those of our ancestors.
>
> But in fact there is an important difference between this account and the traditional theory of humours. On the earlier view, black bile doesn't just cause melancholy; melancholy somehow resides in it. The substance embodies this significance. (188–89)

Clearly, Bishop Reynolds's layered figures for the passions and the body of Christ and for the passions and the bodies of ordinary men (and women) participate in the earlier ontology, in which substance embodies "this" significance. His macrocosmic analogies define the figure for the highly visible vessel of Christ's body no less than the obscured and incontinent body of man (visible in his analogy only as that which borders, without containing,

10. On modern tendencies to think of mental and physical as exclusive categories, Charles Taylor writes: "Much modern philosophy has striven against this kind of dualism. But this is a mode of thought we easily fall into. The onus of argument, the effort, falls to those who want to overcome dualism." See *Sources of the Self: Making of the Modern Identity* (Cambridge, MA: Harvard University Press, 1989), 189.

the seas). More tellingly, at least for the difference that Taylor wishes to describe, is that both bodies analogized by Bishop Reynolds's tropes—whether the perfectly clean body of Christ or the soiled body of mankind—are humoral bodies, earthly vessels defined by the quality and quantity of the liquids they contain.[11] Sin—more precisely, the working of immoderate passion—is like the stirring up of sediment in the ocean; sinlessness is like pure water that can move without becoming muddied. The earth of man's flesh soils even as it is being soiled by the rough action of the sea. Reynolds's logic is that the actions of the passions can be imagined as like the actions of clear liquids only if the body containing them is pure. Christ's body differs from those of ordinary mortals, Reynolds argues, in the clarity of its liquids, the cleanness of its flesh—and the unequivocal instrumentality of its passions. It is this absolute cleanness that allows Christ to experience passions, even strong ones, without being materially changed—dirtied physically and morally—by them. The differences between states of sinlessness and sinfulness, states that post-Enlightenment moderns understand as spiritual and immaterial, are thus imagined as differences in the characteristics of liquids in motion. Reynolds implies that the passions of the sinful body resemble dirt and mire because he imagines the passions to be strongly indebted for their characteristics and their expression to the four humors. As the English Jesuit Thomas Wright puts it in his moral treatise *The Passions of the Minde in Generall*, the passions are "drowned in corporall organs and instruments."[12] Dirt and mire are like sin, but dirt and mire are also like the liquid humors coursing through human flesh. Substance embodies significance; the humors are imbued with moral density and spiritual import; and the passions act within the body just as the forces of wind and waves act in the natural world.

Bishop Reynolds's images are important for the argument of this book because they represent an entirely characteristic expression of seventeenth-century definitions of the embodied passions: what they are in themselves, what they resemble in the natural world, how they operate, and (perhaps most important for students of the history of the emotions) how they are represented in a variety of discourses. That the emotions are given authority and rendered legitimate through the example of Christ establishes a

11. See my description of the liquidity of the humoral body in *The Body Embarrassed: Drama and the Disciplines of Shame in Early Modern England* (Ithaca, NY: Cornell University Press, 1993), 7–13.

12. Thomas Wright, *The Passions of the Minde in Generall*, ed. Thomas O. Sloan (1604; reprint, Urbana: University of Illinois Press, 1971), 7–8. All quotations of Thomas Wright throughout the book are from this edition.

theological and symbolic import for representations of the passions. Yet, I would argue, the passions had an urgent practical character that, for the early moderns, was just as important as their overarching theological significance. In his preface to *Passions of the Minde in Generall*, Wright argues that no man can afford to be ignorant of the passions—especially not the "ciuill Gentleman and prudent Politician," who "by penetrating the nature and qualities of his affections, by restraining their inordinate motions, winneth a gratious cariage of himselfe, and rendreth his conuersation most gratefull to men" (6). The historical context for his emphatic claims of his topic's importance is provided by Susan James, who has argued for the centrality of the passions to early modern culture generally and to early modern philosophical thought in particular: "the interest in the emotions that so pervades seventeenth-century philosophy is itself part of a broader preoccupation in early-modern European culture with the relations between knowledge and control, whether of the self or others."[13] This preoccupation forms part of the narrative of individual and cultural transformation that Norbert Elias has influentially (if somewhat problematically) described as "the civilizing process," by which he meant "the pacification of behaviour and the control of emotions."[14] I have already described some ramifications of the civilizing process with respect to the bodily disciplines of shame in an earlier book, *The Body Embarrassed: Drama and the Disciplines of Shame in Early Modern England*. My interest here, as I specify in more detail later in this introduction, is a broader engagement with a spectrum of emotions including anger and melancholy during a period when, as Taylor suggests, the psychological had not yet become divorced from the physiological.

I focus, finally, on the language of the emotions in Shakespearean drama, taking it as representative of the thinking about the embodied emotions that is peculiar to early modern English culture—though representative in a uniquely rich and influential way. But first it is important to suggest why it matters—in relation to a topic as apparently universal as the emotions—to specify the characteristics both of emotional experience and of emotional expression peculiar to a historical moment. The answer begins with the wonderful observation of Shigehisa Kuriyama that "the history of the body is ultimately a history of ways of inhabiting

---

13. Susan James, *Passion and Action: The Emotions in Seventeenth-Century Philosophy* (Cambridge: Cambridge University Press, 1997), 2.

14. Norbert Elias, *The History of Manners*, vol. 1 of *The Civilizing Process*, trans. Edmund Jephcott (New York: Pantheon Books, 1978); the characterization of Elias belongs to Roger Chartier, "Social Figuration and Habitus: Reading Elias," in *Cultural History: Between Practices and Representations*, trans. Lydia G. Cochrane (Ithaca, NY: Cornell University Press, 1988), 74.

the world."[15] Here he encapsulates the fundamental presupposition of this book. But I would add to this wise sentence the corollary that the history of the embodied emotions is also a history of ways of inhabiting the world, insofar as we inhabit the world physically and psychologically with a set of preferences and affective responses that are—as the best of modern psychological and anthropological research tells us—in part inborn and in part shaped on a minute-to-minute basis by the myriad social and natural stimuli that constitute culture.[16] Ways of inhabiting the world inevitably have a psychological component, as Maurice Merleau-Ponty observes in writing, "Psychology is always brought face to face with the problem of the constitution of the world."[17] I take his statement to mean (among other things) that the nature of an individual subject's phenomenological experience can never be understood properly apart from the social field in which it takes place and thus apart from that social field's governing beliefs about how the world is constituted. The experience of an emotion is thus transactional not only in being a response to a stimulus—whether that stimulus is external or internal, real or imaginary, present or remembered—but also in occurring, almost inevitably, within a dense cultural and social context. And this is true no matter how invisible that cultural or social frame may be, no matter how purely "natural" a stimulus might seem to the perceiver.[18]

Kuriyama himself—pronouncing on the ways of inhabiting the world—provides a powerful description of the diacritical construction of inner and outer worlds in his discussion of ancient Greek understanding of human breath's relation to the wind and of that relation's affective significance. Noting that the word for both breath and wind in classical Greek was *pneuma*, he writes that the Greeks were preoccupied with the wind because "the winds blowing *around* the body were often presumed to be related to the breaths sustaining the life *within* ... When the chorus chants about Antigone, 'Yet from the same winds still / These blasts of soul hold her,' it

---

15. Shigehisa Kuriyama, *The Expressiveness of the Body and the Divergence of Greek and Chinese Medicine* (New York: Zone, 1999), 237.

16. The literature on this topic is voluminous. I have found the following especially useful: Anna Wierzbicka, "Human Emotions: Universal or Culture-Specific?" *American Anthropologist* 88 (1986): 584–94; Amélie Oksenberg Rorty, introduction to *Explaining Emotions*, ed. Amélie Oksenberg Rorty (Berkeley and Los Angeles: University of California Press, 1980), 1–7; James A. Russell, "Is There Universal Recognition of Emotion from Facial Expression? A Review of Cross-Cultural Studies," in *Psychological Bulletin* 115 (1994): 102–41.

17. Maurice Merleau-Ponty, *The Phenomenology of Perception*, trans. Colin Smith (London: Routledge, 1962), 60.

18. On this point, see M. L. Lyon and J. M. Barbalet, "Society's Body: Emotion and the 'Somatization' of Social Theory," in *Embodiment and Experience: The Existential Ground of Culture and Self*, ed. Thomas J. Csordas (Cambridge: Cambridge University Press, 1994), 48–66.

speaks simultaneously of the external winds driving destinies and the swerves of inner passion" (236). The relationship between outer and inner that he describes here is understood to be literal and physical. Its consequence is that for the Greeks the wind had an emotional component and an urgent meaning largely unknown and phenomenologically unrecoverable to us. But—as I insist in this book in some detail and with some urgency—such an understanding of the relation of winds and passions would not have been foreign to the early moderns, thanks to their understanding of the relation of macrocosm to microcosm, of world to body, of the movements of wind or water to the movement of the passions. Their interest in the wind is an instance of the pneumatic character of early modern culture, perhaps especially of early modern affective practice. I want to call this relation of inner and outer—evident not only in the wind but in other physical phenomena—a premodern ecology of the passions. Note the similarity between ancient Greek and early modern representation of the passions: just as passion is wind for Kuriyama's Greeks, so for Bishop Reynolds passion is water—or, more precisely, passion is water moved by wind. The early-seventeenth-century Dominican bishop Nicolas Coeffeteau points to a widespread belief "that as there were foure chiefe winds which excite diuers stormes, be it at land or sea; so there are foure principall *Passions* which trouble our *Soules*, and which stir vp diuers tempests by their irregular motions."[19] A similar oscillation of metaphorical and literal in comparisons between the winds and the passions underlies a tense exchange in Marlowe's *Jew of Malta*. Ferneze, the governor of Malta, greets a visiting bashaw, "What wind drives you thus into Malta road?" and receives the memorable reply,

> The wind that bloweth all the world besides,
> Desire of gold.
>
> (3.5.2–4)[20]

In both epochs, ancient Greek and early modern, passion is a change of inner state knowable *as* and also *by means of* changes, defined as broadly as possible, in the outer world. In such governing beliefs are constituted the link between psychology and the constitution of the world. In such beliefs lies the ecology of the passions.

---

19. Nicolas Coeffeteau, *A Table of Humane Passions*, trans. Edward Grimeston (London, 1621), 31.

20. I quote here from Christopher Marlowe, *The Jew of Malta*, ed. N. W. Bawcutt (Manchester: Manchester University Press, 1978).

In order to construct a historical phenomenology of the early modern emotions, we must begin by understanding that the mind, the body, and the world are always connected through what philosopher Andy Clark describes as a network of "mutually modulatory influences" in a dynamic action of "continuous reciprocal causation."[21] Then we can see the role of the emotions as part of the causal chain, part of the total field, part of how we inhabit the world. This may have been clearer for the early moderns, for whom the question of the passions—their utility, their power, their nature, their number—was, as James claims, a matter of overriding importance. They generally understood the passions "to be thoughts or states of the soul which represent things as good or evil for us, and are therefore seen as objects of inclination or aversion."[22] Depending on the semantic emphasis desired, the nomenclature of the passions varied. Thomas Wright, citing Saint Augustine, outlines the possibilities: "Those actions then which are common with vs, and beasts, we call Passions, and Affections, or perturbations of the mind" (7). He uses these terms synonymously. *Passion* (derived from the deponent verb *patior*) suggested inactivity and suffering; *affection* (from Latin *affectus*) suggested yearning or desire; and *perturbation* (from *perturbare*, to disturb) suggested disturbance. *Motion* was another lexical possibility, as when Iago reminds his gull Roderigo, "We have reason to cool our raging motions, our carnal stings, our unbitted lusts" (*Othello*, 1.3.329–31).[23] Notice, here too in the figure of "unbitted" lusts, the comparison of men to horses.

Such lexical variation may be symptomatic of intellectual confusion about the object in view. Certainly this is a central—skeptical—claim of modern philosophers of emotions, for whom emotions "do not form a natural class."[24] But for the early moderns, the passions precisely *did* form a natural class, indeed a class as natural as the four elements and intimately related to them. Lexical and even taxonomic abundance in this discourse, then, seems to me a mark of respect and wonder, a sign of passion's semiotic richness and ideological reach. Whether passive or tumultuous,

21. Andy Clark, *Being There: Putting Brain, Body, and World Together Again* (Cambridge, MA: MIT Press, 1997), 163.

22. Susan James, 3–5, esp. 4.

23. On the nomenclature of the passions, see Gail Kern Paster, Katherine Rowe, and Mary Floyd-Wilson, introduction to Paster, Rowe, and Floyd-Wilson, 2–3.

24. Certainly this is the claim of Rorty, 1–3; Paul E. Griffiths puts the case more strongly in arguing that because current physical science has not found a role for the "putative kinds of psychological state," there is "an important sense in which the emotions do not really exist." See *What Emotions Really Are: The Problem of Psychological Categories* (Chicago: University of Chicago Press, 1997), 1.

whether the cause of suffering or the motive for action, the passions were "forces that are at once extremely powerful and actually or potentially beyond our control."[25] An excess of emotion—even of the positive emotions of joy or mirth—was understood to be potentially fatal, because, as Wright points out, passions always caused "some alteration in the body" (8). Thus Othello tells Desdemona that his joy at being reunited with her in Cyprus "stops me here" (2.1.197)—"here" being his heart, his chest. What the commonplace comparisons of the passions to winds and oceans tell us as students of the period is just how overwhelming the passions were understood to be. While reason and passion, or reason and sense, were yoked dichotomously, the opposition was hardly equal. Not in experiential terms, but only in semantic ones, did reason successfully oppose the passions. Ordinarily, Wright argues, men allow their reason to yield to passion as the path of least resistance: "after that men, by reason, take possession ouer their soules and bodies, feeling this war [between reason and sense or passion] so mightie, so continuall, so neere, so domesticall, that either they must consent to doe their enemyies will, or still be in conflict: and withall, foreseeing by making peace with them, they were to receiue great pleasures and delights, the most part of men resolue themselues neuer to displease their sense or passions, but to graunt them whatsoeuer they demand" (10). For Wright, there is a kind of biographical allegory at work here in which reason takes possession of soul and body only after the body has already been inhabited by passions and the sense, joined in a league of friendship: "for all the time of our infancy and child-hood, our senses were ioint-friends in such sort with Passions, that whatsoeuer was hurtfull to the one, was an enemy to the other" (9). Reason—the master coming late to an unruly household, the princess on her throne considering the state of her kingdom from a distance—is forever on the defensive, forever seeking domestic peace through appeasement, at times yielding basely to the importunities of passion and sense.

Because I am interested in the intersection of psychology and the early modern constitution of the world, the theoretical heart of this book might best be described as an exercise in historical phenomenology. I consider historical differences in modes of emotional expression between the early moderns and post-Enlightenment inhabitants of the twenty-first century as a means of investigating the possibility of historical differences in modes of emotional self-experience. One determinant of such difference may be

25. Susan James, 11.

found in the psychological materialism—what I call psychophysiology—that governs much early-seventeenth-century thought about the nature of mental and emotional operations. As J. B. Bamborough suggests, "many Elizabethans had difficulty in thinking of an immaterial substance."[26] Thus they posited the existence of animal spirits—bodily substance in its most rarefied form—moving in the neural pathways along the sinews between the body's recalcitrant flesh and its immaterial soul. The role of the spirits to early modern self-experience becomes clearer in chapter 1. For now it is only important to note that early modern theories of behavior needed these spirits coursing through the neural pathways because the categories of experience were not yet constituted by anything named psychology; that place was occupied instead by the passions as experienced by the organic soul.[27] Here, too, substance embodied significance, because there was no way conceptually or discursively to separate the psychological from the physiological. The physical model for what Renaissance philosophers called the organic soul—that part of the tripartite soul governing the emotions—was, Katharine Park has argued, "a simple hydraulic one, based on a clear localisation of psychological function by organ or system of organs."[28] Her description of this fundamental early modern truth is an important one, as becomes clear in the chapters that follow. The organ most in charge of the emotions was the heart—"the seat and Organe of all passions and affections," according to Robert Burton.[29] For Wright, too, the passions were a faculty of the sensitive soul, and the part of the body allotted to their workings was clearly the heart—as proven by the individual subject's experience of its changes: "who loueth extremely, and feeleth not that passion to dissolue his heart? who reioyceth and proueth not his heart dilated? who is moyled with heauinesse, or plunged with paine, and perceiueth not his heart to be coarcted? whom inflameth ire, and hath not heart burning? By these experiences, we proue in our hearts the working of Passions, and by the noyse of their tumult, wee vnderstand the worke of their presence" (32). The language Wright uses here is not a metaphorical expression of emotional tumult but a literal expression of what he understood to happen to a

26. J. B. Bamborough, *The Little World of Man* (London: Longmans, Green, 1952), 30.

27. The term seems to enter the language in the mid-seventeenth century, according to the *OED*, which quotes William Harvey: "*Psychologie* is a doctrine which searches out mans Soul, and the effects of it." The *OED* cites William Harvey as translator of *J. de Back's Discourse* in *Anatomical Exercises* (1653), sig. H8v. I have been unable to locate the original.

28. Katharine Park, "The Organic Soul," in *The Cambridge History of Renaissance Philosophy*, ed. Charles B. Schmitt et al. (Cambridge: Cambridge University Press, 1988), 469.

29. Robert Burton, *The Anatomy of Melancholy*, ed. Thomas C. Faulkner, Nicolas K. Kiessling, and Rhonda L. Blair, 6 vols. (Oxford: Clarendon Press, 1989–2000), 1:145.

heart in the throes of various passions. Its flesh became more moist and tender in the experience of love, its size enlarged in the experience of joy, it contracted in sadness, and its temperature increased in anger.[30] While these events could not be witnessed directly, they could be felt. More to the point, such behavior in the heart made perfect sense in a cosmological model of the world governed by the interaction of the four qualities—cold, hot, moist, and dry. Behaviors were understood as the expression of the interaction of the four qualities, because behaviors were understood to be—at least in part—an expression of the four humors. The forces of cold, hot, wet, and dry constituted the material basis of any living creature's characteristic appraisals of and responses to its immediate environment; they altered the character of a body's substances and, by doing so, organized its ability to act or even to think. "The Minds inclination follows the Bodies Temperature," the jurist John Selden noted in *Titles of Honor*, repeating a Galenic commonplace of the age that recurs as a leitmotif in this book.[31] Heat stimulated action and cold depressed it. Clear judgment and prudent action required the free flow of clear fluids in the brain, but melancholy or choler altered and darkened them. The young warrior's choler gave him impulsiveness and the capacity for rage; phlegm helped to produce his cowardly opposite's lethargy and was responsible for the general inconstancy of women. Youth was hot and moist, age cold and dry; men as a sex were hotter and drier than women.[32] Thus, in Henry Peacham's emblems of the four temperaments, he presents choler as a young man,

> to shew that passions raigne,
> The most in heedles, and vnstaied youth,
>
> (128)

while

> *Phlegme* sits coughing on a Marble seate,
> As Citie-vsurers before their dore.
>
> (129)

---

30. On literalness, see Maurice Pope, "Shakespeare's Medical Imagination," *Shakespeare Survey* 38 (1985): 179.

31. John Selden, *Titles of Honor* (London, 1614), sig. b4.

32. Zirka Z. Filipczak, *Hot Dry Men Cold Wet Women: The Theory of Humors in Western European Art, 1575–1700* (New York: American Federation of Arts, 1997), 14–23, 68–77; and Gail Kern Paster, "The Unbearable Coldness of Female Being: Women's Imperfection in the Humoral Economy," *English Literary Renaissance* 28 (1998): 416.

(See figs. 2 and 3.) Over all these individual qualities arched the defining humoral attributes of geographic latitude—the cold that gave northern peoples their valor, hardiness, and slow-wittedness; the heat that gave southerners their sagacity and quickness of response.[33]

As these generalizations of humoral thought suggest, the qualities were physical, psychological, and even cultural in effect, explaining not only an individual's characteristic responses to circumstances but also those of whole peoples. In the dynamic reciprocities between self and environment imagined by the psychophysiology of bodily fluids, circumstance engenders humors in the body and humors in the body help to determine circumstance by predisposing the individual subject to a characteristic kind of evaluation and response. Such evaluation and response were thought to occasion subtle but important changes in a person's substance—change in the humoral fluids coursing through the body, change in the color and flow of the animal spirits, and change in the temper of the flesh carrying out the heart's commands. This is how the passions altered and were altered by the body. Wright describes the psychophysiological process:

> First then, to our imagination commeth by sense or memorie, some obiect to be knowne, conuenient or disconuenient to Nature, the which being knowne . . . in the imagination, which resideth in the former part of the braine, (as we proue) when we imagine any thing, presently the purer spirits, flocke from the brayne, by certaine secret channels to the heart, where they pitch at the dore, signifying what an obiect was presented . . . The heart immediatly bendeth, either to prosecute it, or to eschew it: and the better to effect that affection, draweth other humours to helpe him, and so in pleasure concurre great store of pure spirits; in paine and sadnesse, much melancholy blood; in ire, blood and choler. (45)

Here, as Taylor suggested, is an example of how substance embodies significance, how psychology and physiology are one: the bodily humors and the emotion that they sustain and move the body to express in action can be lexically distinguished but not functionally separated. For the early moderns, emotions flood the body not metaphorically but literally, as the humors course through the bloodstream carrying choler, melancholy, blood, and phlegm to the parts and as the animal spirits move like lightning from brain to muscle, from muscle to brain. And just as an imbalance of humors causes bodily disease, so an excess of passions causes disease—distemper—

---

33. On geohumoralism, see Mary Floyd-Wilson, *English Ethnicity and Race in Early Modern Drama* (Cambridge: Cambridge University Press, 2003), 23–47.

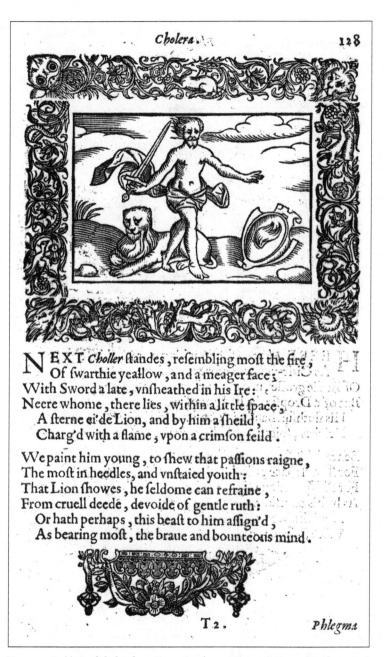

N EXT *Choller* ftandes, refembling moft the fire,
  Of fwarthie yeallow, and a meager face;
With Sword a late, vnfheathed in his Ire:
Neere whome, there lies, within a little fpace,
  A fterne ei'de Lion, and by him a fheild,
  Charg'd with a flame, vpon a crimfon feild.

We paint him young, to fhew that paffions raigne,
The moft in heedles, and vnftaied youth:
That Lion fhowes, he feldome can refraine,
From cruell deede, devoide of gentle ruth:
  Or hath perhaps, this beaft to him affign'd,
  As bearing moft, the braue and bounteous mind.

Figure 2. Emblem of choler, from Henry Peacham, *Minerva Britanna* (London, 1612). By permission of the Folger Shakespeare Library.

H EERE *Phlegme* fits coughing on a Marble feate,
 As Citie-vfurers before their dore :
Of Bodie groffe, not through exceffe of meate,
But of a Dropfie, he had got of yore :
 His flothfull hand, in's bofome ftill he keepes,
 Drinkes, fpits, or nodding, in the Chimney fleepes .

Beneath his feete, there doth a *Tortoife* crall,
For floweft pace, Sloth's Hieroglyphick here,
For Phlegmatique, hates Labour moft of all,
As by his courfe araiment, may appeare :
 Nor is he better furnifhed I find,
 With Science, or the virtues of the mind .

Ad

Figure 3. Emblem of phlegm, from Henry Peacham, *Minerva Britanna* (London, 1612).
By permission of the Folger Shakespeare Library.

in the soul. The difference in humoral disposition even explains why it is that the same stimulus will affect different people in different ways. Wright explains:

> according to the disposition of the heart, humors, and body, diuers sorts of persons be subiect to diuers sorts of passions, and the same passion affecteth diuers persons in diuers manners: for, as we see fire applied to drie wood, to yron, to flaxe and gunpowder, worketh diuers wayes; for in wood it kindleth with some difficultie, and with some difficultie is quenched; but in flaxe soone it kindleth, and quencheth; in yron with great difficultie it is kindled, & with as great extinguished; but in gunpowder it is kindled in a moment, and neuer can bee quenched till the powder be consumed. Some men you shall see, not so soone angrie, nor yet soone pleased, and such be commonly fleg-matike persons; others you haue, soone angrie, soon friended, as those of a sanguine complexion, and therefore commonly they are called goodfellowes: others be hardly offended, and afterward, with extreame difficulty reconciled, as melancholly men: others are all fiery, and in a moment, at euery trifle they are inflamed, and, till their hearts be consumed (almost) with choller they neuer cease, except they be reuenged. (37)

Here, as in Reynolds earlier, we see the operative force of analogy, as Wright uses natural substances and their different reactions to stimuli to explain the differences in the passions and behaviors of individuals. The difference in disposition or complexion—and here Wright's explanation encompasses all four major temperaments—translates into a difference in flesh, a difference (in the reversible logic of humoral theory) visible in behavior. In humoral predisposition, there are physical differences akin to the differences between iron, flax, and gunpowder. Humoral predisposition is an emotional style, a characteristic affect. Fire, a passion in the thermal economy of the soul, is the agent of change. Such analogies work, like Reynolds's, not only to suggest that the passions are strongly embodied, but also to emphasize their naturalness and functionality. Reynolds regards the passions as among the *indifferentia*; they are altered into good or evil "by vertue of the Dominion of right Reason, or of the violence of their owne motions" (41). Wright has a stronger view, explaining the passions as a God-given force in the sensitive soul that works to effect self-preservation—preventing change if possible, effecting it when necessary:

> God, the author of nature, and imparter of all goodnesse hath printed in euery creature, according to his diuine prouidence, an inclination, faculty, or

power to conserue it selfe, procure what it needeth, to resist and impugne whatsoeuer hindereth it of that appertaineth unto his good and conserua- tion. So we see fire continually ascendeth vpward, because the coldnesse of the water, earth, and ayre much impeacheth the vertue of his heate: heauie substances descend to their centre for their preseruation: the Hare flieth from the Hounds; the Partridge hideth her selfe from the talon of the Hawke; and in fine, God hath enabled euery thing to eschew his enemie, and enioy his friend. (11–12)

According to Wright, what distinguishes the workings of the passions from the general workings of self-preservation in all things, including inanimate ones, is that the workings of the natural soul are one—"with one motion eschew their contraries, procure their owne good, and obtaine that they need" (12)—whereas in the sensitive soul common to beasts and men, two appetites are necessary, the concupiscible appetite, with which they "pro- cure the good they desire," and the irascible appetite, with which "they flie the euill they abhor" (12). Wright's conventional distinction between the concupiscible and irascible appetites, derived ultimately from Aquinas, is not very important to the argument of this book; his Aquinian taxonomy of the eleven primary passions matters only in chapter 3 when we turn to his representation of the eleven primary passions experienced by a wolf approaching a sheepfold. What is crucial to remark is his interest—shared by his contemporaries who write treatises of the passions—in placing the workings of the passions within the frame of nature, in defining them as necessary for the business of life: "This delight or payne God imparted vnto vs, that we might thereby be stirred vp to attempt those actions which were necessary for vs, or flie those inconueniences or harmes which might annoy vs" (13).[34]

To the degree that the passions can be understood in this natural frame- work, then, the interpretive force of psychophysiology can be accorded its true importance in the language of the passions. I want to insist that to understand the early modern passions as embodying a historically particu- lar kind of self-experience requires seeing the passions and the body that houses them in ecological terms—that is, in terms of that body's reciprocal relation to the world. Again and again we will see in the following chapters that the representation of emotional experience—often in the form of

34. Such an emphasis on the biological functionality of the passions sounds strikingly like the interest of modern cognitive science in the evolution of the emotions; for a characteristic represen- tation of this argument, see Joseph LeDoux, *The Emotional Brain: The Mysterious Underpinnings of Emotional Life* (New York: Simon and Schuster, 1996).

self-report by characters in the throes of strong feeling—presupposes a
demonstrable psychophysiological reciprocity between the experiencing
subject and his or her relation to the world. The link between inner and
outer is often described in the language of the qualities, since the forces of
cold, hot, moist, and dry not only determine a individual subject's characteristic humors and behaviors but also describe the characteristic behaviors of
other living things—animate and inanimate. This is why scientific descriptions take care to specify characteristic temperatures and combinations of
qualities in every kind of plant and animal. Substance embodies significance not only in human melancholy but in animal melancholy as well.
Indeed, because of the forces of cold, hot, moist, and dry, the passions of the
early modern subject have an elemental character more literal than
metaphoric in force. The passions are the winds and waves of the body, producing internal changes that the subject suffers as if they came from the
outside. This view of the passions aligns them closely to what I have elsewhere proposed as the nature of the humoral body—"characterized by corporeal fluidity, openness, and porous boundaries."[35] The humoral body has
a particular, historically specific relation to its immediate environment, as
when the physician Helkiah Crooke describes all bodies as "*Transpirable*
and *Trans-fluxible*, that is, so open to the ayre as that it may passe and
repasse through them."[36] It is not surprising, then, that the humoral body
should be characterized not only by its physical openness but also by its
emotional instability and volatility, by an internal microclimate knowable,
like climates in the outer world, more for changeability than for stasis.

If this is so, then we can understand why humoral subjectivity would be
characterized by a high degree of emotional lability and why the call for
emotional regulation by self and by external social disciplines such as civil
codes of conduct should assume such an emphasis. It is not merely that
self-control was understood as a good in and of itself—though certainly
there was and is reason to understand it in those terms—but that the internal forces of humors and passions working against it were perceived to be
so strong. In high contrast to the rational-choice theory that underpins so
many contemporary explanations of behavior, the early modern moralists
strongly doubted the force of reason as an encompassing or even an adequate rationale for behavior. As John Sutton remarks, "The body theorised
by early modern neurophilosophers was never just an inert house for a

---

35. Paster, *Body Embarrassed*, 8.

36. Helkiah Crooke, *Microcosmographia; or, A Description of the Body of Man* (London,
1615), 175.

ghostly soul. The body's fluids and spirits, and the traces it conceals, were always active, always escaping notice, always exceeding the domain of the will, always giving shape and flavour to the soul's plans." It is hard, he adds wryly, "*both* to take psychophysiology seriously *and* to see rational inference as the basic characteristic of human cognition."[37] Early modern moralists—writing from their porous humoral bodies, experiencing the volatility of their wriggling animal spirits—are rarely so detached in tone when talking about the relations of reason and passion, about the passions' challenge to the domain of will and soul. Unlike social theorists today, they had no choice but to take psychophysiology seriously, because it was their governing paradigm for theorizing the bodily wellsprings of human behavior.[38] My interest here lies in trying to discover the phenomenological character of early modern experiences of emotion—what passions of many sorts might have felt like in a penetrable body containing wriggling animal spirits, a heart whose blood did not yet circulate, and, perhaps most important, four humors whose attributes of hot, cold, wet, and dry carried enormous emotional, psychological, and what I want to call ecological significance. As Wright points out, a small rise or fall in the temper of the heart sufficed to create significant emotional changes: "although the heart hath more excesse of heate than cold, yet a little melancholly blood may quickly change the temperature, and render it more apt for a melancholly Passion" (35). And the heart was an emotionally demanding organ: "in the hunger of the heart," Wright writes, "the splene, the liuer, the blood, spirits, choller, and melancholly, attend and serue it most diligently" (46).

It is the intellectual dominance of psychophysiology in the early modern period that requires literary historians to accept it as a significant basis for a cultural history of emotion. Recent work in the period has begun to do so, thanks to a rediscovery of the humors as a durably important explanatory force in the cultural history of the body and to a reawakened interest in what I would call the lived practices of early modern cosmology. I would single out, among other examples of such work, Michael Schoenfeldt's *Bodies and Selves in Early Modern England* and Mary Thomas Crane's *Shakespeare's Brain.* Schoenfeldt, too, begins by arguing that in Galenic

---

37. John Sutton, *Philosophy and Memory Traces: Descartes to Connectionism* (Cambridge: Cambridge University Press, 1998), 16–17.

38. Sutton's particular interest is in history of the rarefied animal spirits that moved in the early modern body's neural pathways and carried messages between world, brain, and body. They were certainly involved in the early modern experience of emotion, as Thomas Wright makes clear when he describes "the purer spirits [that] flocke from the brayne by certain secrete channels to the heart" (45).

discourse "the purportedly immaterial subject is constituted as a profound material substance."[39] Like me, he is interested in recapturing the self-experience of the humoral body, but his emphasis is on Galenic discipline as a form of self-empowerment in the struggle for self-control rather than on the early modern experience and representation of the passions per se. I do disagree in part with Schoenfeldt's central thesis about "the empowerment that Galenic physiology and ethics bestowed on the individual" (11). The implication of such phrasing—that all persons are equal under the laws of Renaissance Galenism—simply ignores the realities of social and gender hierarchy everywhere in the period because it mistakenly presumes an unmarked "individual" prior to biological—that is to say hierarchical—classification. Crane's focus is less on the body than on the brain that it houses. For her, one consequence of accepting the materiality of the early modern self is to reintroduce the brain as a word-making organ, hence to reintroduce the authorial brain in all its culturally imprinted particularity as the creative origin of texts.[40] In her work, Shakespeare's brain is both historically unique—a physical fact and organ of creative agency—and culturally representative of how language is formed cognitively through physical and cultural interaction with particular environments. Her use of Shakespeare as representative in this special sense is one that I emulate here.

Like Schoenfeldt and Crane, I take the intellectual dominance of Renaissance psychological materialism as a critical starting point. Unlike them, however, I have found a degree of theoretical empowerment for the emotionally volatile, penetrable humoral self and its reciprocal relations with its environment through a highly specific application of the work of the radical French philosophers Gilles Deleuze and Félix Guattari, specifically their idea of a "Body without Organs."[41] It may seem perverse to yoke Deleuzian theory—with its notorious hostility to dualisms of all kinds—to a hierarchical and emblematic worldview defined by its reliance on analogy and correspondence, sympathy and antipathy. Yet, as they argue, "the BwO is not at all the opposite of the organs. The organs are not its enemies. The enemy is the organism" (158). The early modern body's internal organs differ profoundly from our own, in epistemic as well as in phenomenological

39. Michael C. Schoenfeldt, *Bodies and Selves in Early Modern England: Physiology and Inwardness in Spenser, Shakespeare, Herbert, and Milton* (Cambridge: Cambridge University Press, 1999), 10.

40. Mary Thomas Crane, *Shakespeare's Brain: Reading with Cognitive Theory* (Princeton, NJ: Princeton University Press, 2001), 8–10.

41. Gilles Deleuze and Félix Guattari, *A Thousand Plateaus: Capitalism and Schizophrenia*, trans. Brian Massumi (Minneapolis: University of Minnesota Press, 1987), 153.

terms, because (as Park makes clear) they are assigned psychological functions and thus a crucial role in conscious experience—as it was then articulable—of bodily pleasures and pains. In this respect, the internal organs are essential to representations of the body's self-experience and to early modern self-reports of emotional experience in ways that coincide with the BwO. For in the BwO, "the organs are no longer anything more than intensities that are produced, flows, thresholds, and gradients."[42] Thus I do want to insist that the predominant materialism of early modern thinking and the early modern picture of a world filled with appetites and actively hungry spirits is not at all alien to the fundamental presuppositions about the body's relation to its environment in the Deleuzian Body without Organs. For the early moderns, the power of the passions was a function of the affect-producing organs—the blood-making liver, the hungry heart, the angry gall bladder, and the melancholy spleen. Affects had specific locales, specific points of origin, and thus seem to constitute a paradigm quite foreign to any notion of a body *without* organs. Yet in my reading of them, early modern bodies have an affective immanence and lability supported rather than contradicted by humoral theory, for the reason that affective life was constituted by the humors coursing through the bloodstream and saturating the flesh. It is the immanence of the passions, the power of the passions, that early modern binaries seem intended to counter in a quest for the self-sameness—the manly constancy—so prized by humanist thought. In this book I am interested in the forces understood to threaten that constancy on a moment-to-moment basis—the humors, the passions, the affects, the perturbations of the soul—and to produce the un-self-sameness that is so striking a feature of humoral being-in-the-body. Though humorality is often identified with typologies—the four temperaments, the four complexions—my own reading of humoral discourse finds a much greater emphasis on change and penetrability, on a way of inhabiting the body with keen attention to the winds and waters of its internal climate. Hence Deleuzian deconstruction of such Western binaries as reason and passion, body and spirit, male and female, human and animal cohabits nicely with what I see as the dominant early modern understanding of the material body as phenomenologically indistinguishable from its passions, indeed as constituted by its passions and governed with great difficulty by the rational soul. The model of the Body without Organs is one that seems to me to go far—intuitively, as it were—toward explicating the material embodiment of the passions in pre-Enlightenment thought.

42. Ibid., 164.

My own special aim in this book is to look for traces of a historical phenomenology in the language of affect in early modern drama in order that readers of that drama and other texts of the period may begin to recover some of the historical particularity of early modern emotional self-experience. Without wishing entirely to waive his rights to an idiosyncratic understanding of contemporary psychophysiology, I nevertheless have taken Shakespeare as more representative of his age than not in terms of thinking about the bodily basis of the passions. I believe there must be epistemic limits to the possible sweep of idiosyncratic thought. Even a playwright whom we honor for having greatly expanded the semantic capacities of his native tongue thinks within the intellectual framework of his cultural moment and participates in the cosmological practices of his time. Even if Shakespeare could be held entirely responsible for inventing a psychological vocabulary to represent the experience of affect—and, pace Joel Fineman and others, this is demonstrably not the case in an age known for its enormous literary productivity in a variety of genres—the affects he would wish to describe would arise within an early modern body-soul composite replete with its wriggling spirits, its humors, its complexion, its hungry heart.

I have organized this book into four broad subtopics of the early modern affects, using Shakespeare's plays, and sometimes those of other playwrights, as evidence for what was possible to think and say—among the early modern English—about the experience of embodied emotion, especially when what is expressed seems odd, curious, or requiring explanation for the modern reader. I make no attempt to be inclusive in my choice of play texts or to give full readings of any of the plays I choose to discuss. Occasionally a play discussed in one chapter will return for analysis in another. My method is to use discrete moments and locutions in the play texts as evidence for investigating the phenomenological character of early modern emotion and to contextualize that evidence through reference to early modern moral treatises, medical texts, natural history, and other literary works. The first chapter makes a claim for the literalness of humoral alteration of the body in strong experiences of emotion, especially anger, using specific locutions in *Hamlet* and *Othello* to exemplify the claim. Even in familiar plays—perhaps especially in them, because their language has come to seem so inevitable—there are occasions when the historically different character of an emotional experience has been overlooked. In part this is so because we fail to recognize how the porous and volatile humoral body, with its faulty borders and penetrable stuff, interacts differently with the world than the "static, solid" modern bodily container. And in part it is because, as Katharine Maus has argued, "Renaissance speech habits can make it difficult to know when . . . a bodily analogy is really an analogy; when we are dealing with metaphor and when with a bare statement of fact."[43] But we must struggle against this difficulty if we are ever to recognize the historically specific character of affective discourse. Chapter 2 moves on to the large question of gendered emotions, focusing on early modern narratives of melancholy virgins transformed by love into bold, assertive, independent wives and using the differently tempered experiences of Desdemona, Rosalind, and Katherine Minola as contrasting cases in point. Chapter 3 considers early modern beliefs about the emotional faculties of the soul, given that this "sensitive soul" was shared by humans and animals alike. As I pointed out briefly above, animals had humoral bodies too in this cosmology and were moved to behave and express themselves by the differently proportioned combinations of cold, hot, moist, and dry that constituted the characteristic temperaments and the characteristic flesh of their species. I am interested in how early modern beliefs about animal emotions provide access to the relation between flesh and feelings when bodily fluids—hence bodily temperaments—are shared prominently by men and beasts alike. While it cannot be surprising that anthropo*centrism* is a linchpin in early modern cosmology, the widespread belief in a divinely ordained sharing of bodily humors challenges our easy assumptions that the early moderns would have indulged in thoughtless anthropo*morphism*. The affective behavior of animals, too, constitutes part of the early modern ecology of the passions. Chapter 4 takes up the vexed relation between the social and emotional hierarchies, noting how often in early modern plays upper-class men claim humoral privilege as a matter of birthright and dispute encroachment on their emotional autonomy. Jonson's satiric attack on the humors in plays such as *Every Man in His Humour* and *Bartholomew Fair* is not, as often supposed, an assault against a waning humoral belief system but a critique of socially performative uses of the humors in order to flaunt eccentricity or license unwarranted aggressivity in oneself and others. Shakespeare rarely invokes the humors in Jonsonian fashion, but in characters such as Corporal Nym, Shylock, or Malvolio, humoral thinking is the basis for self-understanding and self-justification in a hostile world. The humors and the display of passions that they support produce a way of life, an explanation for things as they are. The humors recommend themselves to us in exactly these terms, for they offer a glimpse of early modern emotional life with a sharpness and particularity that few other discourses of the period can match.

---

43. Katharine Eisaman Maus, *Inwardness and Theater in the English Renaissance* (Chicago: University of Chicago Press, 1995), 196.

CHAPTER ONE

ROASTED IN WRATH AND FIRE

The Ecology of the Passions in *Hamlet* and *Othello*

To a Red man, reade thy read:
With a Browne man breake thy bread:
At a pale man, draw thy knife:
From a black man keepe thy wife.

Proverbial English rhyme[1]

In this chapter I focus on a few locutions of affect in *Hamlet* and *Othello* in order to determine how such locutions, if properly contextualized in terms of early modern phenomenology, may point to key epistemic changes in subject-object relations. I might have chosen the texts of almost any two Shakespeare plays to make this argument, because the large-scale changes in which I am interested inform affective phrasing everywhere in the plays, which in this respect (as in many others) powerfully reflect their historical and lexical embeddedness. But *Hamlet*, as the canonical text for establishing the possibility and terms of "inwardness" in the late sixteenth century, is useful because of its own large role in the intellectual history of subject-object relations.[2] And *Othello* has the distinction of being the Shakespeare

---

1. See *Oxford Dictionary of English Proverbs*, ed. F. P. Wilson, 3rd ed. (Oxford: Clarendon Press, 1970), 668, subsequently cited as *ODEP*; I am quoting from the rhyme as it appears in Wright, 43.

2. For a thorough discussion of this issue, see Maus. Like me, Paul A. Cefalu finds *Hamlet* uninfluenced by mind-body dualism and laments "the lack of any thorough account of the post-medieval, pre-Cartesian philosophy of mind." But I resist his recourse to modern behaviorist and functionalist theories of mind on the historical ground that they ignore the terms and key

play most profoundly affected by new cultural histories of race, gender, and European imperialism.[3] Clearly it matters to our understanding of such familiar and important plays to read the passions represented in them with historical care. What most impedes our ability to do so, I argue, is our tendency as post-Enlightenment readers—with a residual tendency toward mind-body dualism even in an age of cognitive science—to underestimate the materialism governing pre-Enlightenment thought about the embodied passions and thus to find abstraction and bodily metaphor where the early moderns found materiality and literal reference.[4] Often what is now emotional figuration for us was bodily reality for the early moderns. Their reports on emotional change describe blood rising and falling in temperature and quantity, spleens producing melancholy, and the size and contents of livers or gall bladders determining who will be bold or fearful in an attack. ("For Andrew," says Sir Toby contemptuously of his cowardly friend Sir Andrew Aguecheek in *Twelfth Night*, "if he were open'd and you find so much blood in his liver as will clog the foot of a flea, I'll eat the rest of th'anatomy" [3.2.60–63].) Reports on cognitive operations—on what is happening in the mind in sleep or wakefulness, in passion or calm—speak of smoky vapors ascending from heart to brain, of bodily fumes puzzling thought and darkening judgment. In melancholy, writes Timothy Bright, the "substance of the brayne" drinks plentifully of "spleneticke fogge," whereby his nature is become of the same quality, and the pure and bright spirites so defiled."[5] We must be prepared to accept such reports of mind and body literally in order to track the semantic transformations that overtake bodily locutions as they slowly change from being names for material bodily phenomena such as humor, spirit, and temper to being primarily abstract figurations for the individual psychological characteristics of the disembodied self.[6]

It is true, as Katharine Maus argues and as I acknowledge in the introduction, that "Renaissance speech habits can make it difficult to know when

---

presuppositions of the period. See "'Damnèd Custom . . . Habits Devil': Shakespeare's *Hamlet*, Anti-Dualism, and the Early Modern Philosophy of Mind," *ELH* 67 (2000), 399.

3. *Othello*, too, has been seen as paradigmatic of Shakespeare's development of the "subjectivity effect" by Joel Fineman in "The Sound of O in *Othello*: The Real of the Tragedy of Desire," in *The Subjectivity Effect in Western Literary Tradition: Essays toward the Release of Shakespeare's Will* (Cambridge, MA: MIT Press, 1991), 143–64.

4. See Charles Taylor, 189.

5. Timothy Bright, *A Treatise of Melancholie* (London, 1586), 103.

6. I have made this case before in "Nervous Tension," in *The Body in Parts: Fantasies of Corporeality in Early Modern Europe*, ed. David Hillman and Carla Mazzio (London: Routledge, 1997), 110–11; see also Hillman and Mazzio's introduction to the volume, xx.

... a bodily analogy is really an analogy; when we are dealing with metaphor and when with a bare statement of fact" (196). But these distinctions between analogy or metaphor and bare statement of fact fail to register the importance of analogy to an emblematic way of thinking, still dominant in Shakespeare's lifetime, that made discovery of similitude and resemblance the richest and most direct path to knowledge of the world. Thus the hermeneutic hazards about body analogies that Maus points to, while real enough, only serve to underscore the importance of historical rigor in the phenomenological project of imagining earlier ways of understanding the embodiment of emotion and earlier modes of bodily self-experience. The significance of analogical thought for understanding the early modern emotions is, as I argue in the introduction, that characters' emotions are ontologically coextensive with the particular social and physical environments in which those emotions arise: as one of the six Galenic nonnaturals, the passions or perturbations of mind were fully embedded in the order of nature. Thus to report on an emotion—whether subjectively as experienced or objectively as observed—was, among other things, to describe an event occurring in nature and thus understandable in natural terms. As William B. Ashworth has remarked of Renaissance natural knowledge, early moderns believed that to know the peacock, "you must know its associations—its affinities, similitudes, and sympathies with the rest of the created order."[7] What was true for knowing the peacock was even more important for knowing the emotions of the human body-soul composite, because the stakes were immeasurably higher. For the early moderns, knowledge of emotions required knowing not only about the spleen, the gall bladder, and the liver, which produced various emotions, but also about what in the natural world their organs and emotions most resembled. "I am pigeon-liver'd," says Hamlet to himself bitterly in the second soliloquy, "and lack gall / To make oppression bitter" (2.2.577–78). In order for us to appreciate early modern emotions historically, we must widen the focus from seeing emotions as necessarily originating within an individual body in response to stimulus to seeing how emotions were understood to participate naturally in the fluctuations and variations characteristic of phenomenal life in general. We must especially look for evidence of emotions and the subjectivities they helped to constitute elsewhere than simply within the traditionally privileged ground of a noncorporeal inwardness, that fictional space created and

7. William B. Ashworth, "Natural History and the Emblematic World-View," in *Reappraisals of the Scientific Revolution*, ed. David C. Lindberg and Robert S. Westman (Cambridge: Cambridge University Press, 1990), 306.

maintained by criticism's dematerialized understanding of early modern psychology. This means seeing the characters' relations to their immediate material environments as necessarily governed by a "ceaseless cosmobiologi-cal exchange of vapors between body and world" and hence seeing such rela-tions as themselves constitutive of early psychophysiological truth about self and emotion.[8] It is precisely this relation—between psychophysiology and the physical constitution of the ensouled premodern world—that I want to describe as the ecology of the passions.

The two locutions on which I particularly focus in *Hamlet* and *Othello* (Aeneas's description of Pyrrhus as "roasted in wrath and fire" [2.2.461] and Desdemona's expression of concern that something "hath puddled" Othello's "clear spirit" [3.4.143]) insist on emotion as a physical fact not only in the sense of involving change in bodily substances but also in the sense of occurring objectively as an aspect of physical change in the world. The two locutions form a convenient pair in precisely inverting what they pro-pose as affectivity's relation with the physical environment: the phrase from *Hamlet* representing wrath as a quality of matter dispersed into the natural order, and the phrase from *Othello* introducing natural substances into the deep physical recesses of the embodied self. That these two locu-tions are themselves representative of an ecology of the emotions epistemi-cally foreign to post-Enlightenment habits of thought is the heart of my argument here.

Hamlet, sunk in lethargic melancholy and—with the sudden arrival of Rosencrantz and Guildenstern—perhaps newly apprehensive about the king's plans for him, remembers a play about Dido with nostalgic longing: "One speech in't I chiefly lov'd," he tells the First Player, "'twas Aeneas' [tale] to Dido, and thereabout of it especially when he speaks of Priam's slaugh-ter" (2.2.445–48). For critics, Hamlet's intense focus on this passionate speech has been significant mostly for what it reveals of Hamlet's ambiva-lence about his triangle of parents—represented in the narrated tableau by the mythic surrogates of Pyrrhus, Priam, and Hecuba—and of Hamlet's labile identifications, now with Pyrrhus as revenging son, now with his father and Claudius as the twinned, pitiable objects of parricidal rage, now with his mother as (in his imagination) she watches her son slaughter her husband.[9]

8. I am quoting here from John Sutton, "Porous Memory and the Cognitive Life of Things," in *Prefiguring Cyberculture: An Intellectual History*, ed. Darren Tofts, Annemarie Jonson, and Alessio Cavallaro (Cambridge, MA: MIT Press, 2003), 134.

9. For a good survey of the resemblances, see Robert S. Miola, "Aeneas and Hamlet," *Classical and Modern Literature* 8 (1988): 281–86.

The dramatic resemblances that his request underlines also include those between the ancient city punished for its stubborn harboring of an adulterous woman and a modern court willfully oblivious to the marital scandal in its midst. Mostly, though, it is our knowledge of Hamlet's emotions—themselves a possible projection of or palimpsest for the emotions of that guilt-ridden survivor Aeneas—that interprets his interest in the fall of Troy for us and that mediates whatever meanings we may wish to derive from this latest retelling.[10] But, while Hamlet praises the language of the play—citing one who found it "as wholesome as sweet, and by very much more handsome than fine" (444–45)—the "schoolboy epic" phrases he and the First Player recite from memory have mostly not garnered close reading and respectful attention on their own merits.[11] One reason may be that Marlowe's *Dido, Queen of Carthage*, which Shakespeare in part imitates, has never commanded deep critical attachment.[12] More likely, it is because the red, black, and white palette of Troy's fall here seems so lurid and hyperbolic and because its central tableau of the aged royal couple helpless to defend themselves against attack is so overdetermined in its pathos. Hamlet comes to realize this himself when he reacts to the First Player's involuntary emotional display: "What's Hecuba to him, or he to [Hecuba], / That he should weep for her?" (2.2.559–60).

But students of the early modern affects should note that Shakespeare's version of the fall of Troy (unlike Marlowe's in *Dido*) comes in the key colors and thermal markers of early modern humoralism, as the black-complexioned Pyrrhus, his armor coated with the drying blood of his victims, raises his sword arm over Priam's milky head.[13] (Indeed, if Shakespeare is thinking of Marlowe here, the color scheme comes not from *Dido* but from *Tamburlaine, Part I* when Tamburlaine expresses his states of mind toward the city of Damascus as he moves from mildness to implacability by changing the colors of his tents, flags, and personal equipment

10. The most recent treatments of Shakespeare's Troy include Heather James, *Shakespeare's Troy: Drama, Politics, and the Translation of Empire* (Cambridge: Cambridge University Press, 1997), who does not discuss this speech; and Eric Mallin, *Inscribing the Time: Shakespeare and the End of Elizabethan England* (Berkeley and Los Angeles: University of California Press, 1995). Ned Lukacher does discuss this speech in *Daemonic Figures: Shakespeare and the Question of Conscience* (Ithaca, NY: Cornell University Press, 1994), 132–41, though in terms radically other than my own here.

11. I am quoting Miola, 284, here.

12. For a discussion of Marlowe's *Dido, Queen of Carthage* as Shakespeare's source, see the note to 2.2.437–38 in Shakespeare, *Hamlet*, ed. G. R. Hibbard (Oxford: Clarendon Press, 1987), 227.

13. The color scheme of red, white, and black also features in Petrarchan love poetry, English morris dancing, indoor and outdoor games, playing cards, and ritual observances important in a variety of cultures; see Linda Woodbridge, *The Scythe of Saturn: Shakespeare and Magical Thinking* (Urbana: University of Illinois Press, 1994), 206–64, but esp. 229–31.

from white to red to black.) Shakespeare, in the phrase I focus on below, summarizes Pyrrhus as "roasted in wrath and fire" (2.2.461). Of course, by comparison to Hamlet's famously inexpressible "that within which passes show" (1.2.85), reference to Pyrrhus's wrath would seem to constitute only the barest evidence of psychological inwardness.[14] Pyrrhus utters no words in this inset narrative, let alone words of self-representation pointing to an ineffable interior. References to the cognitive or psychophysiological functions that in early modern texts signal interiority attach to him only by implication. Even though his desires and intentions are terrible in their consequences, he counts for us as a subject hardly at all. In this sense, what Robert Miola has well described as the "peculiar interest and intensity" of the speech derives from the prestige of its literary provenance or the complexity of its framing rather than the charisma of its central figures (284). Yet in a play deeply preoccupied throughout by memory and cognition, Pyrrhus does function for Hamlet and the First Play as a powerful catalyst of memory. He is the main actor in an extended narrative that develops the play's preoccupation with passion and action in its implied contrast between the onlooker Aeneas, who suffers all but does nothing to save the royal couple, and the actor Pyrrhus, unaware of being witnessed, who acts pitilessly with only a moment's silent hesitation. If we transfer our attention from Pyrrhus as an individual subject to the speech's representation of a crucial exchange of attributes between Pyrrhus and his environment, we find evidence of the interiority missing in Pyrrhus expressed by other, epistemically crucial means.

The key to understanding the procedures of such exchange involves recognition of the vitalism that early modern thought about the relation of self to environment tends toward.[15] Aeneas's description of Pyrrhus's movements after he escapes from "th'ominous horse" (2.2.454) is rich in phenomenological detail. Its significance for understanding representations of interiority rests upon the "nested systems of spirits" that enliven the early modern cosmos—the heavens, the environment, the human body, inanimate objects—and make that cosmos above all a theater of pneumatological interaction.[16]

14. Though as David Hillman points out, "in the context of his preoccupation elsewhere in the play with bodily innards, Hamlet's statement can be taken to point to a realm of specifically corporeal interiority"; see "Visceral Knowledge: Shakespeare, Skepticism, and the Interior of the Early Modern Body," in Hillman and Mazzio, 91. See Maus's crucial idea that the whole body interior is involved in the "production of the mental interior" (195).

15. See Owsei Temkin, *Galenism: Rise and Decline of a Medical Philosophy* (Ithaca, NY: Cornell University Press, 1973).

16. I am quoting Sutton, *Philosophy and Memory Traces*, 36.

In *Sylva Sylvarum,* his strange book of physiological musings, Bacon defines spirit as "a natural body, rarified to a proportion, and included in the tangible parts of bodies, as in an integument," and declares that there are "spirits or pneumaticals . . . in all tangible bodies."[17] The operation of these spirits constituted natural law in that the spirits explained the characteristic behaviors not only of animate things, but of inanimate ones as well: "From them and their motions," Bacon argues, "principally proceed arefaction, colliquation, concoction, maturation, putrefaction, vivification, and most of the effects of nature."[18] In this context, "motions" primarily refers to movements and changes in state such as putrefaction or vivification. But in the early seventeenth century, as I note in the introduction, the word also designated emotions—what Iago calls "raging motions" (*Othello*, 1.3.330). Lexical connections between these two meanings (motion as change in condition, motion as affect) occur by means of the spirits, because the pneumatic spirits explained the characteristic actions of all objects as expressions of their innermost desires. Burton, for example, finds love in the behavior of plants toward one another: "In vegetall creatures what sovereignty love hath, by many pregnant proofes and familiar examples may be proved, especially of palme trees, which are both he and she, & express not a sympathy but a love passion . . . they will be sicke for love, ready to dye and pine away" (3:42).[19] For Antonio, in Webster's *Duchess of Malfi,* "loving palms" are the "best emblem of a peaceful marriage, / That ne'er bore fruit divided" (1.1.485–87; see fig. 4).[20] "If such fury be in vegetals," Burton argues, "what shall we thinke of sensible creatures, how much more violent and apparent shall it be in them" (3:43). For the French philosopher Jean Bodin, the presence of desire everywhere in the cosmos was an inspiring part of its design: "What is more noble than the fact that antipathy and contagion, enmities and loves, force and faculty are contained, each with insatiable variety, in

17. Francis Bacon, *Sylva Sylvarum* (1.98), in *Works,* ed. James Spedding, Robert Leslie Ellis, and Douglas Denon Heath, 7 vols. (London: Longmans, 1857–74), 2:381, 2:380. On Bacon's beliefs in spirits, see D. P. Walker, "Francis Bacon and *Spiritus,*" in *Science, Medicine, and Society in the Renaissance: Essays to Honor Walter Pagel,* ed. Allen G. Debus, vol. 2 (New York: Science History Publications, 1972), 121–30. Walker quotes an almost identical passage from *Historia Vitae et Mortis* (122).

18. Bacon, *Sylva Sylvarum* (1.98), *Works,* 2:381. For an excellent survey of the spirits, see D. P. Walker, "Medical Spirits in Philosophy and Theology from Ficino to Newton," in *Music, Spirit, and Language in the Renaissance,* ed. Penelope Gouk (London: Variorum Reprints, 1985), 287–300.

19. I owe the Burton reference to Mark Breitenberg, *Anxious Masculinity in Early Modern England* (Cambridge: Cambridge University Press, 1996), 61.

20. I follow John Webster, *The Duchess of Malfi,* ed. John Russell Brown (Manchester: Manchester University Press, 1997).

VIVITE CONCORDES.

I.

K Omt hier mannen en ghy wyven,
  Die, wanneerje fijt gepaert.
Dickmaels fijt gewoon te kyven,
  Dickmaels toont u wrangen aert;
Leert hier van de boom-gewaffen,
  Leert hier uyt het woefte wout,
Leert op u gefelfchap paffen,
  Siet! dat doet het quaftigh hout.

Let op defe Dadel-boomen,
  Die met beeken afgefneen,
Sijn als bruggen op de ftroomen,
  Mits fy hellen tegen een.
Echte lieden, lieve paren,
  Soo ghy in den Echten ftaet
Liefd en Eendracht kunt bewaren,
  Niet dat u te boven gaet.

Batillius:

P Almarum hinc illinc pontis ceu fornice ducto,
  Amnem intermedium fœmina mafque tegunt
Vltro dum oppofitos mas inde, hinc fœmina ramos
  Curvantes fibi fe confociare petunt,
Ire & in amplexus exoptatofque hymeneos,

Quâ frondofi oculi funt in amore duces.
Iam mihi non aliæ firment connubia flammæ,
  Præferat his omnem non aliunde puer.
Pronubâ jam caftos palma una accendat odores:
  Cedat & ipfa fuas fpinea tæda faces.

Greg. Richterus in Epiftola dedicatoria axiom. Ecclef. ad matrimonium myfticum Chrifti
& Ecclefiæ, hoc ipfum Emblema non minus pie, quàm argute tranftulit.

De naturâ hujus arboris videndus omnino.

Plin. lib. 13. cap. 4. Iohan. Rerum lib. hieroglyph. 50. cap. 10. ubi
Diophanem autorem Græcum, & Georgica Florentini citat, qui multo
de Palina amore confcripfit, eamque contabefcere maris defiderio, quod,
modo radices verfus cum porrigendo, modo verticis in eum proclinatio-
ne, aliisque affectuum fignis non obfcure profitetur.

Figure 4. Loving palm trees, from Jacobs Cats, *Emblemata moralia and oeconomica*, in *Alle de Werken* (Amsterdam, 1658). By permission of the Folger Shakespeare Library.

the innermost entrails [*intimis visceribus*] of metals, plants, and animals?"[21]
We should recognize the force of "entrails" in Bodin's phrase here as literal,
since it is by placing entrails in metals and vegetables that Bodin can find desire in them too: it was in human entrails, after all, that virtue and sin were
located.[22] Bacon, less floridly, describes a tension in all things between their
desire for union with other things and their desire for self-continuance,
what in *Sylva Sylvarum* he abstrusely calls an appetite for "evitation of solu-
tion of continuity." (We could paraphrase this periphrastic obscurity as
"resistance to dissolution.") This appetite of self-love varies by degrees
depending on consistency: hard things, such as iron, stone, or wood, have a
"strong" appetite to resist change and remain themselves, but sticky things,
such as pitch, glue, or birdlime, will "partly follow the touch of another
body; and partly stick and continue to themselves." Such bodies, he notes
somewhat disapprovingly, are usually "ill mixed; and . . . take more pleasure
in a foreign body, than in preserving their own consistence" (*Works*,
2:437–38). Spirits are thus active ingredients in the cosmological structure
of correspondences and analogies, a key part of what makes the appetites of
the body and those of the macrocosm mutually expressive.

Perhaps most important, the spirit realm worked analogically to explain
the psychophysiological constitution of the embodied self, since the pneumatic spirits that organized the universe replenished the life forces of the
human body too, being inhaled into the lungs or absorbed in food and
drink.[23] Thus, in accounts such as Bacon's of things pleasuring themselves
in hybrid unions with other things, the self traversed by desire finds its
own contradictory longings mimicked everywhere by the sympathies and
antipathies that organize and move a desiring universe filled with the strivings of appetite in all things animal, vegetable, or mineral. In such an animated universe, James Bono points out, "Nature is fundamentally playful
and creative; it is, in short, poetic . . . Nature can mimic; it can take natural
forms and make them metamorphose into other shapes; it is inherently
active, transformative, plastic . . . Such transformations and mirroring, then,
display the analogical, metaphorical, and hierarchical structure of the divine

21. From Jean Bodin, *Universae naturae theatrum* (Frankfurt, 1597), sig 4r, translated and
quoted in Ann Blair, *The Theater of Nature: Jean Bodin and Renaissance Science* (Princeton, NJ:
Princeton University Press, 1997), 21.

22. See Hillman, 82, where he quotes Donne's trope in *Devotions upon Emergent Occasions* that
important truths lie hidden in one's bowels "as *gold* in a *Mine*."

23. See Sutton, *Philosophy and Memory Traces*, 36; Walker, "Medical Spirits," 287–88; and Karl
R. Wallace, *Francis Bacon and the Nature of Man: The Faculties of Man's Soul: Understanding,
Reason, Imagination, Memory, Will, and Appetite* (Urbana: University of Illinois Press, 1967), 23–39.

system of nature."[24] Silently but tellingly, this early modern paradigm of nature fills Pyrrhus's poetic environment, like Hamlet's dramatic one, with natural spirits of all kinds working to activate the desires lodged in everything—making things behave as they want and tend to do. For the critic looking for textual traces of historical phenomenology, the spirits grant permission to look for replications of human desire and ways of knowing it elsewhere than merely within an individual subject himself or herself. Here, Aeneas's speech can provide evidence of Pyrrhus's innermost desire not just in a few recognizably direct references to the warrior's affect but also in the whole scope of his body's interactions with the immediate environment. The inward origins and signs of Pyrrhus's behavior, in other words, are redistributed in the details of his rampage through the burning city—how he changes and is changed by the burning city, whose destruction finally becomes a picture not of its own notoriously complicated character, but of the desires of its destroyer.

What I will argue is that, far from being only a set-piece occasion with hermeneutic value because of its metaphorical mirroring of Hamlet's circumstances, Shakespeare's representation of Pyrrhus's wrath here is fully cognate with his representation of affect and interiority elsewhere in the play. Those terms—if we know how to read them correctly—are those of a psychological materialism in which, as Michael Schoenfeldt notes, "the purportedly immaterial subject is constituted as a profoundly material substance" (10). But the substantial self is constructed, as I have just argued, from the same materials as the natural world; this is a chief reason that its appetites are analogous to the appetites animating nature and why—to repeat Merleau-Ponty's observation quoted in the introduction—historical psychology has always to deal with the constitution of the world (60). Even if nature's mimetic playfulness, as Bono suggests, threatens at times to overwhelm order and pattern, resemblances between self and world can never be accidental or without meaning, because the appetites lodged in the self also find expression—if not legitimation—outside the self in a phenomenal world filled with yearning palm trees or ambivalent pitch and birdlime. Indeed the relationship of self to world is less one of resemblance and correspondence than it is of reciprocity or even mutual permeation—what the cognitive scientist Andy Clark has described as "mutually modulatory influences linking brain, body, and world" (163).

---

24. James J. Bono, *The Word of God and the Languages of Man: Interpreting Nature in Early Modern Science and Medicine*, vol. 1, *Ficino to Descartes* (Madison: University of Wisconsin Press, 1995), 184. For more on Ficinian subjectivity, see Gary Tomlinson, *Metaphysical Song: An Essay on Opera* (Princeton, NJ: Princeton University Press, 1999), 11–13.

In Aeneas's narrative, then, this reciprocity of subject and object is signaled first of all by the fateful, multiple connections between Pyrrhus's name, intention, bodily state, and time of day:

> The rugged Pyrrhus, he whose sable arms,
> Black as his purpose, did the night resemble
> When he lay couched in th'ominous horse,
> Hath now this dread and black complexion smear'd
> With heraldry more dismal.
>
> (2.2.452–56)

The red and black color scheme that dominates the whole passage begins first of all in Pyrrhus himself, his name, from the Greek *purros*, meaning flame-colored or yellowish-red. The passage reads almost as if Shakespeare were using the name quasi-allegorically—much as Spenser names Pyrochles in book 2 of *The Faerie Queene*—in order to recognize its relation to choler, even possibly to Pyrrhus's possession of red hair or a red beard. In *The Optick Glasse of Humours*, Thomas Walkington describes the choleric man as "always either orange or yellow visag'd, . . . or a little swarthy, red haired, or of a brownish color; . . . soon provoked to anger, and soone appeased."[25] The color associations of the name may also signal why Hamlet first likens Pyrrhus to the Hyrcanian tiger.[26] The epithet "rugged"— possibly connoting hairiness along with roughness of manner, feature, or mood—might also signal his excess of choler, wrath's drying action on the spirits being involved in the production of hair.[27] Within the framework provided by materialist psychology, Pyrrhus's nature and characteristic behavior are expressed within and without in the mirroring blacks of mind, time, body, and mood.[28] The effect of such mirroring is significant, both rhetorically and literally, as one of *transumption*, a rhetorical figure that designated both the actual transfer of qualities from one place to another and the metaphorical transfer of terms. Physiologically, transumption might refer to the transfer of elements within the body by means of the blood, as when Helkiah Crooke speaks of the "aiery body" being "nourished by blood

---

25. Thomas Walkington, *The Optick Glasse of Humors* (London, 1631), 108–9.

26. The reference comes, however, as Miola points out (282), from Dido's rebuke to Aeneas in *Aeneid*, 4.367.

27. See *The Problems of Aristotle* (London, 1597), sig. A3v: "There is nothing drier then the haires, for they are drier then the bones."

28. For a tantalizingly brief discussion of other key instances of black in the play, see Patricia Parker, "Murder in Guyana," *Shakespeare Studies* 28 (2000): 173.

brought by the Veines" (608). Rhetorically, according to Thomas Wilson, transumption "is, when by digrees wee go to that, whiche is to be shewed. As thus: Suche a one lyeth in a darke doungeon, now in speaking of darkenesse, we understand closenesse, by closeness, we gather blackenesse, and by blackenesse, we judge depenesse."[29] In Wilson's example, to describe a dungeon as dark connotes or even subsumes the other qualities of closeness, blackness, and depth. Here, transumption implies the transfer of analogical attributes—from the darkness of the horse to the darkness of the sleeping city, from Pyrrhus's dark complexion to his black armor. It displays the analogical mirroring that, for the early moderns, expresses the real character of the phenomenal world. Pyrrhus's innermost blackness of purpose—reciprocally produced by and producing a mind darkened by the burning of choler—is not distinguishable from the complexion that is its sign. In this respect, Aeneas speaks of Pyrrhus from well within the ontological terms of the premodern episteme, where, in Charles Taylor's phrase, the substance embodies the significance (189). Pyrrhus's choleric complexion, first replicated in the color of his body armor, participates in the enveloping darkness. For the invading Greek army, such blackness is entirely functional; their plan depends on the night's sympathetic affordance of rage.[30] Thus the conventional moral coloration hinted at in "blackness of purpose" derives not from physiology—where blackness is descriptive—but from Aeneas's antipathetic point of view as the Trojan victim and witness of such sympathetic alignments. That Pyrrhus's blackness mirrors his environment, furthermore, reflects ironically on the "nighted color" of Hamlet's "inky cloak" (1.2.68, 77), which so contrasts with the dominant polychromes of a court no longer in mourning. If Hamlet's refusal—presumably in defiance of a royal edict from Claudius—to cast off this external coloration expresses his desire not to blend in, it also signals his lack of influence on other courtiers. By the same token, while he denies that his inky cloak can denote him "truly," he does not deny the connection altogether between the cloak and his desire to grieve.[31]

The connections that the theory of complexions makes between bodily interior and exterior are also linked to the commonplace analogy of flesh to earth, the analogy that explains why the words we distinguish scriptively as

29. Thomas Wilson, *The Arte of Rhetorique*, ed. Thomas J. Derrick (1553; reprint, New York: Garland, 1982), 350.

30. The Riverside editor assumes that the Greeks have blackened their skin in order to be less visible, a suggestion not followed by other editors; see note to 2.2.452. The reading is possible but does not substantially alter my point.

31. Hillman makes this point (90–91).

mettle and *metal* had yet to be divided. The character of Pyrrhus's embodied disposition—the particular substance of that flesh that reifies his black purpose—has its own hard consistency, its own texture, as if wrathful flesh were the armor of disposition. But Pyrrhus's disposition is not expressed merely by forms of blackness within and without. When Aeneas images the blood of Pyrrhus's victims drying on his body armor ("baked and impasted with the parching streets" [1.2.459]), key transactions are also taking place between Pyrrhus's body, the blood of his victims, and the fire destroying Troy. The imagery invokes not only the landscape of hell but also the inner body-scape of early modern physiology, specifically the concoctions in stomach, liver, and heart that turned food to blood and refined blood to spirit.[32] The blood of "fathers, mothers, daughters, sons" (458) sealed by heat on armor becomes a cruel external replication of internal bodily processes, with Troy's burning streets becoming a kiln to cook the blood of its citizens as food for rampaging Greeks or, analogously, as a forge to create the savage new heraldry of "total gules" burned on the black mettle of Pyrrhus's complexion. The blood of others coats Pyrrhus and seals him, adhering to Pyrrhus's armor—Bacon might say—because like other sticky liquids it has an appetite (or at least a capacity) to do so. His hard rage is met and mimicked by the city's answering fires, which harden him still more—the "coagulate gore" of his victims "o'er-sizing" him, making his body larger in size and fixing or hardening its outline.[33] Even Pyrrhus's eyes are hardened by wrath: the light from the burning streets reflects and is reflected by his "eyes like carbuncles" (463), the mythical stones said to glow from within. This simile, too, is grounded in the earth-flesh analogy and returns in the periphrasis "burning eyes of heaven" when eyes burning in the body metamorphose cosmically into stars. In a futile invocation of the natural order to intervene sympathetically, Aeneas declares that the stars, upon hearing Hecuba's cries, should become moist ("milch" or milky, as in "the milk of human kindness" or the milk opposite to gall [*Macbeth*, 1.5.17, 48]). But the heavens too have become hard and unsympathetic, and if this is a call for rain to douse the fires, the rain does not come.

In Pyrrhus, then, "roasted in wrath and fire" (2.2.461), desire to seek revenge is fed by the burning of blood without and within. To the modern reader, the nicely alliterative phrase seems to bring together different

32. For illustrations of the analogy between cooking and concoction, see the metaphorical tables in Pouchelle, 209–10.

33. Hibbard, in his edition of *Hamlet*, notes that "covered over as though with size" is Shakespeare's usage; see note to 2.2.453.

ontological states, one abstract and general, the other material and particular. But in substituting seamlessly for the bodily substance of choler, "wrath" does not work metonymically as effect substituting for cause. Rather, in Charles Taylor's sense of premodern ontology that I describe in the introduction, it works as significance embodying substance and vice versa. A similar interplay between concrete and abstract, significance and substance, underlies Richard II's address to his quarreling nobles:

> Wrath-kindled [gentlemen], be rul'd by me,
> Let's purge this choler without letting blood.
>
> (*Richard II*, 1.1.152–53)

In the phrase "wrath-kindled," wrath seems to jump categorical boundaries only if we fail to recognize that wrath and choler can function synonymously, that wrath and yellow bile or gall would be purged at the same time. Here, too, Pyrrhus can be roasted by the wrath in his body, because wrath and choler can only be distinguished lexically, not materially. Body and city, subject and object, conjoin; wrath is the hard body's motivating fire, consuming blood and spirits just as fire burns a city; and hardness becomes functionally descriptive not only of Pyrrhus's body but also of the substantial character of his inner state.

In the second half of Aeneas's narrative, when Pyrrhus experiences his famous hesitation, the imagery changes from fire to air, from body to mind, from bodily roasting to mental abstraction.[34] But the effects are no less hyperbolic and overdetermined: first Priam topples tragicomically from the back draft—the "whiff and wind"—of the misplaced first strike of Pyrrhus's "fell sword" (2.2.473); then the city's watchtower, weakened by fire, falls in sympathetic response:

> [senseless Ilium,]
> Seeming to feel this blow, with flaming top
> Stoops to his base.
>
> (474–76)

Puns and tropes pile up insistently at this point, letting rhetorical complexity evoke phenomenological density. In the Folio text's phrase, "senseless Ilium / Seeming to feel," oxymoron promotes prosopopoeia; air currents of whiff and wind return in the pun on "blow." Most interesting is the multiple

---

34. For Lukacher (134–41), this is the heart of the speech.

play on the familiar locution "fell sword"—swords being tempered (like people, liquors, or musical instruments) and thus easily made to participate in humoral discourse. "Fell," deriving from *fel*, Latin for bile or gall, relates metonymically to the bitterness suggested in Pyrrhus's name, coloring, and disposition. The sword—with "fell" as the epithet of its tempering, the mettle of its metal, the signifier of its readiness to cut—is endowed with appetite and humorality, becoming metonymically the complexion of its owner and prosthetically the agent of his arm.

The tight correspondences in the first half of the speech between Pyrrhus's color, rage, the fires burning in Troy, and the temper of his sword lend cosmological emphasis to the global silence that follows Pyrrhus's moment of hesitation:

> for lo his sword,
> Which was declining on the milky head
> Of reverent Priam, seem'd i'th'air to stick.
> So as a painted tyrant Pyrrhus stood
> [And,] like a neutral to his will and matter,
> Did nothing.
>
> (2.2.477–82)

"Will and matter" may be a hendiadys for "purposed business."[35] It is equally likely, however, given the passage's insistence on fire as the outward mirroring of Pyrrhus's inner state, that "matter" could signify body, with Pyrrhus suddenly and mysteriously abstracted from the will that is his purpose and the hardened bodily substance that houses it.[36] Perhaps we are to imagine that the fire roasting him has temporarily consumed itself, has expended its matter:

> But as we often see, against some storm,
> A silence in the heavens, the rack stand still,
> The bold winds speechless, and the orb below
> As hush as death, anon the dreadful thunder
> Doth rend the region; so after Pyrrhus' pause
> A roused vengeance sets him new a-work.
>
> (483–88)

35. Thus Hibbard's note to *Hamlet*, 2.2.472; the role of hendiadys in *Hamlet* has been brilliantly discussed by George T. Wright, "Hendiadys and *Hamlet*," *PMLA* 96 (1981): 168–93.

36. Puns on "matter" and "mother" (*mater*), as Patricia Parker points out, refer to the female body; see *Shakespeare from the Margins: Language, Culture, Context* (Chicago: University of Chicago Press, 1996), 254.

The winds of the passion within his body have, suddenly, blown away, blown elsewhere. It is not surprising that Shakespeare likens Pyrrhus's momentary inaction—his psychic withdrawal from his body's purposes, the replacement of desire by its absence or of wrath by wonder or pity—to the stillness of air before a storm. As we shall see again in *Othello*, metaphors of winds as passions are commonplace, expressive of what Shigehisa Kuriyama has called "the pneumatic character of life" in premodern epistemologies (240). In suggesting that the passions behave like the elements fighting for dominance with their opposite, Thomas Wright employs the metaphor of winds so casually as to suggest its proverbial force: "The Egyptians fought against the Egyptians, the East wind riseth often against the West, the South against the North, the Winde against the tyde, & one Passion fighteth with another" (70–71). In the introduction, I quote Bishop Coeffeteau's citation of a widespread belief "that as there were foure chiefe winds which excite diuers storms, be it at land or sea; so there are foure principall *Passions* which trouble our *Soules*, and which stir vp diuers tempests by their irregular motions" (31). Thus Gertrude describes Hamlet's emotional violence after the closet scene, telling Claudius he is

> mad as the sea and wind when both contend
> Which is the mightier.
>
> (4.1.7–8)

While the linkages described in such passages are typically analogical or—as in the Wright passage—asyndetic in grammatical structure, such linkages nevertheless indicate a strongly physical apprehension of winds as "immanent powers, vivid presences." "Winds sculpted the shape and the possibilities of the body," Kuriyama writes, "molded desires and dispositions, infused a person's entire being" (235).[37] In action they resembled the bodily spirits, so that the royal physician Helkiah Crooke uses meteorology to explain the invisible, instantaneous action of spirits along neural pathways: "their motion is sudden & momentanie like the lightning, . . . or they are like the winde which whiskes about in euery corner and turnes the heauy sailes of a Wind-mill" (824).[38] He is echoed by Descartes, later in the century, who relies upon a meteorological understanding of the inner

---

37. Kuriyama discusses the winds only in relation to ancient sources, but the characterization extends into the early modern period; see Gail Kern Paster, "Pulse, Muscle, Blood, Breath, and Colour," review of *The Expressiveness of the Body in Ancient Greek and Chinese Medicine*, by Shigehisa Kuriyama, *Metascience* 10 (2001): 329–33.

38. See my discussion of this passage in Paster, "Nervous Tension," 114–15.

workings of the body cavity to describe the animal spirits as a "certain very fine wind, or rather a very lively and pure flame."[39]

Such locutions depend for their force on premodern beliefs that the body was filled with moving currents of air in the bloodstream, that the air taken within the body became part of the stuff of consciousness. In Greek tragedy, Ruth Padel argues, belief that air and liquid moved together in the body accounts for the "many images of emotion as liquid swelling, which interact with other images of emotion as rising wind or breath. The two-way, inward and outward movement is an important ingredient of Greek fantasy about innards and their relation with the world" (89).[40] But, as the quotations from Descartes and others suggest, such pneumatic fantasies last well into the early modern period, in part as a function of beliefs about the universal plenitude of spirits of all kinds, in part because of the "pneumatic character" of life itself. According to John Sutton, "Bodily spirits took pleasure in uniting with the sky."[41] It was well known that the Devil, inhabiting the air, had power to alter a body's humors and thus a person's behavior.[42] Burton imagines the Devil being inhaled into the bloodstream in order to work his changes on heart and mind. "The Aire workes on all men," says Burton, "when the humours by the Aire bee stirred, he goes in with them, exagitates our spirits, and vexeth our Soules: as the sea waves, so are the spirits and humours in our bodies, tossed with tempestuous windes and stormes" (1:237).[43]

In *Hamlet*, rather than merely serving the purposes of epic style to inflate Pyrrhus's hesitation hyperbolically, imagery of air stilled naturalizes the sudden cessation of rage in Pyrrhus in order to explain his body's momentary relinquishing of agency to the air that surrounds and flows into it. As Pyrrhus holds his breath, so the air holds his sword ("which seem'd i'th'air to stick" [2.2.479]). The ambiguity of breath—that it moves into and out of the body—allows it to figure what Padel calls "a simultaneously external and internal causality" (91). Here, such riddling of causality occurs

---

39. René Descartes, "Treatise on Man," in *The Philosophical Writings of Descartes*, trans. John Cottingham, Robert Stoothoff, and Dugald Murdoch (Cambridge: Cambridge University Press, 1985), 1:100.

40. For a full discussion of the relation between air and emotion in ancient Greek texts, see Padel, 88–98.

41. Sutton, *Philosophy and Memory Traces*, 34.

42. On the power of demons over bodily humors, see Stuart Clark, *Thinking with Demons: The Idea of Witchcraft in Early Modern Europe* (Oxford: Clarendon Press, 1997), 163. See also Walker, "Medical Spirits," 290.

43. Burton is translating and quoting here from Levinus Lemnius.

when, just as suddenly and mysteriously as he lapsed into distraction, Pyrrhus returns from it to the business at hand:

> so after Pyrrhus' pause,
> A roused vengeance sets him new a-work.
>
> (487–88)

Like changes in weather, the shift of mood seems to penetrate the distracted Pyrrhus from elsewhere (roused from where, roused by what?) in order to spur him to action, or, more precisely, to move Pyrrhus's sword to action. Arm and sword seem coactive not just so that Pyrrhus can accomplish his desire to kill Priam, but so that as working partners in the act, each can express its own agentive desires to move and cut. Bleeding metonymically, effect for cause, not with its own blood but with that of its objects, the fell sword in its remorselessness "now falls on Priam" (492).

This elemental imagery of fire and air, I am suggesting, works to disperse agency from the body out into the environment and back; or, more precisely, to suggest how bodily interiority and affect express themselves environmentally as part of the "vast systems of fluid exchange" between the body and the world.[44] The result is an ecology of the passions peculiar to the psychological materialism of early modern thought, which recognizes the influence of environment on the passions and the effect of human passions on the objective world outside self. This is how and where early modern psychology, because of its material base, dealt with the constitution of the world. Here in the destructive form of wrath, agency is vividly produced and just as vividly decentered, emanating from Pyrrhus's body and its extensions of sword and armor without being specific or exclusive to them, being redistributed outward to a universe of desiring elements and sympathetic affordances. The overall effect is of a subjectivity conceived as unbounded yet as strongly defined by its particular coordinates of time and place—as if at any other time or place, Pyrrhus would be outwardly recognizable yet inwardly different, because he would not be roasted in wrath and fire. To recognize that Shakespeare is describing such a form of subjectivity in Pyrrhus requires turning radically away from any notion of disembodied selfhood toward what the radical French philosophers Gilles Deleuze and Félix Guattari call "the Body without Organs." Theirs is a representation of the body as a distribution of intensities, an immanence of desire: "nothing more than a set of valves, locks, floodgates, bowls, or

---

44. Sutton, *Philosophy and Memory Traces*, 39.

communicating vessels" (153). In the Body without Organs, as in more psychoanalytically orthodox accounts, body and self are constituted by the intensity of their purposes and desires, but in Deleuze and Guattari—as in premodern epistemologies—those forces are dispersed and redistributed to a sympathetically answering object-world, the world in which all desire must find tangible expression and reflection.

To find the specter of Deleuze and Guattari looming over Pyrrhus as Pyrrhus looms over Priam may seem a perversion of Shakespeare's attempt at epic depiction here, yet the deconstruction of selfhood called the Body without Organs shows us how to locate Pyrrhus's inwardness elsewhere, how to name Pyrrhus in action or inaction as an embodied subject spilling beyond the boundaries of organized subjecthood, a subject more like a material site, an intensity of desiring matter or its vacuous absence. As Deleuze and Guattari describe the process: "Flows of intensity, their fluids, their fibers, their continuums and conjunctions of affects, the wind, fine segmentation, microperceptions have replaced the world of the subject" (162). The linkage between early modern cosmology and Deleuze and Guattari, clearly, comes by way of the spirits and the elemental exchanges they enabled. Even though the early modern body is a body *with* organs—indeed organs given discrete psychological functions—the humors filling the body's veins and arteries and the animal spirits racing through the neural pathways give bodily self-experience an immanence very like what Deleuze and Guattari gesture toward. To the modern reader unwilling to recognize the subject-object reciprocity built into an emblematic worldview or to acknowledge the impact upon the subject of what Jean Bodin in the passage quoted above calls the "enmities and loves" contained within the "innermost entrails of metals, plants, and animals," this mode of reading in the case of Pyrrhus may seem uncomfortably allegorical or just plain overwrought. But if we apply my reading of Pyrrhus in a brief digression to his Spenserian counterpart—Pyrochles in book 2 of *The Faerie Queene*—we may see the widening advantages of such reading: the result is not to reduce the character Pyrrhus to an allegorical representation of wrath but to demonstrate how even a stick figure such as Pyrochles may seem less static and unreal once we recognize how the resemblances that interanimate the early modern natural world also govern the narrative practices of Spenserian allegory.[45]

45. The brothers Pyrochles and Cymochles—almost never discussed separately—are usually identified as representations of the Aquinian irascible and concupiscible appetites, respectively; see Schoenfeldt's brief discussion of the brothers (51). On the Aquinian soul, see Susan James, 52–64.

In the ontological reciprocities of Spenserian phraseology, bodily and environmental substances rarely fail to embody significance. The interactivity of self and world that we noted in Shakespeare's depiction of Pyrrhus is also strongly present and even more determinative in *The Faerie Queene*'s portrait of Pyrochles, from the sunbeams glinting off his armor like flames to the hot, choking dust storm he creates by moving through his landscape: he

> prickt so fiers, that vnderneath his feete
> The smouldring dust did round about him smoke,
> Both horse and man nigh able for to choke.
>
> $(2.5.3.3-5)^{46}$

The dynamic interplay between abstraction and materiality so important in Shakespeare's phrase "roasted in wrath and fire" occurs as well in Spenser's description of the choleric knight. The darts that the varlet Atin carries for his master are envenomed "in poyson and in bloud, of malice and despight" (2.4.38.9); Pyrochles' "steed was bloudy red, and fomed ire" (2.5.2.8). Atin describes his master pneumatically as one who "breathes out wrath and hainous crueltie" (2.4.43.8) and explains his own function:

> His am I Atin . . .
> That matter make for him to worke vpon,
> And stirre him vp to strife and cruell fight.
>
> (2.4.42.5-7)

The pun plays on matter as occasion or problem and matter as mere physical stuff—that which makes him "all disposd to bloudy fight" (2.4.43.7). Pyrochles, too, evinces the pneumatic character of life: this matter is the smoldering dust that accompanies Pyrochles as he moves through the world bringing a dispositional mini-environment with him. The self-world interchanges of humoralism allow us to see the motto on Pyrochles' shield, "Burnt I do burne" (2.4.38.5), less as a threat of retaliation for injuries suffered than, in its suggestion of a deterministic physiological and environmental reciprocity, an almost exact parallel to "roasted in wrath and fire."

Of course it is the utter dominance of choler in his nature that makes Pyrochles' interactions with the world a compulsive repetition of combats, exemplifying what (in the context of pneumatic spirits) Bacon sees as the

46. Edmund Spenser, *The Faerie Queene*, ed. Thomas P. Roche (New York: Penguin Books, 1978).

hard body's strong resistance to change or to union with other bodies. Perhaps this strong resistance to being altered or conjoined—the fear of not being hard enough—is why Pyrochles is so horrified by the sight of blood pouring out of his body when Guyon's sword bites "deepe in his flesh" and opens "wide a red floodgate" (2.5.7.9) yet is unable to alter his behavior in any way so as to avoid defeat and injury:

> Deadly dismayd, with horrour of that dint
> *Pyrochles* was, and grieued eke entyre;
> Yet nathemore did it his fury stint,
> But added flame vnto his former fire,
> That welnigh molt his hart in raging yre.
>
> (2.5.8.1–5)

Here, as with "roasted in wrath and fire," the abstract noun "ire" has full material force in the object-world, melting hearts, adding flame to bodily fires, and behaving for all the world like the choler from which, ontologically, it is inseparable.

The behavioral and affective likenesses of Pyrrhus and Pyrochles underscore the humoral grounding in Shakespeare's inset narrative of the fall of Troy and perhaps also, by extension, the governing psychological materialism of the play, even in its representation of Hamlet's famously complex "that within." Despite humoralism's notorious association with physiological typology and its tendency to environmental and physiological determinism, humoral psychology does not preclude complexity. On the contrary, as we have seen, in its attention to the multiple interactions of physical, cultural, and environmental factors, humoral theory is as subtle and complex as any succeeding psychological paradigm; it is "at least as precise and nuanced," says Michael Schoenfeldt, "as the procedures we use to organize and analyze selves" (20).[47] In 2.2, in the bitter second soliloquy that follows the exit of players and courtiers, Hamlet recognizes himself in implicitly humoral terms as the psychophysiological opposite of both the First Player and Pyrrhus, models of passion and action respectively—one as a behavioral model of effective inwardness, the other as a behavioral model of monumental outwardness. The speech is often cited as a model of psychologically infolded complexity as Hamlet examines not only his past and present responses to his predicament but also the discourse of self-examination

47. See also Sutton, *Philosophy and Memory Traces*, 36–43.

itself.[48] Hamlet begins by contrasting himself contemptuously to his social inferior—"this player here"—who so controls his inner bodily processes that he can, as a consequence of listening to his own recitation, flood himself within and without by emotion and cause bodily alteration. He can

> force his soul so to his own conceit
> That from her working all the visage wann'd,
> Tears in his eyes, distraction in his aspect.
>
> $(2.2.553-55)^{49}$

But, though it is harder to see, Hamlet seems to contrast himself as well to the black- and hard-bodied Pyrrhus, who, as we have seen, enacts bodily agency in a form so overheated that it fills the surrounding landscape with its reflection and effects. Instead of Pyrrhus's direct and focused engagement with both the objects that define him and those that oppose him, Hamlet perceives his consciousness removed from contact with the object-world as if by the cold, moist state of sleep. He thus finds himself displaced ontologically from having any direct effect upon his environment—the direct effect to be expected of an early modern prince. But, says Hamlet,

> I,
> A dull and muddy-mettled rascal, peak
> Like John-a-dreams, unpregnant of my cause,
> And can say nothing.
>
> $(2.2.566-69)$

In early English usage, *mettle,* used without qualifiers to describe a person's character, had the positive implication of ardor or spirit—the air-and-fieriness or perhaps the precious metal theoretically innate in the finer natures of princes such as Hamlet. Thus, when Prince Hal compares himself to "bright metal on a sullen ground" (*1 Henry IV,* 1.2.212), he is imagining himself anxiously as inferior alloy.[50] Hamlet's self-comparison may be even more desperate than Hal's, since in contemporary usage *metal* could refer to any kind of matter (especially, says the *OED,* "earthy matter," citing

---

48. The locus classicus for analysis of this speech is Richard Lanham, *Motives of Eloquence: Literary Rhetoric in the Renaissance* (New Haven, CT: Yale University Press, 1976), 133–37.

49. See Crane's powerful discussion of this speech in humoral terms (131).

50. See Stephen Greenblatt, "Invisible Bullets," in *Shakespearean Negotiations: The Circulation of Social Energy in Renaissance England* (Berkeley and Los Angeles: University of California Press, 1988), 21–65.

the phrase "Cressetts of Earthen mettall").[51] In that case, Hamlet is thinking of himself not as a precious-metaled nature muddied temporarily by grief and melancholy, but worse, as nature made of mud itself.[52] Perplexed by his continuing lethargy, Hamlet berates himself here as one whose cognitive faculties are literally darkened (muddied) and slowed by the workings of the melancholy humors bred of grief, lethargy, disappointment, misogyny, and thwarted ambition. Timothy Bright describes the workings of melancholy on the mind: "the instrument of discretion is depraued by these melancholick spirites, and a darknes & cloudes of melancholie vapours rising from that pudle of the splene obscure the clearenes, which our spirites are indued with, and is requisite to the discretion of outward objectes" (102). I will return to the significance of the image of the spleen as puddle in Desdemona's image of Othello's "puddled spirit." Here, Hamlet's scornful, self-directed epithets, with an important social valence lacking in Bright's clinical account, represent the kind of abuse and insult that would be directed from a high- to a low-born man.[53] The descriptors—linking the rascal's sluggish and ineffectual disposition, his "muddy" mettle, to base birth—reconstrue Hamlet's social relation to his world.[54] His lack of purpose and inner strength—his lack of worthy "mettle/metal"—is socially degrading for a king's son; hence it appears to him as a form of psychological servitude, transforming him from prince to "rogue and peasant slave." In this context, to be shamefully "unpregnant of my cause" is to be precisely unlike both Pyrrhus, who fills the space of Troy with his physical monumentality and emotional concentration, and the First Player, who so fills himself with emotional substances that his "whole function" suits "with forms to his conceit" (2.2.556–57).

"For Shakespeare," Mary Thomas Crane has argued, "*pregnant* was a word that named the multiple ways that bodies are penetrated by the external world and produce something—offspring, ideas, language—as a result of that penetration" (159).[55] "To be unpregnant of my cause" is not, then, a

---

51. See *metal* (*OED*, 8), citing a 1903 edition of *Rites of Durham*, by Surtees.

52. Klibansky, Panofsky, and Saxl say that the melancholic was seen as "mud-coloured"; see Raymond Klibansky, Erwin Panofsky, and Fritz Saxl, *Saturn and Melancholy: Studies in the History of Natural Philosophy, Religion, and Art* (London: Thomas Nelson, 1964), 290. Lawrence Babb on pathological grief in the drama is still worth consulting; see *The Elizabethan Malady: A Study of Melancholia in English Literature from 1580 to 1642* (East Lansing: Michigan State College Press, 1951), esp. 104–10.

53. See entries for *rascal* (*OED*, 2).

54. On the relation of mental process to social hierarchy, see Steven Shapin, *A Social History of Truth: Civility and Science in Seventeenth-Century England* (Chicago: University of Chicago Press, 1994), 42–64.

55. Her reference here is to Angelo in *Measure for Measure*.

wholly abstract phrase but one, like "roasted in wrath and fire," in which the bodily matter of pregnant thought presses phenomenologically on the general referent "cause." Pyrrhus is pregnant with desire for slaughter, and the First Player is pregnant with the ideas and emotions generated in his own body when his voice passes through the cavities of his anatomy and he hears himself speak.[56] By contrast, the empty Hamlet sees in himself a failure of effective causation, a failure (we might say) to *be* material enough—in the sense of being pregnant with ideas or language. We might, therefore, change Crane's description of the ideal interaction of self and world from penetration to interpenetration or, better still, to an interpenetration whose fantasized end was consumption. For an early modern upper-class male, the process of becoming pregnant with ideas, or with language, or with "motive and cue for passion" is less the result of penetration by the world than of active consumption of it through ingestion and assimilation. This is what Hamlet imagines himself to have failed at, whether he fantasizes about having to "take" the humiliating consequences of social passivity (having his beard plucked or his nose tweaked, being given "the lie i'th' throat / As deep as to the lungs" [2.2.574–75]) or about lacking the right bodily stuff to lend appetite to killing and revenge. The early modern word for such an appetite was "stomach" (*OED*, 5b). As Bishop Hall comments about the search for humility in a baseborn man, "A Man of lowly stomacke can swallow and digest contempt, without any distemper."[57] The social consequences of such deficits of appetite explain why self-reproach in Hamlet expresses itself as the perception of bodily lack. His withdrawal by grief and disappointment into the inactivity of melancholy means that he is not consuming enough of his world's "stuff" behaviorally, pneumatically. In this he is precisely the opposite of Aeneas's Pyrrhus, that excessive consumer both of his own body and spirits and of the human material of Troy. Hamlet sees himself needing to wake from the dream that is nonconsumption, to breathe in the world and eat it in order to produce blood and choler, the fluids requisite for violent action: "it cannot be / But I am pigeon-liver'd, and lack gall / To make oppression bitter" (576–78).[58] To have such gall—what Pyrrhus, like

---

56. Roland Barthes speaks of the strangeness of hearing oneself speak, the voice "reaching us after traversing the masses and cavities of our own anatomy"; see "Listening," in *The Responsibility of Forms*, trans. Richard Howard (Berkeley and Los Angeles: University of California Press, 1985), 254–55. I owe this reference to Bruce Smith, *The Acoustic World of Early Modern England: Attending to the O-Factor* (Chicago: University of Chicago Press, 1999), 27–28.

57. Joseph Hall, *Meditations and Vows: Divine and Moral*, ed. Charles Sayle (London: Grant Richards, 1901), 98.

58. On the pigeon's (or dove's) proverbial lack of gall, see *A Dictionary of the Proverbs in England in the Sixteenth and Seventeenth Centuries*, ed. Morris Palmer Tilley (Ann Arbor: University

Laertes and Fortinbras, has in spades—is the requisite psychophysiology of physical action, no matter how that action is morally and ethically to be defined.[59] Hamlet here reasons inductively from behavioral deficit to bodily lack, from lethargy to lacking a gall bladder, thus rationalizing his lack of purposive activity, his seeming inability to rouse himself to a murderous revenge. Moreover, in this reciprocal ecology of the passions, to lack a gall bladder oneself is also to fail to spread the bodily entrails of others elsewhere, so that one's own bodily loss translates into a deficit in the natural order: "I should 'a' fatted all the region kites"—birds with big stomachs—"with this slave's offal" (579–80). The prince should feed the birds with the corporeal leavings of his manhunt.

In this depressed interaction between a grief-laden, "muddy" mind and a body physiologically unproductive of the heat and blood required for purposeful action against the usurper king, Hamlet finds a humoral diagnosis, though not an excuse, for his emotional inconstancy:

> The spirit that I have seen
> May be a [dev'l], and the [dev'l] hath power
> T'assume a pleasing shape, yea, and perhaps
> Out of my weakness and my melancholy,
> As he is very potent with such spirits,
> Abuses me to damn me.
>
> (2.2.598–603)

Hamlet sees himself here as too open and vulnerable to influences brought in and through the air, a victim of the pneumatic character of life. But such vulnerability is a constant peril for—indeed almost a natural outcome of—early modern conceptions of subjectivity dependent on the ceaseless interactivity of fluids, spirits, and world to explain behavior and affect. The resulting construction is of subjectivity prone to continual emotional transformation, thanks to the ongoing tumult or even just the continual movements of inner bodily fluids and their exchanges with the world.[60] This is true even of Pyrochles, whose violence constantly expends

---

of Michigan Press, 1950), D574; it was the pigeon's meekness that associated it not only with cowardly men but also with dupes.

59. This is the physiological counterpart to the willfulness that Frank Whigham so brilliantly discusses in *Seizures of the Will in Early Modern English Drama* (Cambridge: Cambridge University Press, 1996), 31–32.

60. On this subject, see Paster, *Body Embarrassed*, 10–11.

and renews itself in characteristic, if monolithic, interactions with his human and physical environment as he forever seeks the old hag Occasion. In *The Anatomy of Melancholy*, the early modern English work most vividly expressive of humoral psychology, the human subject—male or female, melancholy or not—is indeed prey to such constant emotional change. As Burton sees the human spectacle, "Our villages are like mole-hills, and men as so many Emots, busie, busie still, going to and fro, in and out, and crossing one anothers projects ... *Now light and merry, ... by-and-by sorrowfull and heavy, now hoping, then distrusting, now patient, to morrow crying out; now pale, then red; running, sitting, sweating, trembling, halting, &c.*" (1:274). Burton wishes to marry this perception of humoral mutability to a generally tragic view of the world: "Even in the midst of all our mirth, jollity, and laughter, is sorrow and griefe: or if there bee true happinesse amongst us, 'tis but for a time" (1:275). But in humoralism per se, except for the relentless drying and cooling of the aging process, there is no overall pattern or progression from happy to sad within the individual subject. There is only humoral change itself brought about by the continual, reciprocal interaction of body, mind, culture, and the environment.

For the humorally interested reader, other evidence of the psychophysiological reciprocity of self and world—thus ways of reading inwardness otherwise—is everywhere to be found in *Hamlet*. Out of the welter of possibilities in this phenomenologically dense play, I will follow out the sequence of events in the hectic aftermath of Hamlet's staging of *The Murder of Gonzaga*, that scandalous act of dramaturgical insertion, because—like the player's speech about Pyrrhus—it offers up a portrait of wrath (and other key emotions) in ecologically significant terms. The sequence I am especially interested in begins with the wordplay between Hamlet and Guildenstern after Claudius has abruptly halted the play at the instant poison is poured into the sleeping player king's ear. "The King, sir," Guildenstern reports to the momentarily jubilant prince, "is in his retirement marvellous distemp'red" (3.2.299–301). Since the received meanings of distemper included intoxication (*OED*, 4d), Hamlet's reply, "With drink, sir?" may be disingenuous but it is lexically apropos. He facetiously ignores the part he himself has played as cause of the king's distress and makes Claudius himself responsible. The self-defensive jibe is both personal and political, given the disapproval Hamlet has already expressed in 1.4 about the king's sponsorship of public drinking games and the national shame attendant thereon: it

makes us traduc'd and tax'd of other nations.
They clip us drunkards and with swinish phrase
Soil our addition.

(1.4.18–20)

Guildenstern's perhaps surprised, perhaps exasperated correction of the
prince's willful misunderstanding—"No, my lord, with choler"—is probably
intended to clarify and narrow distemper's range of reference and to intim-
idate the prince. The king is not drunk, nor (as Guildenstern might imagine
Hamlet to be hoping) is he fearful. The passion that distempers him is
anger.

It is helpful to recognize that, with no loss of meaning or rhetorical efficacy, Guildenstern might easily have used *anger* to describe Claudius's passion in the first place; in the humoral lexicon, as we have seen, signifier and
substance easily change places. But "choler"—body fluid and raging motion,
yellow bile and anger—keeps Claudius's emotions strongly within the flesh.
Indeed, it is because Guildenstern uses the word "choler" that Hamlet can
continue, with rude semantic pertinence, to taunt him about the king's distemper and his own therapeutic recommendations for curing it: "Your wisdom should show itself more richer to signify this to the doctor, for for me
to put him to his purgation would perhaps plunge him into more choler"
(3.2.305–7). As G. R. Hibbard notes, Hamlet's sardonic reply brings together
three forms of purging—medical, legal, and spiritual—though his reference
to Claudius's physician ensures that medical purgation is the primary sense
operative here.[61] Purgation was, in fact, prescribed for choler. The Puritan
diarist Ralph Josselin records taking syrup of roses for an attack of ague: it
"wrought very kindly with me, gave me 9 stools brought away much
choler."[62] Clearly the physical and the psychological are indistinguishable in
such a self-report. Here, the idea of purgation allows Hamlet both to flaunt
his mock concern for Claudius and to threaten the king indirectly with a
bloodletting, the purgation of bad blood through phlebotomy. The even
more humiliating option—Hamlet's sly implication that Guildenstern
would be stupid enough to ask him, rather than the king's physician, to
administer a cathartic dose to Claudius either rectally or orally—brings us
close to a cluster of early modern health practices and habits of thought. As
I have argued elsewhere, scatology was a primary discourse in the period

61. Hibbard's note to *Hamlet*, 3.2.289.
62. Quoted in Lucinda McCray Beier, "In Sickness and in Health: A Seventeenth-Century
Family's Experience," in *Patients and Practitioners: Lay Perceptions of Medicine in Pre-Industrial
Society*, ed. Roy Porter (Cambridge: Cambridge University Press, 1985), 117.

for the expression of aggression in unequal power relations, especially between men.[63] If bodily fluids are the stuff of emotions, then to alter the character and quantity of a body's fluids is to alter that body's passions and thus that body's state of mind and soul. Here Hamlet, scandalously and powerfully occupying the position of Claudius's doctor, imagines himself both administering a purge to the royal body and refusing to do so, in a humiliation of Claudius doubled and redoubled by the image of Hamlet as the man who can, but will not, heal the body of the king. His purposeful misunderstanding allows the king's body to become the site of a humiliating practical joke, an anally sadistic, involuntary, jest-book purge of the sort that a Scogin or a Skelton might deliver to one of his opponents.[64]

But the performance of the play, for its startled onlookers, has been a penetrative practical joke—an attempted catharsis—of just this psychophysiological sort, capturing the aggressive potential of dramatic fictions to change the minds and bodies of their onlookers.[65] At the end of the second soliloquy, Hamlet declares that he intends *The Murder of Gonzaga* to penetrate the king:

> I'll observe his looks,
> I'll tent him to the quick.
>
>   (2.2.596–97)

"Tent" here not only means to observe him deeply (*OED*, v.1c) in apposition to "observe his looks," but it also means to probe his mind (*OED*, v.4a) to a depth where the probing tool must strike a nerve. A tent was a medical probe, inserted into a wound diagnostically to examine it but also used to keep it open and unable to heal—so humoral therapeutics went—in order for it to express corrupt bodily matter. Here, as with other psychophysiological references, the sense of what will take place in Claudius's mind is a physical one, with the words and actions inserted by Hamlet into the text of the play as a probe intended to make so deep an impression on the king's

63. See my discussions of purging as a form of attack in Paster, *Body Embarrassed*, 113–43; and Gail Kern Paster, "Purgation as the Allure of Mastery," in *Material London Circa 1600*, ed. Lena Cowen Orlin (Philadelphia: University of Pennsylvania Press, 2000), 193–205.

64. The medical and the scatological intermingle promiscuously in these jest books; for examples, see "Selections from *Scogin's Jests*," in *A Nest of Ninnies, and Other English Jestbooks of the Seventeenth Century*, ed. P. M. Zall (Lincoln: University of Nebraska Press, 1970); and *Jest upon Jest: A Selection from the Jestbooks and Collections of Merry Tales Published from the Reign of Richard III to George III*, ed. Bruce R. Wardroper (London: Routledge and Kegan Paul, 1970).

65. Cynthia Marshall, *The Shattering of the Self: Violence, Subjectivity, and Early Modern Texts* (Baltimore: Johns Hopkins University Press, 2002), esp. 106–10.

brain that, tentlike, it will keep the impression open—an immovable, ineradicable memory.[66] (Perhaps the probing is tentlike too in causing Claudius to later describe his deed as if it were a piece of decaying matter: "O, my offense is rank, it smells to heaven" [3.3.36].) During the play, Hamlet sees the effect of his inserted words on his mother also as purgative, when he describes the player queen's scandalous posy ("In second husband let me be accurs'd! / None wed the second but who kill'd the first" [3.2.179–80]) as "wormwood" (181), the bitter-tasting medicine taken internally as a vermifuge to scour the entrails.[67] Later, when he goes to his mother's closet promising to "speak [daggers] to her, but use none" (3.2.396), he imagines her body, like Claudius's, as penetrable but rejects the prospect of physical violence for the verbal substitute.

At this point we can assume that, for both royal onlookers, watching the play has caused an aggravation of choler rather than its release. Certainly it has had the psychophysiological effect on Claudius that Hamlet desired: the sight startles the king into publicly betraying a passion. How to interpret that passion, as fear, anger, or guilt, is precisely the unspoken issue in this dialogue between Hamlet and Guildenstern. As Hamlet's puns and willful misunderstandings in the exchange suggest, the force of his remarks depends upon a commonplace semantic overlap between physiological and political discourses. In 1600 the imbalances or disturbances to which the word *distemper* could refer involved disorder in the body politic as in the natural body, disturbances of climate and air, or general imbalances and a disproportionate mixture of parts. ("Here therefore is the first distemper of learning," says Bacon in the *Advancement of Learning*, "when men study words and not matter.")[68] The linkages among these meanings depend, as we have seen before, on the nested system of spirits in the universe, on the pneumatic character of life. As with so many other events in the play, the disturbance brought about locally by the scandal of *The Mousetrap*—a commotion simultaneously physical, psychological, and political in nature— affects the onlookers' bodies, minds, and sense of well-being. It changes the cultural atmosphere and disturbs the air with its images of murder and poisoning. The spectacle of a player king being murdered by his player

66. The thinking here approximates Descartes's notion of the operations of wonder on the brain, as described by Susan James, 99; see also the account of wonder in Lorraine Daston and Katharine Park, *Wonders and the Order of Nature, 1150–1750* (New York: Zone Books, 1998), 13–17.

67. See Janet Adelman, *Suffocating Mothers: Fantasies of Maternal Origin in Shakespeare's Plays, "Hamlet" to "The Tempest"* (London: Routledge, 1992), 31.

68. Francis Bacon, *The Advancement of Learning* (1.4.§3), in *The Advancement of Learning and New Atlantis*, ed. Arthur Johnston (Oxford: Clarendon Press, 1974), 26.

nephew would thus cause distemper not only in the "real" king but—for different reasons and with a different set of emotions—in the guests invited to the court performance as well, themselves representative of the national culture and the larger body politic. In the context provided by Hamlet's bitter self-reproaches about bodily lack and social passivity in 2.2, the cultural activity of sponsoring a decidedly offensive play represents a form of aggressive appropriation—in psychophysiological terms—of the collective spirits of the court, an attempt to master the visual and auditory field. And indeed we see how instantly inspiriting it is for him to create such a large effect both on his parents and on his social environment. In the aftermath of the performance's abrupt dissolution, he calls with defiant inappropriateness for musical celebration—"come, some music! Come the recorders" (3.2.291–92)—as if attempting to prolong his mastery of the auditory field, to impose his emotional will through music on the air. When Guildenstern asks him to "voutsafe a word with him," the newly energized prince promises, "Sir, a whole history" (296–97). The prince's change in mood from the depression and humiliation of 2.2 to the bold jubilation here is not only easy to spot but also easy to comprehend given the tremendous emotional and phenomenological impact of the aborted production on the entire court. From being "unpregnant of my cause" in social degradation and passivity, Hamlet is now subjectively and affectively full—of desires (for music), of words (a whole history), of threatening wordplay about the king's condition, and even of the pneumatic character of life itself. In a self-report that effectively and precisely reverses the pneumatic imagery of beards plucked and blown in the face, of lies given deep in the throat, he boasts to Guildenstern that he is not a wind instrument at the mercy of those with the breath to play on him: "'Sblood, do you think I am easier to be play'd on than a pipe? Call me what instrument you will, though you fret me, [yet] you cannot play upon me" (3.2.369–72).

But for understanding the ecological significance of Hamlet and Guildenstern's exchange, there are contexts even wider than this pneumatology of the wind and its instruments, contexts that involve the causal networks of body, mind, and world invoked by the words of player nephew Lucianus as he pours poison into the sleeping player king's ear:

> Thoughts black, hands apt, drugs fit, and time agreeing,
> [Confederate] season, else no creature seeing.
> Thou mixture rank, of midnight weeds collected,
> With Hecat's ban thrice blasted, thrice [infected],

> Thy natural magic and dire property
> On wholesome life usurps immediately.
>
> (3.2.255–60)

The incantatory quality of these lines results, I think, as much from the succession of feminine couplet-rhymes as from the demonic imagery. But I am more interested in the cosmology implied and rhetorically constructed by Lucianus's melodramatic set of fatal convergences—first, a correspondence in his body between murderous mind and its physical agents, the "apt" hands; then a correspondence between this body and the natural world that it finds so convenient for its intents. The picture is not the modern one of a disembodied mind instrumentalizing a set of neutral objects—hands, weeds, drugs, time, and the natural world—but, as with Pyrrhus moving through Troy, of a coconspiracy of like material agencies. Political terms of confederacy and usurpation undergird these analogies even as they emphasize the political meaning of the event. Putting Lucianus's mind fully into his body is to see a mind (like Pyrrhus's) blackened symbolically with violent intention and physically with choler or rage; it is to understand hands "apt" in two senses, both as physically capable and as, in effect, morally willing. This human agency is itself met and extended responsively by properties inherent in nature, time, and the "confederate" season. Time "agrees" with the murder not only by affording Lucianus his opportunity but also, in league with the season, by providing times of day when the different properties in life forms would change in response to the natural and cosmological environment. Thus a poisoner collects "midnight weeds"—weeds at midnight, weeds black as midnight—for maximum toxicity, weeds that work metonymically to become the natural symbols of as well as agents for black thoughts.[69] Though the mixture's rankness has presumably been augmented by witchy words, the weeds' toxic cycles belong to them alone in relations of sympathy and antipathy, as their "dire property" and way of being in the world. Their force here depends not only on the literal action of poison on the human body but also—as we have seen in Burton's account of love between palm trees—on conventional understandings of the appetite to do harm or good as it was thought to exist in the vegetal

---

69. The belief in weeds' toxicity at night was proverbial; see "Root of hemlock digg'd i'th' dark" (*Macbeth*, 4.1.25); and [Gerardus], *True Tryall and Examination of Mans Owne Selfe*, trans. Thomas Newton (London, 1602), where the apothecary is asked to examine himself if he "haue superstitiously obserued or fondly stayed for choise dayess or houres, . . . in gathring his herbs or other simples for the making of his drougs and receipts" (51).

world.[70] In Lucianus's words, then, we should recognize the cosmological assumptions common to the multiple puns on distemper, choler, and purgation in the conversation between Hamlet and Guildenstern that takes place so soon thereafter. In both speeches, human passions—here the passion of anger—occur fully within the natural order and take on an elemental force and character contingent upon a fully realized, if only partially articulated, set of correspondences between inner and outer worlds, between the human body and the world in which it feels and acts in continuous, dynamic reciprocity.[71]

These same correspondences inform the scene's rhetorical and emotional climax when Hamlet, picking up the demonic accents and mood of the murderous Lucianus, melodramatically proclaims a correspondence, new in him but familiar to us in the actions of Pyrrhus, between night and his own state of mind:

> 'Tis now the very witching time of night,
> When churchyards yawn and hell itself [breathes] out
> Contagion to this world. Now could I drink hot blood,
> And do such [bitter business as the] day
> Would quake to look on.
>
>   (388–92)

Midnight as represented here is both frightening to the imagination and physically unhealthy, with churchyards yawning up not only ghostly visitors to trouble the conscience but also noxious exhalations to trouble the porous flesh of the humoral body. But even more important for the psychological and physiological correspondences I have been tracing is the literalizing trope of Hamlet's vampirelike bloodthirstiness, in which he expresses a desire for vengeance in imagery reminiscent of Pyrrhus's rampage through Troy. The drink being called for here seems specifically to be human blood, one of the bodily fluids—along with breast milk, urine, and

70. See Pouchelle, 159, and the metaphorical tables on 207–17.

71. As John Sutton points out, disease was understood through "analogies from animal and vegetal worlds in which improper matter intrudes across the seals of the human body"; see "Body, Mind, and Order: Local Memory and the Control of Mental Representations in Medieval and Renaissance Sciences of Self," in *1543 and All That: Image and Word, Change and Continuity in the Proto-Scientific Revolution*, ed. Guy Freeland and Anthony Corones (Dordrecht: Kluwer Academic, 2000), 135. In *Hamlet*, such imagery has already characterized the ghost's report of his own poisoning, when his body becomes "bark'd about" (1.5.71) and treelike with scabby eruptions. And it returns full force in the closet scene when Hamlet describes Claudius as corrupted vegetable matter—"a mildewed ear" of corn "blasting his wholesome brother" (3.4.64–65) and tells his mother not to spread the "compost on the weeds" of lecherous behavior "to make them ranker" (151–52).

mummia—that could be ingested for therapeutic purposes. In medicinal contexts, drinking animal or human blood was widely recommended as a curative for states like sorrow, which cooled and dried the body.[72] In *Three Books on Life*, Ficino recommends it as an antidote to the cooling and drying processes of melancholy old age, to be taken with an equal amount of sugar and wine under a waxing moon.[73] The heat of new blood would contain courage and capacity to act as *its* properties, properties it transmitted to the drinker when ingested. The blood Hamlet speaks of drinking here probably would not belong to Claudius, because Hamlet thinks of it as preparatory to his "bitter business." Drinking blood was proverbially understood as an inducement to homicide. There is a similar passage in Jonson's *Catiline*, when the arch-conspirator seeks to embolden his followers by giving them a cup of wine filled with a slave's blood:

> I'haue killed a slaue,
> And of his bloud caus'd to be mixt with wine.
> Fill euery man his bowle.
>
> (1.483–85)[74]

The blood Hamlet desires here belongs to someone unknown and imaginary—to someone, like Pyrrhus, even more ready to kill than Hamlet now feels himself to be. I read Hamlet's declaration as the psychophysiological expression of a new mood and interest, a material change in consciousness brought about temporarily by the provocative images of the play, Claudius's vehement reaction to it, the sharp exchange with Rosencrantz and Guildenstern, and Gertrude's invitation to her closet. As Hamlet's impulse to drink blood becomes indistinguishable from a desire to shed it, killing becomes a drinking that expresses the moment. The word of the father— the imposition to revenge—overlaps fully with therapeutic protocols, as Hamlet imagines himself suddenly (if momentarily) ready to kill.

My point is that Hamlet's thirst here bespeaks not only the suddenness of his access to rage but also his natural embeddedness in the world and his openness to the cues of time and season, cues he has helped to arrange. He proclaims his readiness "now" for the heart-stimulating, anger-inducing drink of "hot blood." Furthermore, in his promise not to let "the soul of Nero

72. The *ODEP* lists the proverbial expression "Sorrow is always dry" (S656).

73. See Marsilio Ficino, *Three Books on Life* (2.11), ed. and trans. Carol V. Kaske and John R. Clark (Binghamton, NY: Medieval and Renaissance Text Society, 1989), 197, 199.

74. I follow the text of *Catiline* in *Ben Jonson*, ed. C. H. Herford and Percy Simpson, vol. 5 (Oxford: Clarendon, 1937). G. R. Hibbard cites this passage in his edition of *Hamlet*, note to 3.2.373.

enter this firm bosom," to "speak [daggers]" to his mother "but use none" (3.2.394, 396), we should note echoes of the earlier use of purgative discourse. Here, instead of the words and images of a play deeply "tenting" its audience's minds, Hamlet anticipates an aggressive attack of words alone—words as daggers effecting a psychological wounding of his mother rather than the actual wounding he tries not to desire. For such a psychological opening of Gertrude to have the effect of purging her is close to Hamlet's deepest desires in the play—to purify a mother contaminated by sexuality.[75] That Hamlet expresses the need for an external stimulant as he prepares to face the dangerous consequences of his scandalous play seems less important to me than his desire to incorporate the behavioral properties belonging to another's differently tempered blood. We ought, I think, to interpret this new appetite as a sign of release from melancholic depression, the burgeoning of a desire to be ready physiologically and psychologically for an outburst of rage against his mother and for sudden physical action (like stabbing through an arras), the burgeoning of a longing for cure.

But the evanescence of such a transformation goes without saying, on at least two counts. One comes from Hamlet's own sense of how hard won and soon lost any change in temper must be. No sooner has Hamlet himself responded heatedly to the cues of the play than, in the very next scene, watching Claudius kneel, he indulges in a Pyrrhus-like moment of hesitation without a Pyrrhus-like return of choleric arousal. Unlike Lucianus at a similar moment in the passage quoted above, he finds time and season not to be in league with him when he finds Claudius apparently at prayer. The moment—which had seemed so promising for murder when Claudius was reported to be "in choler"—is suddenly not right because of the apparent self-purgation of choler through prayer with which Claudius has preempted his attack. Hamlet's address to his sword—"Up, sword, and know thou a more horrid hent" (3.3.88)—acknowledges the sudden change in atmosphere. It imagines a more "confederate" time and place, imagines too that the weapon, personified like Pyrrhus's fell one, has appetites responsive to and as variable as his own. And the address also presumes a high degree of psychological variability in the mind and body of his opponent, hoping to find him

> When he is drunk asleep, or in his rage,
> Or in th'incestious pleasure of his bed,

75. Adelman, *Suffocating Mothers*, 31–35.

At game a-swearing, or about some act
That has no relish of salvation in't—
Then trip him, that his heels may kick at heaven,
And that his soul may be as damn'd and black
As hell, whereto it goes.

(3.3.89–95)

The irony (obvious to readers of the play) is that Claudius experiences his soul and body, his "bosom black as death" (3.3.67), his "limed soul," as hardened by the effects of murder and fulfilled ambition and with perplexed ambivalence does and does not long for them to be softer:

Make assay,
Bow, stubborn knees, and heart, with strings of steel,
Be soft as sinews of the new-born babe.

(69–71)

The effects of psychological materialism register here in Claudius's metallurgic pun on assay (symptomatic of the flesh-earth analogy), in the buried humoralism that makes young flesh soft and moist, in the overall materialist premise that body might act upon soul to produce affective change. Such would be the self-administration of a physic of kneeling as concomitant to the physic of prayer, both defeated by the condition of a soul "limed" (68)— hence materially altered, Bacon would say—by its sticky appetite for "crown, mine own ambition, and my queen" (55).

For Hamlet at this point in the play, as we learn from his spontaneous murder of Polonius, neither abstaining from killing nor killing itself effects a further hardening into wrath—as it did for Pyrrhus. In Gertrude's closet, after excoriating his mother for the shame of her "compulsive ardure," the lust mutinying in her bones (3.4.86, 83), he begs the Ghost not to look upon him with pity,

Lest with this piteous action you convert
My stern effects, then what I have to do,
Will want true color—tears perchance for blood.

(3.4.128–30)

Tears for blood, weeping for drinking—such are the swift metamorphoses of humoral corporeality. Thus the second count for the evanescence of Hamlet's several transformations in the play comes from humoralism generally, a way of thinking about bodily behavior that—I have argued here—finds it much easier to account for a subject's moment-to-moment fluctuations in mood and action than to account for emotional steadiness and a high degree of psychological self-sameness. In humoralism, even the wrath-roasted Pyrrhus has a moment of material difference from himself before he returns to slaughter, while Hamlet achieves the relative steadiness of mood that critics have often noted only after leaving Denmark for a indeterminate space of time. Psychological self-sameness presupposes disembodied consciousness, not the humoral subject's full immersion in and continuous interaction with a constantly changing natural and cultural environment. From this point of view, the volatility that characterizes Hamlet's behavior and moods until his return from the aborted trip to England is to be understood less as a striking feature of his disembodied personality and more as a humoral inevitability, given the myriad complexities of his predicament as Shakespeare represents them. Early modern behavioral thought understood such complexity and used humoralism and the pneumatic character of life—at least in part—to explain them.

It is only with great difficulty, I have been suggesting, that we can read the early modern passions *as from within* an early modern embodied consciousness. We might begin to do so if we could imagine for a moment, as Hamlet does, what it might be like to want to drink hot human blood. But this recognition of phenomenological difference can arise even with locutions that, because they now seem metaphorical, reproduce literal, early modern understandings of the bodily core of affective expression. Again, as with *Hamlet*, I want to start with a familiar passage from *Othello* and work outward to see how such locutions may offer glimpses of phenomenological alterity important for our understanding of early modern interiority and affect.

In act 3, scene 4 of *Othello*, Desdemona expresses bewilderment over the sudden transformation in her husband's behavior. "My lord is not my lord," she tells Cassio and Iago, "nor should I know him / Were he in favor as in humor alter'd" (3.4.124–25). Her distinction here between "favor" and "humor"—the lack of change in Othello's external appearance contrasting strongly with a profound alteration of mood within—is something more specific than the Renaissance commonplace describing the gap between "a socially visible exterior and an invisible personal interior."[76] For Desdemona follows this observation with an explanation tending toward medical diagnosis:

---

76. I am quoting Maus, 12.

Something sure of state . . .
Hath puddled his clear spirit.

(140, 143)

Desdemona's reference to Othello's puddled spirit presents semantic transformation in handily encapsulated form. Because her words yield readily to
abstract paraphrase—"surely something has troubled Othello's calm disposition"—modern readers have no trouble responding with sympathetic
understanding to Desdemona's general point that her husband's characteristic way of meeting the world is no longer the same. Any possible misunderstanding of her words could be remedied by the *Oxford English
Dictionary*'s definitions for the homely verb *to puddle*: meaning 3a is "to
make water muddy or dirty," while just below, in 3b, *puddle* means "to mud-
dle, confuse, to sully the purity or clearness of." For the *OED*, figurative and
literal meanings of *puddle* coexist in such close proximity that the graphic
image of a shallow body of water being dirtied disappears readily behind an
abstract idea of mental or emotional confusion. The difference between the
two meanings seems entirely obvious to us, because—despite the advent of
new cognitive paradigms about emotions as neurochemical events—conceptual boundaries between the psychological and the physical, between
subject and object, still obtain.

But the firm inscription of such boundaries has yet to occur for early
modern characters such as Desdemona. For them, emotional and physical
transformations are ontologically inseparable: substance embodies significance and vice versa. While the strong connotations of incorporeality that
"spirit" has for us make it most natural to interpret the word at this moment
in *Othello* in abstract terms as "a particular character, disposition, or temper
existing in, pervading or animating a person . . . ; a special attitude or bent
of mind" (*OED*, 8a), early modern usage marks a difference. Even the words
of this definition—words such as "temper" or "bent" of mind—are modern
abstractions from once material bodily phenomena, so that the definition of
"spirit" contains the historical processes I am seeking to make clear. As we
have seen, multiple connotations of corporeality existed for "spirit," not
only the pneumatic spirits that Bacon located in all things, but physiological
spiritus as well, the medical term referring to those three vaporous fluids—
natural spirits, vital spirits, and animal spirits—that were concocted out
of blood and inspired air and that served as "the source of all activity in
the living body."[77] When Desdemona wonders what in the world has

77. Park, "Organic Soul," 469.

caused her husband's sudden anger—whether "something . . . Either from
Venice, or some unhatch'd practice / Made demonstrable here in Cyprus"
(140–42)—she uses "spirit" to mean all of Othello's faculties (cognitive, emotional, and physical) and hence his characteristic bodily habitus. She constructs his mind as a physical place where the clear fluid of bodily spirit has
become stopped when it should flow out, a place containing turbid wastewater that befouls what it should rather cleanse and irrigate. Since puddles
tend to collect in low places (the word *puddle* being derived from the Old
English word *pudd*, meaning ditch or furrow), her picture of the puddled
spirit points to the animal spirits inhabiting the complex enfoldings
and cavities of the brain. But for proper working, the animal spirits needed
above all to be transparent. In perturbations, says Felix Plater, "*some matter
mixt with the Spirits* doth cloud obscure, darken the animal Spirits which
ought to be bright clear lucid and most pure."[78] Thomas Walkington argues,
"where there is a fulnes and repletion of infected and malignant humors,
where the subtill spirits be not onely tainted but even corrupted with puddle humors . . . the cleare chrystalline and rarified spirits can by no means
brooke, as beeing disturbers of their noblest actions" (97). Bright argues that
in the person "where that naturall and internall light is darkened, their fan-
sies arise vayne, false, and voide of ground: euen as in the externall sensible
darkenes, a false illusion will appeare vnto our imagination" (100). While
Desdemona does not know the efficient cause of Othello's transformation,
her language suggests that she is thinking here in material terms about how
passions—perturbations of the soul—work within the body. Thomas
Fienus, the great Louvain professor of medicine, explains: "through the
emotions the humors and spirits are borne upwards, downwards, within
and without . . . Since the imagination produces change by means of the
emotions and the emotions produce change by means of the natural movement of the heart and by means of the movement of the humors and
spirits, the imagination does also."[79]

In the great activity of spirits moving between heart, brain, and body
lie the effects and the expression of all passions—especially, perhaps,
those passions of melancholy and anger, which, as Desdemona knows,
puddle the spirit and darken the mind. Burton remarks that as the heart,

78. Felix Plater, Abdiah Cole, and Nicholas Culpeper, *A Golden Practice of Physick* (London:
Peter Cole, 1662), 31–32; also quoted in Stanley W. Jackson, *Melancholia and Depression: From
Hippocratic Times to Modern Times* (New Haven, CT: Yale University Press, 1986), 94.

79. Thomas Fienus, *De viribus imaginationis* (1608), quoted in Theodore M. Brown, "Descartes,
Dualism, and Psychosomatic Medicine," in *The Anatomy of Madness: Essays in the History of
Psychiatry*, vol. 1, *People and Ideas*, ed. W. F. Bynum, R. Porter, and M. Shepherd (London: Tavistock,
1985), 48.

humors, and spirits "are purer, or impurer, so is the Minde, and equally suffers, as a Lute out of tune, if one string, or one organ be distempered, all the rest miscarry" (1:373). For Othello, the physical consequence of passion is that solubility—the early modern mantra of physical and emotional health—is imperiled by something aversive penetrating him from without to alter what he knows and what he is. In this sense, we might think of him as "pregnant" with Iago's cause. That aversive thing (which we know to be Iago's slanderous insinuation) causes the characteristically smooth, untrammeled flow of his body's clear fluids to slow, stop, congeal, and putrefy and, in so doing, to transform him from a calm into a jealously angry man. As Thomas Wright explains, the "Passions ingender Humours, and humours breed Passions" (64). Change of humor in Othello, then, occurs in a bodily register that is indistinguishably physical, psychological, and emotional. And it occurs in a semantic register in which, as we saw earlier in the case of black bile and choler, emotional change *resides* in internal bodily alteration. When this happens, the *OED*'s two meanings for the verb *to puddle* collapse into one, because, for all the early moderns, a confused and disordered spirit is not just metaphorically *like* a dirty puddle but really *is* a dirty puddle in the psychophysiological landscape of the brain.

Desdemona's imagery—of powerful feeling as a fluid changing in color from clear to dark and in motion from flowing to stopped—defines the onset of Othello's passion as the onset, literally, of psychosomatic disease. Such imagery represents ways of thinking about the "living, impassioned mind" that lead as far back in time as fifth century Greek tragedy or even Homer.[80] And the imagery also works to link Shakespeare's text, almost directly, to the ancient medical authorities whose views of the workings of the human body-soul composite and its interaction with the world still constituted dominant physical, psychological, and ideological truth in early modern Europe. It cannot be surprising, then, that both ancient poets and early modern ones "represent emotion as Hippocratics represent the causes and symptoms of disease: [as] internal liquid 'falling,' 'dripping,' flooding in and to the innards."[81] Once again, we need to remember that the physical model underlying ancient and early modern psychology is "a simple

80. Padel, 85; see also Richard Broxton Onians, *The Origins of European Thought about the Body, the Mind, the Soul, the World, Time, and Fate* (Cambridge: Cambridge University Press, 1951), 44–65.

81. Padel, 85. On the continuities between ancient and early modern physiological paradigms, see Kenneth D. Keele, "Physiology," in *Medicine in Seventeenth Century England*, ed. Allen G. Debus (Berkeley and Los Angeles: University of California Press, 1974), 148.

hydraulic one, based on a clear localisation of psychological function by organ or system of organs."[82]

The trace of such medical discourse in Desdemona's language localizes Othello's spirit in these terms. It entails the difficult knowledge that the dark puddle that has formed so disastrously in Othello's mind signifies peril—simultaneously physical and psychological—to the smooth functioning of all his faculties of agency. And the peril is especially fraught for those powers of cognition and speech that depend crucially on the clear flowing of the animal spirits from the cavities of the brain out to the body's organs. Because the onset of passion altered a subject's cognitive powers, his capacity to see and know, the puddling of Othello's "spirit" means the darkening and dirtying of Othello's world as Othello perceives and represents it to himself: "the Passions," says Wright, "not vnfitly may be compared to greene spectacles, which make all things resemble the colour of greene; euen so, he that loueth, hateth, or by any other passion is vehemently possessed, iudgeth all things that occur in fauour of that passion" (49). But the spectacles of Othello's passion are not green; they are much darker ones that give him a world-altering darkness of vision, mood, and representation.

To understand Desdemona's account of Othello's transformation in these terms allows us to see the work of physiology rather than metaphor elsewhere in the play. In 2.1, for example, having just been reunited with Desdemona in Cyprus after surviving a terrible storm at sea, Othello finds expression overwhelmed by joy: "I cannot speak enough of this content," he tells his wife. "It stops me here; it is too much of joy" (2.1.196–97). He speaks in part of the rhetorical inexpressibility of great joy, but mostly of joy's physiological effects. Wright explained why extreme joy could cause fainting or even death in these terms: "if the passion of pleasure be too vehement, questionles it causeth great infirmitie: for the heart being continually invuironed with great abundance of spirit, becomes too hot and inflamed, and consequently engendreth much cholericke and burned blood: Besides, it dilateth and resolveth the substance of the heart too much, I[n] such sort, that the vertue and force thereof is greatly weakned" (60). And he goes on to relate a story from Plutarch about Roman mothers who died for joy upon seeing their sons return home safely from battle.

The onset of emotion—a rush of spirituous blood to the heart—so floods Othello's being, so dilates his heart and swells the lungs, that for a moment he feels breathless, speechless. It "stops me," he says, "here"— pointing (I would argue) to his heart, his chest. The joy, being immoderate,

---

82. Park, "Organic Soul," 469.

feels dangerous enough to make Othello almost prefer leaving the calm of reunion and returning to the violence—of weather, Turks, and before that the angry father—that had separated them:

> If after every tempest come such calms,
> May the winds blow till they have waken'd death
>
> . . . .
>
> If it were now to die,
> 'Twere now to be most happy.
>
> (2.1.185–86, 189–90)

We have found meteorological commonplaces something like this in *Hamlet* when Aeneas likens Pyrrhus's hesitation before the murder of Priam to the stillness in the air before a storm or when Gertrude likens Hamlet's rage to the contention of wind and rain. Related associatively to the hydraulic modeling that links organs and psychological functions, such imagery derives ultimately from Hippocratic writings on the human body's susceptibility to air and waters. Thus Wright, describing physiological impediments to virtue, likens inconstancy to wind and sea: "This inconstancy raigneth not onely ouer the soule, at diuers times, as now the Sea ebbeth, now floweth, now is tempestuous, now calmed, but at the self same time it will, and will not . . . not vnlike to two contrary winds which at the self-same time tosse the clouds, one beneath, another aboue" (336). Edward Reynolds, bishop of Norwich, makes a similar comparison between weather and the passions in order to advocate the mean of bodily temperance: "As in the Wind or Seas, (to which two, Passions are commonly compar'd) a middle temper betweene a quiet Calme and a violent Tempest, is most serviceable for the passage between Countreyes; so the agitations of Passion, as long as they serve onely to drive forward, but not to drowne Vertue, . . . and run onely in that Channell wherewith they are thereby bounded, are of excellent service, in all the travaile of mans life" (60). In *Antony and Cleopatra* a similar understanding of the meteorology of passions informs Enobarbus's wry comment about Cleopatra's spectacular displays of emotion: "We cannot call her winds and waters sighs and tears; they are greater storms and tempests than almanacs can report" (1.2.147–49).

But Othello's language at this moment demonstrates how dangerous it is to compare strong feelings to the winds, for he imagines a marital weather of gusts and calms only, being blown about by passion and stopped by an ecstatic but deadly increase of joy. As we noted earlier with Pyrrhus's sudden change from abstraction back to wrath, to figure strong emotion as a surge coming from *somewhere else*, somewhere external to the self, not only disclaims any sense of possession of one's own feelings, but it also portrays the self as passively victimized by them. The meteorology of love here is just the kind of extreme weather in which there can be no safe passage between countries, no comfortable intercourse between husband and wife, no ongoing traffic of ordinary, domestic life. Othello's implication—that great passion is as humanly uncontrollable, unpredictable, and potentially devastating as violent weather, and causally as external to the self—prompts the alarmed Desdemona to invoke the only possible protection against it, the vision of a succession of divinely ordained days:

> The heavens forbid
> But that our loves and comforts should increase
> Even as our days do grow.
>
> (2.1.193–95)

To recognize the conventionality of such meteorological thinking about the passions is not thereby to underestimate its significance for early modern phenomenology, but to point again to the pneumatic character of premodern life and the humoral subject. Othello's language of being stopped "here" at the heart, like Desdemona's image of the puddled spirit, directs our attention inward, to representations of humoral transformations occurring in and through the movements of the passions. As joy floods the heart and stops the breath, so anger burns the body's interior—roasts it in wrath and fire—and blackens the fluid spirits of agency. Thus, in 2.3, emerging from his wedding chamber to calm the brawl that has broken out among the night watch, Othello becomes enraged by his men's refusal to tell him what has caused it. At that moment, he warns them, his heart's blood is heating in anger, and the sooty excrements formed in that central bodily furnace ascend to the brain to darken the rational faculties situated there:

> Now, by heaven,
> My blood begins my safer guides to rule,
> And passion, having my best judgment collied,
> Assays to lead the way.
>
> (2.3.204–7)[83]

---

83. "Collied" is the reading in F, "coold" in Q1. What I take to be Q's misreading is a plausible compositor error, but the meaning that results is exactly the opposite and makes no sense in terms of early modern physiology.

Here, as before with "puddled," meaning takes us literally to the body rather than to the disembodied psyche. "Collied," meaning blackened with coal dust or begrimed, tends to be missed by readers led astray by editorial tendencies to see Othello's phrase as metaphorical or responding to what they see as racist irony—the black man's unconscious acknowledgment of his innately intemperate disposition.[84] But, as Mary Floyd-Wilson has pointed out, the equation of blackness and passionateness was far from inevitable, because the temperament associated with blackness was susceptible to contradictory interpretations. Humoral tradition, which linked black skin to a "cool, dry, dispassionate complexion," sometimes allegorized blackness as a sign of constancy and wisdom. Emerging racial stereotypes, by contrast, linked blackness instead to an innate propensity to rage (132). Desdemona clearly subscribes to the former view when she denies the first signs of Othello's jealousy, telling Emilia,

> the sun where he was born
> Drew all such humors from him.

> (3.4.30–31)

But as we have seen with Pyrrhus roasted black as his purpose, choler "blackened" the consciousness of anyone caught in its grip. As Jacques Ferrand points out, melancholy came in three varieties; one was located in the "hypochondries" or upper belly, another spread through the body in the veins, and the third "arises from black choler engendered in the brain."[85] Othello's declaration of physiological change here seems the kind of warning to be expected from a commander facing the insubordinate silence of his men. And the racially threatening irony of the collying of his judgment is available in the play only retrospectively, once Othello, the dispassionate black man, has changed into the emerging modern stereotype—the gullible and jealous black man too easily moved to kill his wife.

There is more telling evidence of immoderate passion's physical effects on Othello's bodily spirits in the long sequence in 3.3, first when

84. See Norman Sanders's note on 2.3.186 in Shakespeare, *Othello*, ed. Norman Sanders (Cambridge: Cambridge University Press, 1984). Sanders glosses "blood" as "anger" so that his accurate gloss for "collied" as "darkened, blackened" seems equally figurative. Here again the *OED* defines the verb *to colly* as having literal and figurative meanings—blackening with coal dust, begriming and blackening in character, darkening—and quotes this line from *Othello* as illustrating figurative meaning. On the inversion of reason and passion in this speech, see also Parker, *Shakespeare from the Margins*, 49.

85. Jacques Ferrand, *A Treatise on Lovesickness*, trans. Donald A. Beecher and Massimo Ciavolella (Syracuse, NY: Syracuse University Press, 1990), 236.

Desdemona begins her suit to Othello on behalf of Cassio and later when Iago has thoroughly imbued Othello with doubt and jealousy. Desdemona presses her husband as to when he shall receive Cassio to hear the banished officer's suit for reinstatement:

> When shall he come?
> Tell me, Othello. I wonder in my soul
> What you would ask me that I should deny,
> Or stand so mamm'ring on.

$$(3.3.67-70)$$

Mammer, says the *OED*, means "to stammer, mutter," or "to vacillate, waver, be undecided." Here again the separated modern meanings—differentiating between the mental act of indecision as cause and the bodily act of disrupted speaking as effect—belie an early modern conceptual fusion. This fusion—the reciprocal, ontological expressiveness of mind and bodily organs—explains why the major physical sign of Othello's crisis of faith in Desdemona is a disruption of speech leading to loss of consciousness. As the passage of the spirits between his body and mind becomes increasingly agitated, Othello's behavior registers the literally inflammatory effects of Iago's graphic images of Desdemona's infidelity. Othello feels his bosom swell with its freight of bodily passion (3.3.449); we witness his increasing inarticulateness, the agonized burst of phrases that express the throes of passion and loss of rational control. "Why do you speak so startlingly and rash?" Desdemona asks in bewilderment as he interrogates her about the whereabouts of his handkerchief. "Is't lost? Is't gone? Speak, is't out o'th'way?" he demands in abrupt, staccato questions (4.1.79–80). Othello, for his part, cannot believe that images alone, produced only by the internal senses—thoughts unmotivated by external reality—could have such physical power over him: "Nature would not invest herself in such shadowing passion without some instruction. It is not words that shakes me thus. Pish! Noses, ears, and lips. Is't possible? Confess? Handkerchief? O devil!" he exclaims (3.4.39–43) before falling into what the Folio stage direction calls "a trance."[86] Iago's delighted reaction—"Work on, / My medicine, [work]!" (43–44)—suggests that, in the destruction he has accomplished, the physical and the psychological are inseparably implicated. Such misrecognition is, as we know, at the heart of Othello's jealous sickness, the consequence of

---

86. Q1's "*He fals downe*" captures the stage action as well, but without diagnostic implication. *Trance*, according to the *OED*, is derived from the French verb *transir*, meaning to pass, to depart, but also to be numbed by fear and cold.

the manifold physiological changes worked by what Iago calls the "poison" of "dangerous conceits," which "with a little act upon the blood / Burn like the mines of sulphur" (3.3.325–29), heating the blood—thickening, blackening, collying it.

Ironically (if unsurprisingly), Othello's profound misrecognitions of Desdemona, Iago, and Cassio do not prevent him from reporting the physical changes within himself in terms strikingly like Desdemona's image of the darkly puddled spirit. Othello has localized his love for Desdemona in his viscera, has held it within his body. His heart, in this respect as in others, is specifically an early modern one—its function understood not in post-Harveian terms as a pump, but rather as a capacious receptacle of blood and feelings. As Galen describes this action, "the heart, itself, having all imaginable attractive faculties, snatches and, as it were, drinks up the inflowing material, receiving it rapidly."[87] In storing blood and spirits, it also stored, as Robert Erickson has noted, "thoughts and secret feelings or one's inmost being"; it was "the source of desire, volition, truth, understanding" (11). With respect to the heart's other basic capacity, that of discharging blood, ancient and early modern discourses compared it to a "fountain, maintaining the vital economy of the body."[88] Both images—the heart as receptacle and the heart as fountain—haunt the jealous husband's perception and experience of his own fatally damaged affections. Once Othello is convinced of Desdemona's infidelity, what he comes to find unendurable is an acute sense of being repelled by his own viscera, being alienated from them or—even worse—being discarded by his own bodily substance as if he and his affections had become a standing pool of excrement: "Had it pleas'd heaven," he tells her,

> To try me with affliction, had they rain'd
> All kind of sores and shames on my bare head,
> Steep'd me in poverty to the very lips,
> Given to captivity me and my utmost hopes,
> I should have found in some place of my soul
> A drop of patience; but, alas, to make me
> The fixed figure for the time of scorn
> To point his slow [unmoving] finger at!
> Yet I could bear that too, well, very well;

87. Galen, *On the Usefulness of the Parts of the Body*, trans. Margaret Tallmadge May, 2 vols. (Ithaca, NY: Cornell University Press, 1968), 316. I owe this reference to Robert A. Erickson, *The Language of the Heart, 1600–1750* (Philadelphia: University of Pennsylvania Press, 1997), 7–8.

88. Erickson, 15.

> But there, where I have garner'd up my heart,
> Where either I must live or bear no life;
> The fountain from the which my current runs
> Or else dries up: to be discarded thence!
> Or keep it as a cestern for foul toads
> To knot and gender in!
>
> (4.2.47–62)

Much of the imagery in this painful passage finds metaphorical equivalents of Othello's anguish in scriptural allusion and features of the natural landscape—with "sores and shames" alluding to such punishments as blisters inflicted as a test on Job or as a plague on the Egyptians, poverty as a pool of abjection, the imagery of fountains and cisterns coming from Proverbs 5:15–18.[89] But, though clearly metaphorical in character and structure, the scriptural and natural imagery actually works to support the natural facticity of the emotions and the body as the source, site, and means of the emotions' occurrence. For here, as before in this play and everywhere in the period, affect itself and the affect-laden events being metaphorized are understood as liquid states—shame is a rain, poverty a steeping pool, patience a drop, and life itself the water running from a fountainhead or standing in a cistern.[90] At least two of the afflictions Othello says he would have preferred to being cuckolded are understood as physically transformative—the literal shame of skin disease or the near equivalent of shame in other forms and the poverty that, like steeping liquors, washes, or dyes, exacts a transformation—physical, social, and psychological—of the victimized subject. Other images bespeak the same conceptual fusion of matter and feeling, of body and psyche, that we have seen earlier in the play's characteristic locutions of strong emotion. Even more important, given what I have been arguing about the reciprocity governing the analogical relations of humoral self and world, Othello understands his emotions and the natural decay of a dried-up fountain or a toad-infested cistern to be mutually expressive, reciprocally significant. He feels the receptacle that is his heart polluted and fouled by the death of his passion, just as a body of water is

---

89. See Sanders's notes to *Othello*, 4.2.58–61. He quotes the Geneva version of Prov. 5:15–18: "Drink the water of thy cistern . . . Let thy fountain be blessed, and rejoice with the wife of thy youth."

90. The *OED* cites as a figurative use of *steep* a line from Chapman's translation of the *Odyssey*: "She . . . sweete sleepe / Powr'd on each wooer; which so laid in steepe / Their drowsie temples, that each brow did nod" (2.29). But sleep, understood to result from vapors rising to the brain, was a wetter state than being awake; hence the trope of being steeped in sleep is not entirely figurative.

fouled by the presence within it of decaying matter. This image of love decaying in a cistern may be conventional; in *Macbeth* this is precisely how Malcolm, testing Macduff by pretending to be morally unfit to govern Scotland, describes a sexual voluptuousness without bottom:

> Your wives, your daughters,
> Your matrons, and your maids could not fill up
> The cestern of my lust.
>
> (4.3.61–63)

Here in Othello, the significance of the figure again derives from a historical phenomenology: in a porous body, whose passions are literally elemental and whose affections are borne materially within the bodily cavity, damage in the relation to the beloved other is experienced as a thoracic wound. Thus the jealous Leontes announces that while Hermione lives, "my heart will be a burthen to me" (*Winter's Tale*, 2.3.206). In this context his fear that there is no "barricado for a belly," that "it will let in and let out the enemy" (1.2.204–5), refers not only to his conviction of his wife's infidelity but also to fears for his own bodily integrity. As David Hillman has remarked, "Leontes's refusal to acknowledge his wife's integrity is akin to a repudiation of his own interior, a visceral response to knowledge that leaves him feeling that the 'centre' of his body is in need of protection from encroaching knowledge" (95).

Leontes' experience of affliction in marriage helps us to read Othello's meaning here—to comprehend his failed husbanding of self and Other and, more important, to understand his crucial reference to "there, where I have garner'd up my heart" as pointing not to Desdemona herself, but to the love-relation with her that he holds in his own viscera within the storage space of his heart. Such an interpretation is, admittedly, counterintuitive for the modern reader, for whom "there" probably refers to Desdemona herself as Othello's now alienated domestic possession—the wife's body as "a storehouse, a geographical space, and finally as an aberration of nature."[91] But, as we shall see below, images of monstrous reproduction in the period need not refer to the female body or, indeed, to the female reproductive organs at all. What Othello is describing here is the self-alienated state of his *own* feelings, not Desdemona's, his sense of having lost wholesome self-possession and self-knowledge to another way of being in the world that is neither

---

91. John Drakakis, "The Engendering of Toads: Patriarchy and the Problem of Subjectivity in Shakespeare's *Othello*," *Shakespeare-Jahrbuch* (Weimar) 124 (1988): 74.

vital nor sound. The underlying psychophysiological ideal remains one of bodily solubility and transparency of fluids—both of which he signifies metaphorically as lost. What he reports instead is the death, corruption, or loathsome stagnation not within Desdemona's body (the absent presence in this speech) but in the wellsprings and pools of emotion that are his own viscera. His is a sense (I want to argue) peculiar to the psychological materialism of the early modern period, when organs had psychological functions and still located and organized feelings. It is a sense especially acute at a moment in the history of bodies, minds, and souls when the boundaries between inside and outside the body were more porous, when bodily fluids carried the full weight of a character's destiny, and, most important, when dense networks of "continuous reciprocal causation" linked body, mind, culture, and the physical world.[92] This is why Othello can imagine his viscera as an internal landscape, his organs and his vital fluids working within the internal economy of his body much as the features of a domestic landscape work in the natural world, a landscape with granaries and cisterns to store solid and liquid nourishment, with fountains or springs to move water from place to place—or not. This is why Othello can imagine wholesome affection itself as a bodily store, like that of foodstuff, to be consumed and replenished over time or to be transformed—here tragically—through the bodily workings of melancholy and rage.

Othello's dread of embodied emotion as a dark, murky, standing water in which toads knot and gender is thus no less a fear of what emotion hides from view than of what it expresses. Indeed his expression of fear is powerfully similar to what motivates Desdemona's figure of puddled spirit; it registers in a vehemence foreign to us but understandable in the early modern cultural imaginary, at a time when bodily fluids and the waters of nature were elementally unified and reciprocally expressive and when natural signs were theological encodings. Fear of stench and the odor of decay—stench not as symptomatic but as causative—was widespread in early modern Europe. Hydrology in the period saw standing water and the bad, miasmic air that it caused as a particular danger.[93] According to Thomas Dekker, such water was responsible for the great plague of 1603:

92. Sutton, *Philosophy and Memory Traces*, 40.

93. On the ideological valences of the civic water supply, see Jonathan Gil Harris, "This Is Not a Pipe: Water Supply, Incontinent Sources, and the Leaky Body Politic," in *Enclosure Acts: Sexuality, Property, and Culture in Early Modern England*, ed. Richard Burt and John Michael Archer (Ithaca, NY: Cornell University Press, 1994), 203–28. On the deep-seated fear of stench and mud, see Alain Corbin, *The Foul and the Fragrant: Odor and the French Social Imagination* (Cambridge, MA: Harvard University Press, 1986), 22–34.

From standing Pooles . . .
From boggs; from ranck and dampish Fenns,
From Moorish breaths, and nasty Denns,
The sun drawes vp contagious fumes.[94]

The idea of standing water as breeding contagion and disease is well
established in moral and theological discourses, where literal and symbolic meanings overlap and blend. The mid-sixteenth-century homily "A
Fruitfull Exhortation to the Readyng and Knowledge of Holy Scripture,"
for example, compares Scripture as "the welle of life" to the "stinkyng
podelles of mennes tradicions."[95] For Bishop Reynolds, water emblema-
tizes the action of the passions on the spirit and puddles stand as the
symbol of manifest corruption: "for what water more sweet," he asks
rhetorically, "than that of a Spring, or what more thick or lothsome, than
that which standeth in a puddle, corrupting it self" (60). And when
Burton, with characteristic lugubriousness, comes to imagine the terrible
uncertainties of mortal existence, the trope of filthy puddles occupies a
prominent place in the list of existential horrors: "the world it selfe is a
maze, a labyrinth of errors, a desert, a wildernesse, a denne of theeves,
cheaters, &c. full of filthy puddles, horrid rocks, precipitiums, an ocean of
adversity, an heavy yoke, wherein infirmities and calamities overtake and
follow one another as the Sea waves" (1:273). It is thus a simple semantic
extension for the heart damaged by sinfulness to be imagined as a container of foul liquids, "a foul sink of all atheism, sodomy, blasphemy,
murder, whoredom, adultery, witchcraft, buggery." And the roiling of
those foul liquids within the body's hidden recesses, according to the
New England Puritan Thomas Shepard, resembles nothing so much as
the hidden depths of a standing pool: "thou feelest not these things stirring in thee at once . . . but they are in thee like a nest of snakes in an old
hedge. Although they break not out into thy life, they lie lurking in thy
heart; they ar there as a filthy puddle in a barrel, which runs not out,
because thou happily wantest the temptation of occasion to broach and
tap thine heart."[96]

---

94. [Thomas Dekker], *News from Graves-End* (London, 1604), sigs. C3v–C4.

95. "A Fruitfull Exhortation to the Readyng and Knowledge of Holy Scripture," in *Certain
Sermons or Homilies (1547), and A Homily against Disobedience and Wilful Rebellion (1570): A
Critical Edition*, ed. Ronald B. Bond (Toronto: University of Toronto Press, 1987), 61.

96. Thomas Shepard, *The Sincere Convert* (1641), in *The Works of Thomas Shepard*, 3 vols.
(Boston: Doctrinal Tract and Book Society, 1853; reprint, New York: AMS Press, 1967), 1:28. I owe
this reference to Richard Rambuss, *Closet Devotions* (Durham, NC: Duke University Press, 1998), 57.

But even here in the heated tones of preacherly warnings, we must be careful not to assume that figurative discourses displace literal ones, or that the perceived danger of the puddles inside and outside the body was based on mostly wrong scientific reasoning. Analogies between an emblematically understood physical world and human physiology made puddles outside and puddles inside the body reciprocally and horribly coexpressive. Nashe in *The Terrors of the Night* likens filthy puddles to cognitive confusion much as Desdemona did, in terms strikingly like Othello's agonized terms of self-alienation here: "And even as slime and dirt in a standing puddle engender toads and frogs and many other unsightly creatures, so this slimy melancholy humor, still still [*sic*] thickening as it stands still, engendreth many misshapen objects in our imaginations ... Our reason even like drunken fumes it displaceth and intoxicates, and yields up our intellective apprehension to be mocked and trodden under foot by every false object or counterfeit noise that comes near it."[97] The horror for Nashe may be, as it is for Othello, the great uncertainty of physical process—with the standing puddle not just harboring toads and frogs but spawning them out of its own muddy substance.[98] Puddles and the toads in them, then, were iconic of that which was to be loathed: in *Troilus and Cressida*, Ajax hates a proud man "as I do hate the engendering of toads" (2.3.158–59). In *The Duchess of Malfi*, Antonio expresses his disdain for the melancholy Cardinal with these words: "the spring in his face is nothing but the engendering of toads" (1.1.158–59).[99] But it seems that the figure is rarely used, as it is here, to describe an aspect of oneself. For Othello it is the cistern of self that produces toads out of its own filthy psychophysiological substance.

At the beginning of the seventeenth century, it was still possible to believe that creatures spawned by puddles could spawn in the human body as well.[100] Thus a puddle was loathsome not only in itself; it was even more loathsome because the creatures engendered in its murky depths could multiply horribly in the bodies of those who slaked their innocent thirst in precisely the wrong places: "how comes it to passe," asks the naturalist Edward Topsell, "that in mens stomacks there are found frogs & toades?

---

97. Thomas Nashe, *The Terrors of the Night*, in *The Unfortunate Traveller and Other Works*, ed. J. B. Steane (Harmondsworth, UK: Penguin, 1972), 217.

98. On the theological literature involving toads, see Mary E. Robbins, "The Truculent Toad in the Middle Ages," in *Animals in the Middle Ages: A Book of Essays*, ed. Nona C. Flores (New York: Garland, 1996), 25–47.

99. Webster, *The Duchess of Malfi*.

100. Perhaps because they were thought to be venomous, toads were proverbially loathsome; see *ODEP*, 826–27.

I answer that this euill hapneth vnto such men as drinke water, for by drinking of water, a toades egge may easily slip into the stomack, & there being of a viscous nature, cleaueth fast to the rough parts of the ventricle, and it being of a contrary nature to man, can neuer be digested or auoyded."[101] In these theological images of the sinful body as a filthy sink and in the bodily horrors that, according to Topsell, happen to the unwary thirsty man may lie a gloss for the imagery of Othello's extraordinary, agonized self-perception in this passage. His love for Desdemona now seems to him like the ordinary thirst of a man who drinks water only to find a once unimaginable danger in this ordinary act of human appetite and need. Othello had stored affection in his heart as the good husbandman stores food in his granary or water in his cistern, "there where I must live or bear no life."[102] But sexual disgust and shame turn him against such fundamental acts of social and domestic self-perpetuation, transferring to socially sanctioned appetites and lawful reproductive sexuality the loathsomeness reserved for the knotty engendering of toads, acts of reproduction imagined to take place in—and because of—the befouled cistern that constitutes even as it houses the affections of the embodied self.

Modern readers recognize that these images of monstrous reproduction in a befouled inner landscape represent Othello's tragic internalization of the alienated account of his and Desdemona's sexual union, an account that, from the very beginning of the play, Iago has promulgated in order to bring about his enemy's destruction.[103] We have begun to recognize the significance of race, color, and geography as historical constructs deeply implicated in this tragic action and in the course of its reception. What we have tended not to see is how early modern physiological discourse determines the language of passion in *Othello*, undergirding the play's construction of gender, racial, and ethnic differences with a discourse of embodied passions in which all the play's early modern bodies—black and white, male and female, Florentine and Venetian and Moor—participate because it is the discourse in which all these early modern subjects necessarily think about the psychological sources of their own and others' behavior.

I wish to emphasize that to recognize the common referentiality of physiological discourse in the play is not to take away from the play's racial

101. Edward Topsell, *The Historie of Serpents* (London: Isaac Jaggard, 1608), 190–91.

102. These images of the domestic economy link this passage to the conventional association of the husband's labor and his cuckolding; see Douglas Bruster, *Drama and the Market in the Age of Shakespeare* (Cambridge: Cambridge University Press, 1992), 47–55.

103. See, for example, Michael Neill, "'Unproper Beds': Race, Adultery, and the Hideous in *Othello*," *Shakespeare Quarterly* 40 (1989): 383–412.

stigmatization or its construction of the bodily alterities by which the play's discourses of race and gender are naturalized. Nor by identifying the onset of Othello's passion in humoral terms can Othello's murder of Desdemona be exonerated. Humoralism cannot describe why Iago hates Desdemona but only how the currents of extreme emotion work to alter Othello's body and darken his judgment. In the ancient imagery of feeling as flow, of affections as the differential currents of liquid states, our attention is directed inward to the contents of Othello's body and soul, as he reports to Desdemona not on anger (which seems to me mostly discarded now) but on a sense of bodily degradation that ironically echoes and substantiates from within her earlier sense of his darkening of spirit. For Desdemona, that darkening was projected as transforming and occupying the interior spaces of a beloved other. It is Othello's tragedy to experience and describe this awful, life-destroying darkening directly, within himself. He imagines that inner bodily decay and death as what seems most loathsome—as toads multiplying in the dark and fetid fluids of his own damaged viscera, as corruption generated within the self's dark recesses.

Like the image of Pyrrhus roasted in wrath or fire or that of Hamlet wanting to drink hot blood, the image of the dark puddle makes legible the overarching unity of physical and psychological in early modern behavioral theory. If Pyrrhus's wrath exemplifies evidence of inner qualities distributed out into the phenomenal environment, the image of Othello's puddled consciousness brings the fetid materials of the outside world into the innermost recesses of self and mind. All of these references deepen the quality of our attention to the phenomenology of the passions because they stand as evidence of the unity of the physical and the psychological everywhere else in the canon.

CHAPTER TWO

LOVE WILL HAVE HEAT

Shakespeare's Maidens and the Caloric Economy

The Galenic commonplace that "the Minds inclination follows the Bodies Temperature" had particularly disastrous consequences for early modern constructions of the psychophysiology of women.[1] Men's bodies were thought to be hotter and drier, women's bodies colder and more spongy. This was not a difference that applied universally: most theorists believed that some men, especially old or melancholy ones, were colder than some women. But generally, as part of the order of things, females started off their lives colder in temper than males of the same age and, with rare exceptions, stayed that way.[2] As the royal physician Helkiah Crooke noted in 1615 after surveying the biological evidence for the relative heat of the sexes, "We conclude . . . that . . . men are hotter then women . . . as well in regard of the Naturall Temper, as that which is acquired by diet and the course of life" (276). For Crooke—and for other thinkers, as we shall see—women's coldness was both natural and environmental, an innate feature compounded by the action of the six Galenic nonnaturals (air, diet, rest and exercise, sleeping and waking, fullness and emptiness, and the passions) summed up casually in his phrase "acquired by diet and the course of life." Indeed, depending on the significance we wish to see in Crooke's use of the word "acquired" as meaning that which is added, purchased, or sought out,

---

1. Selden, sig. b4; but the idea is often repeated with slight variations in wording.

2. For a summary overview of these differences and a useful application of them to art historical materials, see Filipczak, 68–77.

women's coldness was important enough in the scheme of things to collapse the great binaries of innate and acquired, voluntary and involuntary.
Women begin colder than men and, Crooke implies, continue to be so
whether passively through the permanent effects of humoral predisposition
or actively in a more or less self-damaging acquisition of coldness.

This totalizing theory of human agency and affect, masquerading as the
facts of sexual difference, can be tracked in the humoral discourses of
drama. The subtending consequences of the heat differential registered first
of all in the part that hot and cold played in the hierarchical order of things,
in the associations of heat with life and cold with death. Even in the nineteenth century, the great biologist Claude Bernard, for example, could
explain the theory of vital heat by saying, "heat is a condition essential to
the manifestation of the phenomena of life. The heat which has its source
in the interior of the organism, in man and in warm-blooded animals,
explains how their vital activities remain free and independent, within limits, of external climatic variation."[3] "This descriptive statement would have
been as acceptable to the ancients as it is to the modern physiologist,"
Everett Mendelsohn has noted. Vital heat brings warm-blooded animals a
degree of physical autonomy from the environment unavailable to cold-
blooded species. But the crucial difference between ancient and modern
understandings of vital heat is that for the ancients and their early
modern followers, heat was thought to be an innate, inherent property of
warm-blooded animals, a motive power originating in the heart and responsible for growth and generative functions, for digestion, movement, sensation, and thought.[4] Note Bernard's association of body heat with such
value-laden terms as *independence* and *freedom of activity*. Aristotelian
taxonomies ranked all species thermally, distinguishing among the temperatures implied in observable modes of reproduction and the resulting
degree of perfection of their offspring. Among the warm-blooded species,
rank accrued as a function of blood attributes such as temperature, consistency, purity, or turbidity. The ranking privileged humans as animals with
the warmest, purest blood, but—as we will see below and again in chapter
4—humoralism used differences in consistency and temperature of blood
to *distinguish between* human beings as well.

In humoralism, the coldness and sponginess of female flesh, relative to
the flesh of men, become traits of great ethical consequence by explaining

3. Claude Bernard, *Leçons sur la chaleur animale*, trans. and quoted in Everett Mendelsohn,
Heat and Life: The Development of the Theory of Animal Heat (Cambridge, MA: Harvard University
Press, 1964), 1n.

4. Mendelsohn, 1n, 8, 11–13.

the sex's limited capacity for productive agency, individuality, and higher reasoning. As with everything else in this cosmology, states of consciousness and cognitive awareness were ranked in terms of cold/hot, moist/dry. Waking consciousness was thought to be a hotter and drier state than sleep; rationality was less cold and spongy than irrationality. This is why—as I suggest in chapter 1—Hamlet berates himself as a "muddy-mettled rascal," unable to think clearly and purposefully or to act decisively. His John-a-dreams' lack of animal spirits means a dampening and loss of conceptual potency—a becoming "unpregnant of my cause" (2.2.567–68)—as well as a feminizing cowardice.[5] But men other than the "muddy-mettled," being hotter than most women, were thought to have better perceptual and cognitive apparatuses—better hardware and software—and were able to report more rationally and reliably about the world.[6] The relative heat in bodies thus becomes a paradigmatic case of Judith Butler's argument in *Bodies That Matter* that "sexual difference ... is never simply a function of material differences which are not in some way both marked and formed by discursive practices."[7]

Indeed, meaningful beliefs about female humorality were so persistent that, even at the end of the seventeenth century, William Congreve could regard female coldness as a force antithetical to individuality itself: "Methinks something should be observed of the Humour of the Fair Sex; since they are sometimes so kind as to furnish out a Character for Comedy. But I must confess I have never made any observation of what I Apprehend to be true Humour in Women. Perhaps Passions are too powerful in that Sex, to let Humour have its Course; or may be by Reason of their Natural Coldness, Humour cannot Exert it self to that extravagant Degree, which it often does in the Male Sex."[8] Here—and from the creator of *Way of the World*'s Millamant, no less—we see the meaning of the term *humor* as applied to women at an interesting point in its development from early modern bodily fluid to post-Enlightenment mental abstraction. For Congreve, "true" humor means singularities of disposition, style, and address—what "shews us as we *are*"—or, as he goes on to explain using the

---

5. On Shakespeare and other early moderns' usages of the word *pregnant*, see Crane, 159–61.

6. Shapin, 86–89.

7. Judith Butler, *Bodies That Matter: On the Discursive Limits of Sex* (New York: Routledge, 1993), 2.

8. Congreve to John Dennis, July 10, 1695, in *William Congreve, Letters and Documents*, ed. John C. Hodges (New York: Harcourt, Brace, 1964), 183. I owe this reference to Katharine Streip, " 'Just a Cérébrale': Jean Rhys, Women's Humor, and Ressentiment," *Representations* 45 (Winter 1994): 117.

universal male pronoun, "A singular and unavoidable manner of doing, or saying any thing, Peculiar and Natural to one Man only; by which his Speech and Actions are distinguish'd from those of other Men" (180, 182). By preventing humor from displaying itself, then, women's passions obliterate in them the individual distinctiveness that Congreve finds natural in all men. Even in his alternative explanation—that humor does not display itself fully in women "may be by reason of their Natural Coldness"—women's cold temperature tamps down individuality by preventing the free flow of bodily humors necessary for its real expression. For Congreve, repeating an old misogynistic saw in somewhat new or obfuscated terms, the dominion of passion over reason in women produces a changeability inimical to the self-identity he equates with having "true" humor. Women's passions, then, is just another term for temperamental inconstancy. The emotional volatility of inconstancy seems to be a threat, rather than an incentive, to the production of individuality in speech and action, to "a singular manner of doing, or saying any thing"—because, in this view, the psychophysiological basis of individual distinction not only is gendered but also requires a constancy synonymous with heat. As we shall see, women are capable of the hotter passions but not of the laudable, steady heat that produces either manly constancy or the great distinctiveness of "extravagant" humor.

It is worth noting that Congreve's exclusion of women from the full range of human individuality repeats in a late-seventeenth-century idiom the same exclusion from the full range of temperaments that we see in medieval depictions of the four humors reproduced by Klibansky, Panofsky, and Saxl in *Saturn and Melancholy* (297–303).[9] The late-fifteenth-century German calendar woodcuts that they cite offer emblematic images of sanguine, choleric, phlegmatic, and melancholic man in isolate pairs with an accompanying female figure whose signifying function is to provide a neutral social background for the men's temperamental self-display (see figs. 5–8). What the woodcuts represent most clearly is the correlation among heat, gender, and conceptions of agency. The ideal heat of the sanguine man, for example, signified by wooing, takes on engenderment even as it ostentatiously displays its own self-sufficiency. As a motion arising from within a self-sufficiency of desire and vitality, the sexual heat of the sanguine man does not require response from his female partner and does not get it. This disparity in agency and self-signification is even more extreme in the depiction of choler, where, as display of agency increases with the

---

9. They discuss several sets of German calendrical illustrations (reproduced in plates 80–82, 84–85, 87–90), one of which I include here (figs. 5–8).

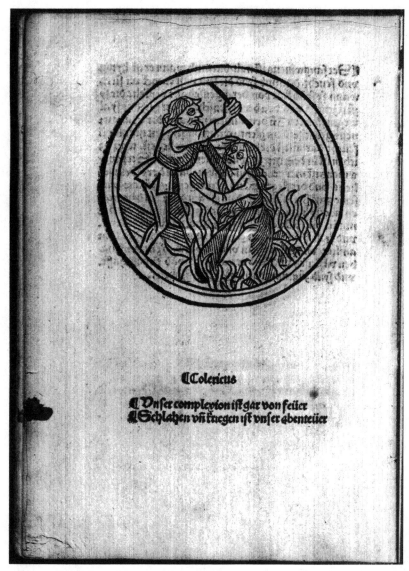

Figure 5. Medieval woodcut of choler, from the *Deutsche Kalender* (Ulm: Johann Schäffler, 1498). By permission of the Pierpont Morgan Library, New York (PML 23170, woodcut 1).

heat of the furious man, it recedes in the woman accompanying him. The man of choler, surrounded by flames, beats a woman kneeling helplessly at his feet. It is the function of the women here to *lack* temperament even as they lack agency, for to possess either would be to complicate the outlines of temperamental male display.

Figure 6. Medieval woodcut of sanguine, from the *Deutsche Kalender* (Ulm: Johann Schäffler, 1498). By permission of the Pierpont Morgan Library, New York (PML 23170, woodcut 2).

Female temperament makes an appearance in the woodcuts where we would expect it to, in the depictions of the colder melancholic and phlegmatic complexions. Even here, however, in the depiction of melancholia, attention is drawn to the abject figure of the scholar, his head in his

Figure 7. Medieval woodcut of phlegm, from the *Deutsche Kalender* (Ulm: Johann Schäffler, 1498). By permission of the Pierpont Morgan Library, New York (PML 23170, woodcut 3).

hands.[10] The emotional state of the spinster who accompanies him, if it signifies at all, is hard to read. Only in the depictions of the phlegmatic temperament do women take on a fully functional signifying role as men's

10. The association of melancholy with the scholarly life is traditional; see Juliana Schiesari, *The Gendering of Melancholia: Feminism, Psychoanalysis, and the Symbolics of Loss in Renaissance Literature* (Ithaca, NY: Cornell University Press, 1992), 112–41.

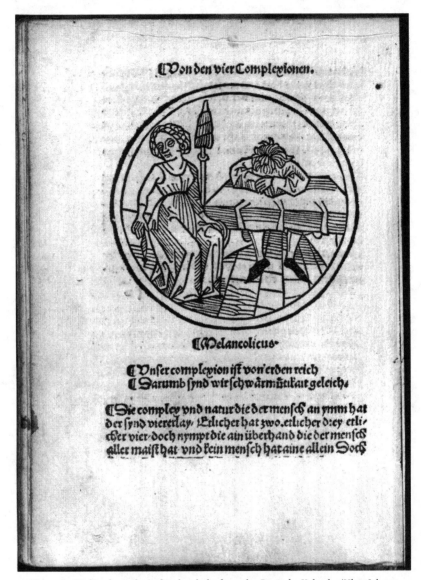

Figure 8. Medieval woodcut of melancholy, from the *Deutsche Kalender* (Ulm: Johann Schäffler, 1498). By permission of the Pierpont Morgan Library, New York (PML 23170, woodcut 4).

equals in temperament, here with a woman playing a harp while her companion plays a lute. Humoral men signify themselves as fully, if conventionally, different from one another, say these illustrations; women help them to do so. Men's behaviors reveal themselves to be predominantly sanguine, choleric, phlegmatic, or melancholic. Women's humorality, occluded in the depictions of sanguine or choleric man, marginally present in melancholia, and fully expressive only among the phlegmatics, fails to signify, because *normative* humoral woman is temperamentally constrained, and such behavioral oppositions as might be implied by temperamental un-self-sameness are here kept out of view.[11]

Admittedly, the opposition in Congreve's account between passions and humors—between the bodily forces that erase individuality and those that produce it—takes us away from an earlier moment when the passions and humors were thought to be so closely allied as almost to be functionally indistinguishable. As Thomas Wright explains in *The Passions of the Minde in Generall*, the "Passions ingender Humours, and humours breed passions" (46). But Congreve's implication that female coldness prevents women from having the internal warmth and quickness of spirits necessary to activate, produce, and most of all maintain individual distinctiveness suggests that the consequences of women's coldness may be global indeed. For Congreve, women's natural coldness excludes them from creative participation in the full range of individual variation and expressiveness, excludes them from the "Diversity of Humour" that Congreve finds "diffused throughout Mankind" (183)—where mankind is the male part of it.

In this chapter I want to suggest how such bodily phenomena as humor, spirit, and temper become performative of versions of femaleness even in contexts where, to us, discourses of sexual difference and the body itself seem barely to be in play. The psychophysiology of early modern thought means that embodiment is everywhere assumed in affective discourse, just as bodily references always assume an affective context or consequence. My interest here, as elsewhere in this book, is partly in detailing the somatic (hence sexualized) basis of phenomena we often relegate to the nonsomatic realm of mood and affect. And it is partly in offering a materialist way of locating bodiliness within the equivocal history of ostensibly female emotions. Like other contemporary playwrights, Shakespeare found in language of the humors and their four qualities of cold, hot, moist, and dry a discourse for signaling the relationship within his characters between embodied emotion and perceptible behaviors, between the mind's inclination and the body's temperature. Extremes of emotion correlate with extremes of temperature. And within these extremes, the doctrine of female coldness imposes itself as a behavioral norm—an ostensible natural limit—governing the appropriateness of affectivity in female characters not only under

---

11. For other illustrations in this tradition, see Filipczak, 14–27.

a given set of dramatic or social circumstances but as a matter of overall obedience to the thermal paradigms of nature. Thus, the social intention deeply, if obscurely, imbricated in the thermal economy not only grants affective privilege to men over women, as we might expect in such a patriarchal biology, but it also works to dampen the emotional expressiveness and claim to individuality theoretically granted to women as a whole. Such is the burden of the fifteenth-century woodcuts and of Congreve's dismissal of individual distinctiveness in women.

We will see in chapter 4 how the correlation between the social hierarchy and the affective hierarchy works to organize men's relations with each other. Here, I propose to show the discourse of female humoralism at work by contrasting selected representations of female melancholy and female rage, mostly, but not exclusively, in Shakespearean drama. My intention is not to cover the whole field of such representation—clearly an impossible task—but rather to point out some textual instances where the language of the humors acts as a deep, hence misrecognized, organizing structure for representations of female affectivity. Within these texts, I propose, female humorality and the overarching argument from heat signify powerfully in the representation of the actions and emotions of female characters—especially, though not exclusively, in the romantic comedies and in those tragedies, such as *Othello*, that depend heavily on the generic shapings of romantic comedy.[12] There, the journeys of figures such as Rosalind and Desdemona from maidenhood to the heterosexual enclosure of marriage are marked by dramatic emotional changes from sadness and inactivity to a bold adventurousness hardly predictable from their first appearances. In *Taming of the Shrew*, by contrast, it is Katherine's excessive choler, uncontained and unsocialized, that Petruchio must regulate—a process complicated and underscored by the play's emphasis on his own humoral imbalance. If her taming entails his self-taming, the play nonetheless endorses his retention of choler as a prerequisite to, and the biological basis of, male mastery.

It is the dramatic representation of the nature and causation of behavioral and expressive changes in Desdemona, Rosalind, and Katherine Minola that I want to track here for what such changes reveal of buried assumptions about female affectivity more generally. In doing so, I will implicitly take issue with one of the foundational arguments of feminist criticism of these plays—namely, that the final commitment to marriage

---

12. Susan Snyder, *Comic Matrix of Shakespeare's Tragedies: "Romeo and Juliet," "Hamlet,"* *"Othello," and "King Lear"* (Princeton, NJ: Princeton University Press, 1979), 3–14.

inaugurates a diminishment of the freedom and unconstraint that Shakespeare's cross-dressed and other heroines briefly experience in their trajectory from maidenhood through courtship and marriage.[13] Humoralism allows us to see the contours of a different trajectory, perhaps specific to the period, in which the onset of sexual maturity in girls and their passage to wifehood are understood to involve a significant increase of bodily heat and of the aggressive agency such heat entails. I argue that in a cosmology where "the Minds inclination follows the bodies temperature," these characters' passages from young womanhood into marriage involve— indeed almost require—a psychophysiological transformation that is easy for us to misrecognize or undervalue, thanks to the post-Enlightenment dematerialization of psychological process and insistence on self-sameness in the representation of character. While the terms of my description may make the nature of this transformation seem analogous to the chafing and "sexual friction" that Stephen Greenblatt has written about with respect to many of these same characters, the psychophysiological changes I refer to here are really quite different, in being a literal description of bodily transformation from the inside out, from the mind's inclination to follow the body's temperature. In Greenblatt's account, the awakening of female protagonists such as Rosalind and Viola to heterosexual desire—figured as and coinciding with their cross-dressing as Ganymede and Cesario—brings them closer to the conditions of biological maleness and proves the trenchancy for the early moderns of Thomas Laqueur's one-flesh, one-sex model of sexual difference.[14] As Laqueur points out, Galen describes the female genitalia as an inverted simulacrum of male genitalia: "think first, please, of the man's [external genitalia] turned in and extending inward between the rectum and the bladder. If this should happen, the scrotum would necessarily take the place of the uteri, with the testes lying outside, next to it on either side."[15] From this, Laqueur and Greenblatt posit a model of gender fluidity in the early modern period in which maleness and femaleness, rather than being organized into the great binaries that we generally refer

13. On this rich topic, see, for example, Jean E. Howard, "Scripts and/versus Playhouses: Ideological Production and the Renaissance Public Stage," *Renaissance Drama*, n.s., 20 (1989): 31–49; or Theodora A. Jankowski, *Pure Resistance: Queer Virginity in Early Modern English Drama* (Philadelphia: University of Pennsylvania Press, 2000), 114–35, both of whom accept that marriage operates almost entirely as a constraint on early modern women.

14. Stephen Greenblatt, "Fiction and Friction," in *Shakespearean Negotiations: The Circulation of Social Energy in Renaissance England* (Berkeley and Los Angeles: University of California Press, 1988), 66–93; Thomas Laqueur, *Making Sex: Body and Gender from the Greeks to Freud* (Cambridge, MA: Harvard University Press, 1990), 25.

15. Galen, 2:628.

to as "opposite sexes," occupy different points along a sliding continuum of genital difference.

But, as I have argued elsewhere and will continue to argue here, genital difference is only the most evident sign in the period of a more pervasive source of difference between men and women—the heat differential that described women's inferiority in terms of their place on the thermal scale of nature.[16] Here, I want to argue that the biological warming of Shakespeare's cross-dressed and other female characters—as represented by the trio of characters on whom I will concentrate—occurs within a "natural" paradigm of femaleness. In Rosalind and Desdemona, this warming registers not as a masculinizing threat to sexual difference but rather as their powerful emergence from a condition of physical and emotional lassitude, understood not quite *as*, but *in terms of* female—indeed virgin—melancholia. In the contrasting example in *The Taming of the Shrew*, Kate—introduced as a humoral subject distempered by too much heat—must be cooled in order to be socialized as a wife. The change wrought in her is a product of Petruchio's transformation of her environment through manipulation of the six Galenic nonnaturals of air, diet, rest and exercise, sleeping and waking, fullness and emptiness, and the passions. Only through an active intervention in her body's relation to its environment can Petruchio achieve Kate's emotional subordination to him, impose wifehood on her, and bring her coercively to the recognition of her place in the world. Of course, given what we see of the emotional independence and verbal power that Shakespeare gives such wives as Adriana in *The Comedy of Errors* or the Windsor wives or even Bianca and the newly remarried widow in *Taming of the Shrew*, this narrative is perhaps best seen as a humoral fantasy. That fantasy comes in parodic form, of course, in Jonson's *Epicoene* where Morose looks for a silent, indeed virtually mute, virgin and marries her, only to be horrified, immediately after the marriage ceremony has apparently been celebrated, by the torrents of loud language that come from her mouth. The fantasy—as these examples suggest—is one with deep roots in early modern cosmological thought about the nature and behavior of women, and hence it is well worth detailing one more time, first by looking at the paradigm of virgins' melancholy and its

---

16. See Paster, "Unbearable Coldness." For other critiques of Laqueur and Greenblatt, see Patricia Parker, "Gender Ideology, Gender Change: The Case of Marie Germain," *Critical Inquiry* 19 (1993): 348–49; Janet Adelman, "Making Defect Perfection: Shakespeare and the One-Sex Model," in *Enacting Gender on the English Renaissance Stage*, ed. Viviana Comensoli and Anne Russell (Urbana: University of Illinois Press, 1998), 23–52; and Valerie Traub, *The Renaissance of Lesbianism in Early Modern England* (Cambridge: Cambridge University Press, 2002), 191–95.

literary effects and then by observing its opposite in the choleric distemper of Kate.

As frequent references to young women's green sickness make clear, the early moderns identified in certain young women a disease not only both physical and emotional in character, but also (as we have little difficulty in noticing) thoroughly ideological in its cultural underpinnings. The disease emerged in the sixteenth century, probably, as Helen King argues, thanks to the coincidence of two textual events: the rediscovery of the Hippocratic text *On the Diseases of Virgins* and the publication in 1554 of Johannes Lange's *Medicinalium epistolarum miscellanea*.[17] In English, green sickness is first mentioned in Andrew Boorde's 1547 *Breviary of Helthe*, as a form of jaundice; by 1559, however, in William Bullein's *A Newe Boke of Phisicke called the Gouernment of Health*, it has become a disease specific to young women.[18] In his case history written in epistolary form, Lange diagnoses the illness of a friend's marriageable daughter as "the virgin's disease"—a condition most easily remedied either by venesection or by marriage. The disease prevailed from the sixteenth to the nineteenth century—eventually becoming known as chlorosis or the "special anaemia of young women."[19] My concern here is not so much with the disease per se—since a medical diagnosis of green sickness is rarer in drama than passing references to it might suggest—as with the larger question of female humorality with which green sickness, as a particularly dangerous outbreak of female humors, is thoroughly entangled. If for Congreve, women's lack of heat prevents them from developing distinctiveness in writing, address, and social demeanor, young women's cold humorality in Shakespeare produces behavioral traces of a pathology— traces that are part of what desire must act upon, psychophysiologically, and disperse. As Thomas Wright declares, "loue will haue heat, and sadnesse cold, feare constringeth, & pleasure dilateth" (35). Bishop Reynolds

---

17. Helen King, *Hippocrates' Woman: Reading the Female Body in Ancient Greece* (London: Routledge, 1998), 194–95. As King notes (268n13), Lange's text was published in Basel in 1547 and expanded and reissued in 1560. His discussion of green sickness was popularized and became widely influential in Schenck von Grafenburg's *Observationum medicarum, rararum, novarum, admirabilium, et monstrosarum libri*, published in Frankfurt in 1600. I quote from the Latin text of "Epistola XXI" in Johann Lange, *Epistolarum medicinalium* (Frankfurt: Andreas Wechel, 1589), 100–104; and from the English text in Johann Lange, "Epistola XXI: De morbo virgineo," from *Medicinalium epistolarum miscellanea* (Basle: J. Operinus, 1554), reprinted in *Classic Descriptions of Disease*, ed. Ralph H. Major (Springfield, IL: Charles C. Thomas, 1932), 488–89.

18. Helen King, 193.

19. Ibid., 188.

concurs: "Love . . . consists in a kind of expansion or egresse of the heat and spirits to the object loved" (74).

Lange's description of the "virgin's disease" had the effect of widely reintroducing a disease originally identified in the Hippocratic corpus and thereby promoting a syndrome recognizable for three centuries thereafter. Since early modern physicians "believed that all diseases were known to the ancients," the virgins' disease could not be new in itself.[20] In effect, it had always existed and only needed to be rediscovered. But what immediately strikes the modern reader in Lange's letter to the distressed father of a green sick maiden is the utterly conventional homosocial context out of which both the disease and its diagnosis emerge—advice from a doctor to his good friend (addressed in the Latin text as Achates) about why the friend's newly marriageable daughter is spurning eligible suitors: "You will have complained to me, your faithful companion that your first born daughter, Anno [sic], & now sad, is desired in marriage by many suitors, of great excellency and illustrious birth, and also with an abundance of wealth, descended by ancestry from your forebears not from your inferiors; whom you are compelled to refuse because of the weakness of your daughter" (488). In Lange's subsequent description of the girl's condition, the social and the physiological intertwine. Anna is newly or even suddenly sad, but her symptoms seem strictly physical: her once rosy cheeks and lips have dramatically paled, "as if exsanguinated"; any movement causes the girl's heart to tremble and the arteries of her temple to pulsate, while the more vigorous activities of dancing or stair-climbing produce severe respiratory difficulties. She loathes food, especially meat, and her legs and ankles swell at night. But the symptoms themselves are quickly subordinated in Lange's text to a diagnostic, significant test of medical expertise. For in response to the father's report that many doctors have failed to understand the girl's symptoms or to agree on the nature of her disease, Lange seems openly contemptuous: "I marvel that old physicians do not know the cause & nature of the disease" (488). Far from being mysterious, the disease is easily readable, because it belongs not to a striking individual case of sudden and inexplicable distemper but to a generic state already known to the ancients. It belongs, that is, not to an individual patient named Anna but to a broad category of person, the marriageable virgin. Indeed—despite the dramatic quality of the symptoms—the disease itself seems to be less a disease than a condition, so that its very namelessness seems to be a trait of the class of person subject to it: "Nor has this disease a proper name, as much as it is peculiar to virgins, might indeed

20. Ibid., 195.

be called 'virgineus'" (488). And, Lange goes on to insist, this disease is a common one, attacking "virgins, when now mature they pass from youth to virility." (The Latin text here simply says that Anna is "iam maturae," so that the English translator's strong choice of "virility" bears the now obsolete meaning of sexual maturity, "the power of procreation; the capacity for sexual intercourse" [*OED*, 2].) It is in part the father's inexperience with marriage-age daughters and old doctors' unfamiliarity with Hippocratic medicine—Lange leads us to infer—that makes the problem so hard to diagnose.

My point is not so much that poor Anna's suffering has become the occasion of a homosocial competition among physicians in a diagnostic game of reading femaleness as it is that Anna's subsumption as individual patient into a more or less predictable biological and reproductive category works to dispossess her of that suffering—certainly as her own to signify but also as her own to bear. Like the coldness of temperament in Congreve's analysis of "the Fair Sex," Anna's disease de-individualizes her and makes her body expressive not of its own symptoms but of young femaleness in general. That is, the very symptoms that separate her from the happier, stronger girl that she used to be align her with a new and socially more difficult cohort, the reluctant virgin. Thus virgins' disease cannot be separated from the twinned social demands on fathers and daughters that underlie it: demands on the fathers to release their daughters to suitors, demands on the daughters to release themselves from a reluctance whose nature seems indeterminately physical and emotional.[21]

The particular urgency underlying the letter, of course, is that Anna is sought after by the very kind of suitors most attractive to a father—well-born young men of means ("virtutem integritae ac stemmatis claritate, opumque facultatibus" [100]). As Lange goes on to note, the father has come to him for an "opinion of the disease of the girl, and dependable advice concerning marriage" (488). It is obvious to the modern reader that what is missing here is the patient's own narrative, her own case history. Any reference to her anxiety concerning her state of health has been subsumed into the father's concern, and there is no reference to her own interest in marriage in general or her "many suitors." Perhaps we are to suppose that, like Juliet learning of Paris's existence for the first time from her mother and nurse, Anna has neither seen nor heard of them on her own. Instead the list of physical symptoms works like a Petrarchan blazon to isolate the girl's physical features one

21. Anna and her father thus occupy the culturally difficult terrain identified by Lynda Boose in "The Father's House and the Daughter in It: The Structure of Western Culture's Daughter-Father Relationship," in *Daughters and Fathers*, ed. Lynda E. Boose and Betty S. Flowers (Baltimore: Johns Hopkins University Press, 1989), 19–74.

from another and to bestow an almost autonomous agency on the refractory parts—the stomach loathing food, the trembling heart, the dyspnea that "seizes" her while dancing. Furthermore, because diagnosis here is really social categorization, recognizing Anna's "virility" is to identify marriage as a medical cure and thus remove it from the arena of individual choice, the sphere of personal desire. What makes Anna's disease an accessory of her sex, of course, results from a combination of factors related to female physiology and what seems to be an anatomical straitening peculiar to virgins. In Lange's account, menstrual blood, produced by the liver, flows to the womb but cannot flow out of it because of the womb's "narrow mouths," "thick & crude humors" (488), and the blood's thickness.[22] Anatomy conspires with physiology, and structure with temperature, to make the young virgin's body incapable of expelling its bloody waste products. The blood then flows back to its source, flooding the viscera and even reaching the head, where it produces "imaginary terrors of spectres" ("epilepsiam, & delirium" [103]).

At this point, narratives of female melancholia often recount a rapid descent into the symptoms of madness visible in overtly lovesick maidens such as the Jailer's Daughter in *Two Noble Kinsmen* or the grief-struck Ophelia.[23] But if we stay for the moment with the powerful physical symptoms of the green sick maiden whose illness does not take such spectacularly pathological forms, we watch medical diagnosis harp on a daughter's body clogged with the viscous fluids of its own reproductive maturity, weighed down by its own new ripeness. The heart trembles with the effort of moving and refining cold, thick blood; the temples beat when the blood, moving up into the head, threatens delirium. We might call the green sick maidens, like the depressed and inactive Hamlet, "muddy-mettled"—their thoughts are disordered, their judgments impaired. How else could they refuse such eligible suitors? To call this a disease of suppressed menses understates the real nature of the problem, because the blood does not disappear, become absorbed or consumed; rather, the thick, humor-filled, unexpressed blood goes elsewhere in the body to places where it does not belong. Though Lange does not say so, this redistribution of menstrual blood would probably be understood as particularly damaging, given the excremental associations of menstrual blood in general and of suppressed menses in particular.[24] As is so often the case in humoralism, the virgin's body poisons itself—distempers itself, makes itself weaker—with its own fluids. In this

22. On the demonization of menstrual blood as excremental, see Paster, *Body Embarrassed*, 81.

23. See Carol Thomas Neely, "Documents in Madness: Reading Madness in Shakespeare's Tragedies and Early Modern Culture," *Shakespeare Quarterly* 42 (1991): 315–38.

24. Paster, *Body Embarrassed*, 81.

respect, virgins' disease is a classic version of pollution in Mary Douglas's terms—a disease of matter, here biological matter, out of place.[25] And the urgency of properly responding to this disease has to do with daughters' notorious propensity to affect their own cures by falling in love with the wrong kind of suitor. As John Harington puts it in *The Metamorphosis of Ajax*, "if the parents bestow them not, they will bestow themselves."[26]

Helen King has pointed out that there are several contradictions in Lange's half-Galenic, half-Hippocratic account of virgins' disease, especially the pallor of a body deemed plethoric—overfull of unexpressed blood (196–98). But for me, the contradictions are less telling than the overarching irony: the very blood that is the social and biological sign of the virgin's maturation has become the site and origin of a disease of self-poisoning. We saw in chapter 1 that humoralism presupposes a constant and dynamic interchange between self and environment, with the passions engendered by and engendering the humors not only involved in a person's current state of health but, as one of the six nonnaturals (along with diet, air, rest and exercise, sleep and waking, fullness and emptiness), existing objectively as a force in the natural world. For Anna, two changes in her immediate environment have inexorably converged: the new production in her maturing body of menstrual blood requiring expulsion and the new presence in her social world of "many suitors" desiring her in marriage. The appearance of the menses is itself productive of psychological change: according to Lange, virgins "are afflicted with imaginary terrors of spectres, especially when the menses appear, for before this, they are not at all badly affected" (488). It is difficult for us to resist extrapolating the possible nature of these terrors. Perhaps we might want to hypothesize Anna's fear of or distaste for a future that includes sexual penetration, reproduction, and child-birth.[27] But for Lange, if the one physiological change is the source of disease, social interpellation is the source of cure: "I instruct virgins afflicted with this disease, that as soon as possible they live with men & copulate" (489). For if the disease should happen to bypass them in puberty, it will strike later on "unless they have been married" (489). As stated here, the remedy does not involve the satisfaction of desire, since desire is a term suppressed in this diagnosis. The remedy proposed is almost more structural than anything else, part of what Valerie Traub has seen as the "sex-positive" climate of early modern Europe.[28]

25. Mary Douglas, *Purity and Danger: An Analysis of the Concepts of Pollution and Taboo* (1966; reprint, London: Ark, 1984), 125–26.

26. John Harington, *A New Discourse of a Stale Subject, Called the Metamorphosis of Ajax*, ed. Elizabeth Story Donno (New York: Columbia University Press, 1962), 65.

27. Traub, *Renaissance of Lesbianism*, 95.

28. Ibid., 80.

But in fact, marriage is not the only cure for virgins' disease, as Lange himself acknowledges. A less life-altering cure would be venesection, "if nothing hinders," and (since the disease is one of suppressed menses) a dose of medicines designed to bring on menstrual flow, thin the viscous humors, and open up the obstructed body. It is the equation of these two apparently unlike remedies—phlebotomy or marriage, even marriage as a form of phlebotomy—that returns our attention to the alien psychophysiology that subtends the entire discussion of virgins' disease. If the obstructedness of the virgin's body seems merely a mechanical or even structural fault, the thickness of her blood alerts us to the disease's larger affective implications that—I would argue—involve the virgin's relation to her whole environment. From this point of view, the superiority of marriage to phlebotomy is that, in Lange's sex-positive thinking, the social cure of marriage subsumes the merely medical cure of phlebotomy. The virgin's obstructed body is opened up through sexual penetration; the coldness of her humors is relieved by the physical activity of sexual intercourse; the plethora of blood is relieved by the expression of female seed; and the father adds a well-born suitor to his extended family or, in an alternative construction, lessens the burdens of his own household by one daughter. In such a scenario, individual choice of sexual partner—which goes so entirely unstated here as not to exist for Lange at all—need play no part. Indeed, it is the irrelevance of individual desire to this analysis—not the massive authority of Hippocrates—that may provide the best explanation of why virgins' disease becomes so prevalent once the Hippocratic text has been recovered. For in fact, because of its origins in uterine dysfunction, virgins' disease cannot really be separated from other disorders uneasily distributed among the emotional, psychological, and gynecological—most of which were also attributed to menstrual disorders. This slippage among gynecological diseases is why the great seventeenth-century physician Thomas Sydenham prescribes "the steel pills, or powder, ordered in the hysteric passion" to be taken for virgins' disease, "in a dose adapted to the age of the patient."[29] Since in the seventeenth century the hysteric passion was sometimes associated with the womb's imagined tendency to move up or down within the body, its relationship to a blood disorder such as green sickness is not immediately obvious. But the overlap between Sydenham's two therapies implies that femaleness per se is the subtending summary diagnosis in these two diseases. The prescription for a warming and strengthening

29. Thomas Sydenham, *The Entire Works of Dr. Thomas Sydenham*, ed. John Swan (London, 1742), 607.

dose of steel pills in both cases suggests that the question is women's relation to vitality itself.

Note, for example, how many of the symptoms of virgins' disease suggest inactivity and lethargy: heaviness of the body, lassitude in the legs, drowsiness. Others, such as heart palpitations, the fevered pulse, difficulty in breathing, and perverse appetites, describe both the breakdown of the body's regulatory mechanisms and physical problems in its relation with the natural world. The latter is especially evident in the green sick maiden's relation to food—either a general aversion to food like Anna's or the odd cravings often mentioned in diagnosis, as in Sydenham's listing of "an unnatural longing for such things as are noxious, and unfit for food" (606). Helen King wants to leave open the possibility that Anna's aversion to food could express her more or less rational choice to lessen her body's production of blood—whether to discourage the production of menses and thus avoid plethora or to forestall the onset of sexual maturity altogether and thus rid herself of unwanted suitors or an unsought destiny in marriage (202). But the longing described by Sydenham for "such things as are noxious, and unfit for food" cannot be rationalized in those terms and seems to me to signify a cultural perception that the virgins' disease involves a skewed relation to the object world—a perverse misclassification and misuse of things—as well as a skewed relation to the social world. For in effect, Anna's symptomatology works like a refusal of the social goods that the father's place in the world makes available to her—namely, the many well-born suitors flocking to the paternal household who invite her toward the complicated pleasures and responsibilities of physical and social maturation within the constrained terms and expectations of early modern elders.

When Robert Burton turns in 1621 to a description of virgins' melancholy in *The Anatomy of Melancholy*, the overarching social context of the disease becomes even clearer, for the simple reason that—unlike Lange and Anna's father—Burton is deeply interested in the role played by individual desire in the etiology of the disease and is careful to render its social specificity as well. Burton's classification of this melancholy seems to include but not be restricted to green sickness, since he does not use the term *green sickness* nor mention the odd food cravings sometimes thought to be part of the symptomatology. He also refers in passing to "many other maladies . . . incident to young women" (1:414), but they all proceed from the single cause of "those vitious vapours which come from menstruous blood" (1:416), "that fuliginous exhalation of corrupt seed, troubling the Braine, heart and minde" (1:414). According to Burton, virgins' melancholy rarely afflicts working women, because they can "qualifie and divert" such painful feeling through hard work and physical labor without the need for medical assistance: "seldome shall you see an hired servant, a poore handmaid, though ancient, that is kept hard to her worke, and bodily labor, a course country wench troubled in this kinde" (1:416). *Qualify* in this context is a physiological term referring to the body's refinement of its fluids through exercise:[30] the heat produced by the laboring body and its consumption of the extra blood would work to warm and thin the lowborn virgin's otherwise congested blood and humors, relieving her of the physical symptoms so devastating to the higher born. Virgins' melancholy thus belongs to "noble virgins, nice gentlewomen, such as are solitary and idle, live at ease, lead a life out of action and imployment, that fare well in great houses and Joviall companies, ill disposed peradventure of themselves, and not willing to make any resistance, discontented otherwise, of weake judgement, able bodies, and subject to passions" (1:416–17). Burton reserves pity for women who "out of a strong temperament, innate constitution, are violently carried away with this torrent of inward humours, & though very modest of themselves, sober, religious, vertuous, and well given (as many so distressed, maides are) yet cannot make resistance" (1:417). In the hydraulic system of early modern emotions, such women are flooded with the thick bodily fluids of sadness—a torrent of inward humors—and can thus hardly be expected to withstand them.

Much in Burton's description of virgins' and widows' melancholy boggles the historical imagination, beginning with the almost comic snobbery of his implication that subaltern women were too simple and coarse by nature to feel this melancholy and could qualify or refine the thick humors of menstrual blood and sweat them out of their bodies through labor. And Burton himself admits that his experiential credentials for knowing women are not above reproach: "Into what subject have I rushed," he exclaims in an odd burst of self-interruption, "What have I to doe with Nunnes, Maids, Virgins, Widowes? I am a bacheler my selfe, and lead a Monasticke life in a College" (1:417). Despite such drawbacks, however, his serious and sympathetic account of virgins' melancholy is in fact a model of humoral description and includes enough rich social and medical detail to remind us of the explanatory force of Galenic thought for the analysis of behavior and feelings. Burton begins by describing the physical symptoms—the state of the

---

30. Heat may be qualified; the *OED* cites Andrew Boorde's *Breviary of Helth* (1547): "Qualyfie the heate of the Lyuer ... with the confection of Acetose" (8a); the strength or flavor of a liquid may be qualified, as in Nashe's *Prognostication*, "A Cuppe of Sack ... so qualified with Suger, that they proue not rewmatick" (*OED*, 11; *Prognostication*, 152).

virgins' organs, fluids, body parts, and skin—before listing the corresponding emotional symptoms. When the melancholy humor stirs and flies upward from its seat in the spleen, we are told, burning in the midriff and heartstrings follows. Sometimes these virgins cannot sleep and sometimes they have terrible dreams; they dislike every object and crave solitude. Now their head aches, now their heart. Suffering at times from heat, from wind, or from thirst, they "are weary of all" (1:415). Here, as elsewhere in Galenism, great systematic complexity is applied to the classification of bodies, temperaments, and illnesses. The seven "natural" factors innate to the body of every individual have to be considered as well as the six non-naturals of diet, sleep, rest or exercise, fullness or repletion, air, and passions or perturbations of mind. What we need to appreciate here (as noted in chapter 1) is how much Burton's model depends upon, even as it represents, a continuous, dynamic reciprocity within and outside the body in question. All the factors involving body, mind, and emotions interact with each other and with an environment construed holistically to include both the physical world and the sociocultural context. What is clear amid the proliferation of melancholic symptoms is the direct interaction between the body and its immediate surround, between the "torrent of inward humours" and the malady's social expression, between the painful beating of a virgin's heart and what we would call its superstructural causality. Finally Burton takes up the cause of "all such distressed parties" (1:417) by zeroing in, with an almost Althusserian ferocity, on the subtending social cause of this illness—the patriarchal enforcement of women's sexual obedience and its repressive consequences. He writes vehemently, "Must I needs inveigh against them that are in fault, more then manifest causes, and as bitterly taxe those tyrannizing Pseudopolititians, superstitious orders, rash vowes, hard-hearted parents, gardians, unnaturall friends, allies (call them how you will), those carelesse and stupid overseers, that out of worldly respects, covetousnesse, supine negligence, their owne private ends . . . can so severely reject, stubbornly neglect & impiously contemne, without all remorse and pitty, the teares, sighes, groanes and grievous miseries of such poore Soules committed to their charge" (1:417).

What seems remarkable, overall, in this description of virgins' melancholy is not so much the mixture of prescience and belatedness in Burton's social analysis as it is the forceful construction of an ideologically totalized environment. This is an environment where humors, organs, sighs, winds, distempers, high birth, ease of living, lack of occupation, parents, guardians, and enforced vows of chastity meet to act upon and within the female sufferer. Within the Galenic logic of this construction, mind and body suffer together and reciprocally in what modern philosophy of mind calls a process of "continual reciprocal causation"—a process in which "mutually modulatory influences [link] brain, body, and world, with causal coupling between all the components."[31] External physical and cultural factors thus work together with bodily humors and passions to produce melancholy distress—or, in the case of the hardworking subaltern women with no time for brooding, to avert it. Furthermore, this vision of an illness that in cause and expression is both social and medical, emotional and physical, allows Burton to recommend—like Lange but far more sympathetically—a series of cures that are themselves both social and medical, emotional and physical. These range from diet, phlebotomy, and physic to the purgative physical disciplines of labor and exercise, to the purgative emotional disciplines of religion, to the overarching social remedy, "the best and surest remedy of all . . . to see them well placed, and married to good husbands in due time" (1:416).

What I want to emphasize here is precisely the paradigmatic wholeness of Burton's global vision of virgins' melancholy—the humoral logic of moving from the torrent of inward humors within the afflicted virgins to the repressive social structures acting upon them. Burton, like Lange, de-individualizes the disease and emphasizes the role of congested humors in its causation; there are no individual case histories here of the kind (anonymous and often apocryphal) that he sometimes offers in his taxonomy of melancholy, no stories of named sufferers of virgins' melancholy. Even so, his insistence on its social specificity as a product of the frustrated desires of young leisured women without purpose and activity in their lives makes the sexual remedy of a happy marriage only part of a socially enriched picture of personal growth and individual fulfillment through the moderation of passions and the increase of socially purposive activity. Like physical labor, marriage becomes an activity that qualifies and diverts the thick humors bred of idleness and lack of purpose. Marriage functions as a metonymy of social purpose and worth, rather than the reverse. The satisfaction of desire works with an alleviation of idleness and inactivity that Burton silently equates with the attainment of marital station. It is thus Burton's wholeness of vision here that allows us to see female affectivity and female bodiliness as mutually descriptive and mutually causative even in texts, as I said at the start of this chapter, ostensibly concerned with meanings other than the psychophysiology of emotions.

31. Sutton, *Philosophy and Memory Traces*, 40.

Indeed, Burton's description of virgins' melancholy is useful whether or not we wish to accept the somewhat archaic terms of his impassioned social analysis, his bachelor's idealization of what marriage might mean for young wellborn women, and whether or not we are willing to imagine virgins' melancholy as anything resembling a discrete pathological state. It was nearly axiomatic in early modern cosmology that women's condition relative to men's was passive rather than active and that their natures (unless otherwise specified) were essentially phlegmatic.[32] But in medical or philosophical texts, the description of such traits is never simply biological, since they are used tautologically both to explain and to prove the limitations of female faculties and agency, as the Belgian physician Levinus Lemnius points out: "For they that be cold (because they be fearful and dasterdly) neuer yet ... deserued tryumph for any worthy exploit done, neyther dare to geue the onset and enterpryse, to any thinge wherin is any great difficulty, daunger, or odde singularity."[33] In his chapter on sexual difference, the English royal physician Helkiah Crooke limits the value of women's agency by distinguishing between the temporary body heat that an excited female might experience under great provocation and the self-sustaining hot temper of the normatively active male: "those that are angry, pettish, fretfull or wantle [i.e., unsteady, fickle] ... are cold; but those that are wrathfull are hot. If therefore Women are Nockthrown or easily mooued of the hindges, that they haue from their cold Temper, and from the impotencie and weaknes of their mind, because they are not able to lay a law vpon themselues" (276).

The key distinction here is a semantic one masquerading as a biological one, since Crooke wants to insist that the anger of women or other phlegmatic types must not be confused with the wrath of the stout-hearted man: "Anger is a disease of a weake mind which cannot moderate it selfe but is easily inflamed, such are women, children, and weake and cowardly men, and this we tearme fretfulnesse or pettishnes: but Wrath which is *Ira permanens* belongs to stout heartes" (276). The difference, according to Crooke, is one of temper, of sudden and intense flare-ups of reactive female heat subsiding back into primordial cold. Crooke works hard to contain the ontological possibility of female heat, because to accept a high degree of normative variation in female heat would produce differences of temperament between one woman and another and would thus threaten the axiomatic

32. Paster, "Unbearable Coldness," 44–45; see also Ian Maclean, *Renaissance Nature of Women: A Study in the Fortunes of Scholasticism and Medical Science in European Intellectual Life* (Cambridge: Cambridge University Press, 1980), 30.

33. Levinus Lemnius, *The Touchstone of Complexions* (London, 1581), 45.

differences of temperament that secured the hierarchical relation between all women and all men. It becomes necessary for him to ascribe powerful rises in affect to temporary caloric derangements of exclusively female events, such as maternity, which could be diagnosed as disease states anyway. This way, the cold temperament of woman is separated by nature from the emotional privileges and behavioral sanctions granted to the hotter sanguine and choleric temperaments: "the loue [women] beare to their yong addeth spirits and courage vnto them, and therefore that is rather to be accounted woodnes [insanity or extreme passion] then fortitude . . . We say therefore that Females are more churlish and fierce, but not stouter or stronger hearted" (276).

But Burton seems to reverse this circular logic in humoral thinking and to explain young women's cold and melancholic distemper not as the simple cause of their physical inactivity, lack of productivity, and passivity but rather as the complicated result. Desperate sadness seems to him symptomatic of those idle gentlewomen of strong temperament who have the intelligence and leisure to dwell on the relative powerlessness that social privilege in them entails. Their idleness becomes the space of reflection, the occasion for passion. He presents their frustration as compounded of something subtler and more superstructural than merely sexual deprivation (however central such deprivation may be to his and others' analysis). In this, we might note parenthetically, he is far more progressive than Freud, who understood neurasthenia, in men and women, as wholly sexual in origin.[34] Burton's analysis also allows us to see virgins' melancholy as a disease of social frustration on the part of the afflicted virgins and social aspiration on the part of the parents and elders who try to keep them well fed, idle, and socially unproductive.

In Thomas Middleton's *A Chaste Maid in Cheapside*, for instance, the city wife Maudlin Yellowhammer sees green sickness in her daughter's melancholy behavior, especially as compared to her own behavior at the same age:

> You are a dull maid o'late, methinks;
> You had need have somewhat to quicken

---

34. See Elizabeth A. Wilson, "Melancholic Biology: Prozac, Freud, and Neurological Determinism," *Configurations* 7 (1999): 407. To be fair, however, as Wilson argues, Freud postulates "a melancholic ontology of pain, hemorrhaging, and wounding within which psychical forces and somatic forces are mutually and constitutively obliging" (411). I owe this reference to Douglas Trevor.

Your green sickness—do you weep?—a husband!
Had not such a piece of flesh been ordained,
What had us wives been good for?—to make salads,
Or else cry'd up and down for samphire.
To see the difference of these seasons!
When I was of your youth, I was lightsome
And quick two years before I was married.[35]

Moll is asked whether she has practiced her virginals and rebuked for having neglected her dancing lessons. These are the activities reserved for this daughter of aspirant merchant-class parents, even as the scene (set in a goldsmith's shop) shows us Mrs. Yellowhammer herself as a woman of business, presumably watching over the shop in her husband's absence. It is the place of business from which she tries to remove her daughter and place her instead within a domestic interior where virginals are to be played, dancing masters to be anticipated, and future husbands to be received.

The key to Maudlin's resort to a medical idiom lies in her desire to misrecognize Moll's unhappiness as symptomatic of disease and hence susceptible to a generic remedy—"a husband," the husband of her own choosing, not Moll's—rather than the frustration of individual desire with a specific object in view (as we soon learn to be the case). The unsympathetic mother scolds her daughter for lassitude and heaviness, for disappointing her ambitious parents' hopes for marriage to a knight:

You fit for a knight's bed!
Drowsy-brow'd, dull-eyed, drossy-spirited.

(12)

Embedded here is the same social philosophy that lies behind Hamlet's social equation of low birth and muddy mettle (though a social philosophy here adjusted to the aspirations modeled by the rich Yellowhammers and typified in their name).[36] Indeed, the heavy alliteration of disparaged attributes calls attention to the bodily model and the pathology being evoked, preparing us for the emphasis throughout the rest of the play of female

35. Thomas Middleton, *A Chaste Maid in Cheapside*, ed. R. B. Parker, the Revels Plays (London: Methuen, 1969), 1.1.3–11.

36. In the *OED*, *yellowhammer* refers not only to the bird, but also contemptuously to a person, especially a jealous husband. Middleton's name picks up these associations but also, through metonymy, the tool for goldsmithing, here itself golden (or at least yellow) in color.

symptomatology.[37] Moll's lethargy is symptomatic of green sickness in terms much like Lange's—and for an equivalent reason. The depressed Moll is hardly "fit for a knight's bed!" The mother's quasi-diagnostic language should draw our attention to "drossy-spirited" not only for its near equivalence to *Hamlet*'s "muddy-mettled" but here—in a goldsmith's shop—for the specific association of dross with the scum thrown off by metals in melting. Bodily process was, in the period, associated with concoction, with heat transforming substance in a series of increasingly refined purifications. The mother sees her daughter's spirits—what animates her flesh, what enlivens her bodily fluids—as excrement, sees her flesh as too, too solid, impure, and heavy for a high-born suitor.

But as we saw in chapter 1, the analogy of flesh to metal/mettle is close to commonplace in the period. These are the terms, for example, in which Prince Hal couches his anxiety about his worth as lineal heir to a tainted throne, seeing himself ambivalently as "bright metal on a sullen ground" (*1 Henry IV*, 1.2.212) that will

> show more goodly and attract more eyes
> Than that which hath no foil to set it off.
>
> (214–15)

But Moll's physical and emotional heaviness—understood as the same—lowers her in social station, says Mrs. Yellowhammer cruelly; it aligns her with the heavy metals. It is as if, with such heaviness, she is betraying a social environment itself implicitly figured as purer metal:

> You dance like a plumber's daughter and deserve
> Two thousand pound in lead to your marriage,
> And not in goldsmith's ware.
>
> (1.1.21–23)

Perhaps Mrs. Yellowhammer wishes to shame Moll into a better relationship to her surroundings, for Moll's drossy heaviness skews what her mother imagines as a proper relationship to such an aspirant, gold-filled environment; it bespeaks a lack of appetite itself perverse in such a bountiful place. When Mr. Yellowhammer enters and seeks to reconcile mother and daughter, he does so by naturalizing and softening Moll's imperfectness. That is, he tries to change the governing analogy of what Moll is like from metal to textile:

37. See my discussion of the play in Paster, *Body Embarrassed*, 52–63.

As there is no woman made without a flaw,
Your purest lawns have frays and cambrics bracks.

(35–36)

But Mrs. Yellowhammer returns the conversation to metals and a mechanical remedy familiar from Lange: "But 'tis a husband solders up all cracks" (37). In fact, as we soon learn, Moll's sadness stems directly from her parents' insistence that she marry the unsuitable rakehell Sir Walter Whorehound rather than the penniless Touchwood Junior, with whom Moll eventually elopes. The maternal diagnosis of green sickness is thus critiqued from within the play, in terms like Burton's, by the action's insistence on Moll's active sexual appetite and a heaviness produced by parental constraint and the prospect of a deeply undesirable marriage. It is true that in Moll, subjectivity is more a sketch than fully developed interiority; but what is notable for my purposes here is Middleton's efficient representation of the conditions in which green sickness as a social disease might be said to flourish even among the middling ranks—physical inactivity and the inclination of overbearing and socially aspirant parents to diagnose pathology in a daughter's sexual reluctance that is easily explicable by other means.

The environmental complexity in Burton's account is thus ratified, in brief, in the brilliant social dialogue of Middleton's opening scene between Moll and her parents. More to the point, this complexity is inherent in early psychophysiology, which permitted minute environmental, cultural, or physical changes to have transforming effects on the humoral subject (including the melancholic virgin). In this respect, the passions, while only one of the six nonnatural factors constantly at work on body and mind, were understood to operate in the body as the winds and waters operated on the natural world. Thomas Wright explains how a change in the passions could work so radical a change in individual cognition, judgment, and behavior as almost to constitute metamorphosis: "wee may compare the Soule without passions, to a calme sea, with sweet, pleasant, and crispling streames: but the passionate, to the raging gulfe, swelling with waues, surging by tempests, minacing the stony rockes, and endeauouring to ouerthrow Mountaines: euen so, Passions make the Soule to swell with pride and pleasure; they threaten wounds, death and destruction, by audacious boldnesse and ire: they vndermine the mountaines of Vertue with hope and feare; and in summe, neuer let the soule be in quietnes, but euer, eyther flowing with pleasure, or ebbing with paine" (59). As the extravagance of Wright's tropes suggests, humoral explanation found it much easier to

account for a subject's moment-to-moment or day-to-day variations in temper and behavior than to account for emotional steadiness or even perhaps
for a high degree of psychological self-sameness. This was especially true
for those known to be inconstant—that is, women and effeminate men.
This is clear in Crooke's distinction between the sudden flare-ups of female
heat versus the "*Ira permanens,*" which belongs to "stout heartes" (276).
Furthermore, it took only a minor change in internal temperature to produce powerful alterations of behavior. Wright explains that the heart is
"prepared by nature to digest the blood sent from the liuer" but that a given
individual's heart, either by nature or by circumstance, would not necessarily have the "temperature which all passions require; for loue will haue
heat, and sadnesse cold, feare constringeth, & pleasure dilateth" (35). From
this point of view, the heaviness and lassitude of reluctant virgins—as
Burton suggested—is symptomatic of a sense of powerlessness and productive of their physical coldness rather than the reverse. But when spurred on
by a passion, the humors acted upon the heart to bring it to the temperature
required to propel a given emotion or course of action. Wright points out
that "although the heart hath more excesse of heate than cold, yet a little
melancholly blood may quickly change the temperature, and render it more
apt for a melancholly Passion" (35). A little discouragement, in other words,
has swift and significant consequences.

Most early modern philosophers emphasize the overwhelming influence of the humors and passions on the soul, both for good and for ill. They
insist on the enormous difficulty the rational soul experiences in trying to
govern the unruly internal organs and fluids only ostensibly at its command. Thomas Wright argues that for the sake of an inner peace, most subjects allow their reason to serve their passions: "after that men, by reason,
take possession ouer their soules and bodies, feeling this war so mightie, so
continuall, so neere, so domesticall, that either they must consent to doe
their enemies will, or still be in conflict: and withall, foreseeing by making
peace with them, they were to receiue great pleasures and delights, the most
part of men resolue themselves, neuer to displease their sense or passions,
but to graunt them whatsoeuer they demand" (10). In such accounts, as
noted in the introduction, the humors and allied passions are accorded so
much power that calm rationality ceases to be the most characteristic aspect
of human cognition. Instead, humoral discourse advances the argument
that emotional volatility—even if, or especially if, derogated and moralized
as inconstancy—is a historically important, deeply gender-inflected variable
in early modern constructions of seventeenth-century moral philosophers,
and the contest between reason and passion opens out to participate in a

variety of different narratives. This is the story of what Norbert Elias so influentially named "the civilizing process"—the slow struggle to pacify and regulate the emotions that Elias saw as characteristic of early modern society.[38] It is the civilizing process that becomes an enriched historical context for my returning to green sick virgins and to the urgent passionateness— the torrent of inward melancholic humors—that motivates their despair. I do not wish to exaggerate this sadness, as Burton does; to lexicalize it, as Lange does; or to reduce it to *furor uterinus*, a disease of the womb only.[39] But I do want to take the humoral context of women's sadness seriously whenever that mood is evoked, even fleetingly, in fictional texts. When used to introduce a character, and especially when depicted as floating free of any immediate cause, sadness becomes crucially performative of female coldness and passivity—of what was characterized as innate female lack but that we might recharacterize more sympathetically as culturally occasioned female loss. And the discarding of initial sadness is a sign of the nature of the affective and bodily changes imagined to occur when young female protagonists are aroused, through the workings of desire, to their ostensible biological (and patriarchal) destiny as wives and mothers.

I want to suggest here that this pattern of initial sadness discarded for love works, psychophysiologically, as an example of early modern thinking about the female life cycle, especially about the reciprocal interactions among habits of mind, body, passions, humors, and environments—that is, all the variables thought to be working constantly on the subject to alter what she thought and felt, how she behaved. To admit the influence of all environmental factors—but especially, perhaps, the role of the passions and the humors—might work to account for the noticeable transformations that regularly occur in Shakespeare's unmarried female protagonists. Often they change in state and disposition, from the quiet, often sad passivity that Burton associates with solitary idle gentlewomen brooding on their own powerlessness to a bold adventurousness demonstrated by secret marriages, elopements, and cross-dressing. In the context provided by Lange and Burton, three of Shakespeare's female protagonists may serve as representative cases in point, with Desdemona and Rosalind anchoring a discussion of virgins' melancholy and Katherine Minola providing a contrasting example.

38. For a recent critique of Elias as painting a too "linear process of inhibition," see Anna Bryson, *From Courtesy to Civility: Changing Codes of Conduct in Early Modern England* (Oxford: Clarendon Press, 1998), 10–14, esp. 14.

39. Laurinda Dixon, *Perilous Chastity: Women and Illness in Pre-Enlightenment Art and Medicine* (Ithaca, NY: Cornell University Press, 1995), 11–58.

To recognize this change in the case of Desdemona, we must consider
the possibility that Brabantio is neither merely wrong nor deceived about
the "tender, fair, and happy" daughter he describes as

> so opposite to marriage that she shunn'd
> The wealthy curled [darlings] of our nation.
>
> (*Othello*, 1.2.66–68)

Did we not know that the description referred to one who had already
eloped with a Moorish general, indeed that the words are spoken to the
trangressing suitor himself, such a description might remind us of Lange's
description of Anna. And since at this early point in the play, Brabantio's
daughter (like her new husband) has yet to be accorded a proper name, we
might see the conventionality of this description as part of Shakespeare's
larger narrative strategy to delay naming his two central figures as long as
possible in order to play with the very ideas of conventionality and individuality as the charged parameters of social judgment and evaluation. In the
play, the difference between Brabantio's household and the situation
implied by Lange's description of Anna and her unhappy father is that
there is no evidence that widower Brabantio—at least before her elopement
and now at this moment of outraged retrospect—regretted his daughter's reluctance to entertain suitors. He describes Desdemona's domestic
circumstance without self-consciousness as a "guardage" that she would
not freely have left behind. The irony here, then, is that if Desdemona's
prior state of virginal reluctance has been cured—in Lange's terms—by
marriage, that cure is portrayed here as a kind of bad medicine. Brabantio
exclaims,

> Judge me the world, if 'tis not gross in sense,
> That thou hast practic'd on her with foul charms,
> Abus'd her delicate youth with drugs or minerals
> That weakens motion. I'll have't disputed on
> 'Tis probable, and palpable to thinking.
> I therefore apprehend and do attach thee
> For an abuser of the world, a practicer
> Of arts inhibited and out of warrant.
>
> (1.2.72–79)

Brabantio turns Othello into a version of the Venetian mountebank—an
"abuser of the world"—though one allowed inside the house under false

pretenses, to practice on a guarded Venetian woman, much as Volpone with "Scoto's oil" will later practice from a makeshift stage erected in public space on the guarded and married Celia. In Othello's account of Desdemona's response to his autobiographical narrative, we are shown a young woman awakening to, or being reminded urgently of, female lack, dispossession, inactivity. She becomes a young woman more closely resembling the green sick virgin:

[I] often did beguile her of her tears,
When I did speak of some distressful stroke
That my youth suffer'd. My story being done,
She gave me for my pains a world of [sighs],
She swore, in faith 'twas strange, 'twas passing strange;
'Twas pitiful, 'twas wondrous pitiful.
She wish'd she had not heard it, yet she wish'd
That heaven had made her such a man.

(1.3.156–63)

Is Desdemona weeping before she hears Othello's story as well as when she hears it? Does she wish not to hear it because it reminds her of her own powerlessness and inactivity, the limitations of her life under guardage? We can recognize Desdemona here, at an early stage of desire and certainly before her initiation into sexual experience (whenever that may be said to happen), as aroused from maidenly withdrawal and melancholy by the heat of her passion for Othello and for the imagined world of action he brings into her guardage. Even if we acknowledge that these contrasting portraits of Desdemona by Brabantio and Othello represent the clear self-interest of each speaker, that self-interestedness too would repeat a diagnostic paradigm in which the conditions of female subjectivity are described from the outside—with one speaker discounting the factor of individual desire, the other highlighting it. Brabantio is Lange's concerned father, though he does not identify Desdemona's reluctance to entertain suitors as a symptom of disease. When he later represents her to the Senate, she more closely resembles the green sick virgin:

A maiden never bold,
Of spirit so still and quiet that her motion
Blush'd at herself; and she, in spite of nature,
Of years, of country, credit, every thing
To fall in love with what she fear'd to look on!

It is a judgment maim'd, and most imperfect,
That will confess perfection so could err
Against all rules of nature.

(1.3.94–101)

Wisely, Othello assumes the point of view later expressed by Burton, representing Desdemona with a sense of powerlessness and lack of purpose in her father's household. Even if the motherless Desdemona—unlike Burton's inactive virgins—has "household affairs [that] would draw her hence," Othello implies her lack of interest in them.[40] To Othello's narrative she would "seriously incline." The household affairs, he says, she would "with haste dispatch" in order to hurry back "with a greedy ear" to "devour up my discourse" (1.3.146–50). This figure of aroused aural desire is a famous one, though it has not been seen in the context provided by medical accounts of the melancholy maiden's general listlessness and aversion to food. In Othello's view, Desdemona seems to lack appetite for the responsibilities of her father's household, a lack demonstrated as well as remedied by her hunger for his own narrative. In this sense, her appetite for an exotic narrative is only a slight displacement of her appetite for the exotic subject in that narrative. He—or marriage to him—becomes the cause of a new vitality in her, vitality ready to make its escape from a purposeless existence, to dispose of itself. But the contradiction represented in these two accounts of Desdemona is subtle, for Brabantio must on the one hand portray his daughter as uninterested in eligible Venetian suitors—hence, according to the green sick narrative, victim of a deficiency and disorder of appetite—and on the other accuse Othello of having persuaded his otherwise happy daughter to elope only by means of perverting her appetite with

some mixtures pow'rful o'er the blood,
Or with some dram (conjur'd to this effect).

(1.3.104–5)

Here, it is in the father's interest to try to deny his daughter's interest in suitors in order to protest against the particular marriage-as-remedy that her husband now claims to have effected. But psychophysiological transfor-

40. Natasha Korda makes this point in *Shakespeare's Domestic Economies: Gender and Property in Early Modern England* (Philadelphia: University of Pennsylvania Press, 2002), 148.

mation by means of desire would account for the newfound agency that
Desdemona demonstrates in the boldness of her speech before the Senate
when she expresses an appetite that does not seem to distinguish between
her husband and the wayfaring life he has previously led:

> That I [did] love the Moor to live with him,
> My downright violence, and storm of fortunes,
> May trumpet to the world.

(1.3.248–50)

Because at this point the audience is, like the Senate, being asked to
approve Desdemona's choice and hence accept her decision to elope as the
only means to effect it, we tend to reject the possibly negative implication
of this newly aroused taste and desire. But Iago seizes upon this possibility
as the basis for his persistent construction of a narrative of disordered
female appetite in which Desdemona is increasingly implicated. Using the
idiom of early modern misogyny and its characterization of female inconstancy, Iago describes Desdemona's new appetite as a natural development
of womanhood, even as he echoes Brabantio's judgment that for her to
desire Othello can only be a perversion of appetite: "She must change for
youth; when she is sated with his body, she will find the [error] of her
choice" (1.3.349–51).

My point here is not to incline toward Brabantio's or Othello's account
of Desdemona but rather to insist on the possibility that, in humoral narratives of the reluctant virgin, an early modern audience would have a framework for recognizing and normalizing the social transformation in her
from still, quiet maiden to boldly articulate wife. This resolves the contradiction between the two men's accounts, allowing us to see Brabantio and
Othello as not representing her only through the powerful lenses of their
own self-interest rather than describing Desdemona herself; such a framework opens up a hermeneutic space for the thermal transformations
wrought by desire. The two described behaviors would mark the thermal
difference between women married and unmarried, between virgins before
the onset of desire and women—married or not—in its throes. Such a
transformation would account not only for bold Desdemona before the
Senate but also for the sophisticated Desdemona who banters with Iago
while waiting for Othello's ship to arrive and especially the determined
Desdemona who promises to Cassio that she will perform the intercession
he requires of her "to the last article" (3.3.22). In Edward Snow's nice

phrase, she speaks in "the voice . . . of a free, ethically empowered subject."[41]
In Desdemona's naive expectation of success—"I give thee warrant of thy
place," she tells Cassio (20)—we may find (beyond the obvious dramatic
irony) something of a new wife's overconfidence in her powers. As the wife
of a husband who declares that the content he feels upon being reunited
with her is

> so absolute
> That another comfort like to this
> Succeeds in unknown fate
>
> (2.1.191–93)

she may understandably regard herself as the new center of Othello's world
and behave accordingly. Her overconfidence has been anticipated in Iago's
two remarks to Cassio on Desdemona's likely power to help him—the cynical assessment that "Our general's wife is now the general" and the insight
that "she holds it a vice in her goodness not to do more than she is
requested" (2.3.315–16, 321–22).

But if we give full weight to the taming language she employs in
describing how she will work upon Othello, we do not really need Iago's
help to see Desdemona as feeling herself endowed with social purpose
through a predictable alteration in temperature and temperament accompanying marriage, her new adventurous life, and her dramatic change of
scene. What she promises Cassio to effect is very nearly a wholesale transformation of her husband's domestic environment, since she pledges to
"intermingle every thing he does / With Cassio's suit" (3.3.25–26):

> My lord shall never rest,
> I'll watch him tame, and talk him out of patience;
> His bed shall seem a school, his board a shrift.
>
> (22–24)

To "watch him tame"—to tame him by preventing him from sleeping—is to
use the means employed by falconers in taming their wild birds for domestic use. In *Taming of the Shrew*, as we shall see below, Petruchio keeps Kate
awake and starves her as part of a Galenic strategy of overall environmental

---

41. Edward A. Snow, "Sexual Anxiety and the Male Order of Things in *Othello*," *English Literary Renaissance* 10 (1980): 406.

manipulation designed to remove choler and lower the body's temperature. He, too, sees himself as a falconer taming a falcon—but what Desdemona promises here, scandalously, is a strong reversal of gender roles in which she becomes Othello's tamer, tutor, and confessor. The absoluteness of her promise to Cassio may imply that she regards Othello's censure of him as prompted by excessive choler, or perhaps—in these promises to tame and school him, to make his dinner table a confessional—that she regards her husband as requiring emotional regulation, penance, and forgiveness. Even before Cassio has asked for her intervention, Emilia tells us that

> The general and his wife are talking of it,
> And she speaks for you stoutly.
>
> (3.1.43–44)

Either Desdemona must disagree with Othello on the justness of Cassio's punishment, or she wishes to test her own new environmental powers as wife.

Shakespeare does offer a glimpse of Desdemona's notion of taming strategies in the scene when she begins to intercede for Cassio and displays a verbal persistence bordering on aggressiveness, refusing to accept Othello's repeated demurs for appointing a time to see Cassio and finally seeking to shame him for his hesitation by calling it "mamm'ring"—that is, stammering or hesitating:

> When shall he come?
> Tell me, Othello. I wonder in my soul
> What you would ask of me that I should deny,
> Or stand so mamm'ring on.
>
> (3.3.67–70)

She accuses her husband here of lacking the generosity of spirit that she herself would display to him, should he ask a similar favor. In doing so, she courts the kind of blame that, in *The Comedy of Errors*, the Abbess (rather unfairly) directs at Adriana while accusing her of causing the Ephesian Antipholus's madness:

> It seems his sleeps were hind'red by thy railing,
> And thereof comes it that his head is light.
> Thou say'st his meat was sauc'd with thy upbraidings,

Unquiet meals make ill digestions,
Thereof the raging fire of fever bred,
And what's a fever but a fit of madness?

(5.1.71–76)

To make this connection between Desdemona and Adriana is not to accuse either wife of shrewishness, and not to become one of those critics whom Carol Neely has accused of almost blaming Desdemona for causing her own murder.[42] Desdemona does not participate in the psychophysiological transformation of Othello that occurs as a result of Iago's insinuations. Desdemona has little chance in the play's foreshortened time scheme to put her Cassio project into action, and by the end of this scene, Othello has already begun to be—in her unwittingly euphemistic phrase—"not well" (3.3.289). By the end of the next scene, Desdemona has recognized in him the transformation, the puddling of his spirit, that I focus on in chapter 1, and her boldness of spirit has begun to shrink from the onset of his anger. By the time they are together in their bedchamber, Desdemona has retreated before her husband's sudden, inexplicable rage and violence and must now plead for her own reinstatement in Othello's affections. Her recalling (in 4.3) her mother's lovesick maid Barbary and her plaintive singing of Barbary's song may help to reinforce our sense of her return to a withdrawn and melancholy state, as she faces the sudden, inexplicable loss of her husband's love and her own intimations of mortality. The early sense of female lack that inspires Desdemona to wish "that heaven had made her such a man" (1.3.163) returns here. Her identification with the lovesick Barbary suggests a recursive identification with her own early powerlessness as a maiden in her father's house, especially when she sings the plaintive, self-despairing line, "Let nobody blame him, his scorn I approve" (4.3.52). One irony of her circumstance, as critics have long suggested (though not in the context of the narrative of the reluctant virgin), is that in the final scene her husband wants, in effect, to return her to that state of virginal reluctance. In his fatal approach to her bed, he looks with pained desire upon "that whiter skin of hers than snow, / And smooth as monumental alablaster" (5.2.4–5)—a pallor and coldness complexly associated not only with a sleeping woman, but (I am suggesting) with the reluctant virgin he found not long before in Brabantio's house.[43] The irony we may

42. Carol Thomas Neely, *Broken Nuptials in Shakespeare's Plays* (New Haven, CT: Yale University Press, 1985), 106.

43. For this argument, see Valerie Traub, "Jewels, Statues, and Corpses: Containment of Female Erotic Power in Shakespeare's Plays," *Shakespeare Studies* 20 (1988): 225–27.

now add to the overwhelming ironies of the end of the play is that in her fear of her husband and nostalgia for a safer time in her life, Desdemona has already begun to retreat to that earlier affective state of female pallor and reluctance associated with the unmarried woman.

What I also want to emphasize here is how the early modern narratives of the reluctant virgin and disordered female appetite work to entangle Desdemona in Iago's insinuations, even as those narratives help to account for the transformations in Desdemona that we witness in comparing her father's portrait of her as reluctant virgin to the new wife who stands in brilliant self-explanation before the Senate begging to leave for Cyprus and who, once there, rashly promises to change her husband's mind about an act of military discipline. If the Senate cleared Othello of the act of poisoning "this young maid's affections" (1.3.112), it did not quite relieve Desdemona from carrying the burden of misogynistic narratives of women's propensity, beginning in maidenhood, for disorders of the appetite. After all, Iago's predictions to Roderigo echo in a virulent form the misogynistic narratives of disordered female appetite, a disorder that Iago proposes as natural: "When the blood is made dull with the act of sport, there should be, [again] to inflame it and to give satiety a fresh appetite, loveliness in favor, sympathy in years, manners, and beauties—all of which the Moor is defective in. Now for want of these requir'd conveniences, her delicate tenderness will find itself abus'd, begin to heave the gorge, disrelish and abhor the Moor; very nature will instruct her in it" (2.1.226–34).

Here, in this cynical prolepsis, Desdemona's earlier delicacy and reluctance are made to turn against her; her reported lack of appetite for any suitor returns in a distorted form as she is imagined to disrelish the suitor she chose and look for another one. "If she had been bless'd," Iago tells Roderigo contemptuously, "she would never have lov'd the Moor" (252–53). It is all the more interesting, in this context, that when Iago describes Cassio's attractiveness to Desdemona, he sums it up by noting that he "hath all those requisites in him that folly and green minds look after" (2.1.246–47). Greenness of mind calls up contradictory explanations—unripeness and immaturity of judgment (*OED*, 8c) or vitality and youthfulness (*OED*, 7).[44] Both options could serve Iago here, whether he wants to criticize Desdemona for having chosen Othello in the first place or imagine that she will be led by her now-aroused appetite to exchange objects of desire. Thus Cleopatra similarly defends her youthful choice of Caesar as lover by describing it as one made in

---

44. The Riverside edition glosses *green* here as "youthful, lusty," while the Folger Library edition, like many others, prefers "unripe and immature."

My salad days,
When I was green in judgment, cold in blood.

$$(1.5.73-74)^{45}$$

Iago's imputation of greenness of mind to Desdemona would, in any case, justify her change in object choice. But more to my purposes here, the term identifies her judgment as being biologically determined—the mind's inclination following the body's temperature. Iago builds systematically on Brabantio's suspicion about the nature of Desdemona's appetite, describing in soliloquy her newfound power in marriage as "her appetite" that

shall play the god
With his weak function.

$$(2.3.347-48)$$

He reminds Othello of Brabantio's public portrait of his daughter, as if that initial reluctance to marry another Venetian, followed by the spectacular transgression of her choice, implied a perversion of appetite that now leads her to adultery:

Not to affect many proposed matches
Of her own clime, complexion, and degree,
Whereto we see in all things nature tends—
Foh, one may smell in such, a will most rank,
Foul disproportions, thoughts unnatural.

$$(3.3.229-33)$$

It is Iago's harping on likeness of "clime, complexion, and degree" as a characteristic of ordinary appetite and desire that cues us to the psychophysiological basis of his accusation here—and to the cultural narratives of disordered female appetite that, as we have seen, attach to humoral discourse. His suggestion is that Desdemona's choice of Othello represents a perverse response to or interaction with her environment—clime, complexion, and degree—considered in a totalizing way. Her rejection of her proper relation to the social goods of this environment—metonymized by eligible suitors—is thus not unlike that of Lange's Anna or of Moll Yellowhammer. Iago reminds Othello of Brabantio's belief that the apparent perverseness of

45. Cleopatra describes herself then as moist and cold like salad—the green mind's inclination following the cold body's temperature, indeed the mind being "green" because of the cold body's temperature.

her choice was due to an intervention by Othello in the workings of Desdemona's appetite—but Iago succeeds in leading Othello to accept instead that it was "nature erring from itself" (227). Othello's taking her hand in the next scene builds on the implied diagnostics at work here, when he finds it "hot, hot, and moist" (3.4.39)—the moist heat of the hand betraying a rise in the body's temperature.[46]

Desdemona ignores, or chooses not to recognize, the threatening implication of this thermal representation here, since Othello goes on more reassuringly to call the hot, hot, and moist hand "a good hand, / A frank one" (43–44).[47] Desdemona accepts her hand as a symbol of intention and an agency located firmly within the body: "'twas that hand that gave away my heart" (45). But perhaps we should imagine that her palm is in fact sweaty: she is anxious about the lost handkerchief, has made a point of stoutly denying to Emilia and herself the increasingly obvious possibility that Othello is jealous, and has decided to press Othello hard on the subject of Cassio:

> I will not leave him now till Cassio
> Be call'd to him.
>
> (32–33)

Indeed, as new wife in love with her husband, as new wife testing out her powers over that husband, as new wife endowed with an agency symbolized for the moment by Cassio's suit, Desdemona would have no reason to shrink from a diagnosis of "hot, hot, and moist." As Thomas Wright insists, "loue will haue heat and sadnesse cold, feare constringeth, & pleasure dilateth." Even so, this may be the last moment in the play when Desdemona feels the warmth of happiness in marriage and the expansion of ethical agency that her still-new change of status seems to have created in her. Her decision to continue her suit on Cassio's behalf feels to us disastrous, if not dispositive—given what we have seen of Iago's rapid success in convincing Othello of her infidelity. It is the first sign of real fear in her that, under Othello's angry questioning, she lies about the loss of the handkerchief: "It is not lost; but what and if it were?" (83).[48] Certainly it is a sign of loss of confidence in the life of adventure that she welcomes the Senate's orders, as

---

46. See Traub, "Jewels, Statues, and Corpses," 223.

47. See Harry Berger Jr., "Impertinent Trifling: Desdemona's Handkerchief," *Shakespeare Quarterly* 47 (1996): 238, on her reasons to ignore the obvious evidence of Othello's jealousy.

48. Ibid., 240.

delivered by Ludovico, for them to return to Venice: "[By my troth], I am glad on't" (4.1.238)—words that Othello misconstrues as her pleased response to the news of Cassio's assignment as new governor of Cyprus. But perhaps even more indicative of Desdemona's affective retreat from wifely confidence and boldness is the note of strong self-remonstrance that she strikes in accepting Othello's treatment of her:

> 'Tis meet I should be us'd so, very meet.
> How have I been behav'd, that he might stick
> The small'st opinion on my least misuse?
>
> (4.2.107–9)[49]

Emilia's exclamation "Here's a change indeed!" (106) encompasses all the affective reversals under way, including an affective transformation in Desdemona herself. She cannot find an answer to Iago's question "How is't with you?" (110). "I cannot tell," she replies, and goes on to express wistful nostalgia for childhood, a regressive desire to be a daughter again and in the protective climate of her father's guardage:

> Those that do teach young babes
> Do it with gentle means and easy tasks.
> He might have chid me so; for in good faith
> I am a child to chiding.
>
> (4.2.111–14)

But her memory of her dead mother, her identification with the servant Barbary, and her singing of the lovesick maid's song revise her nostalgia for her youthful home and self, allowing the Venetian house to include within its emotional boundaries a wider history of sexual betrayal and even madness (since Barbary's love "prov'd mad / And did forsake her" [4.3.27–28]). Her question to Emilia about the possibility of married women's infidelity—distinguishing sharply between the kind of sexual forsaking that one might expect of men, but not of women—is itself a kind of retreat into childlike naïveté. It is sharply at odds with the sophistication of her quayside banter with Iago in 2.1, which presupposes, at the very least, knowledge of misogynistic lore—what she calls "old fond paradoxes to make fools laugh i'th' alehouse" (2.1.138–39).

---

49. See Korda, 149, on Desdemona's resemblance here to the tamed Kate at the end of *Taming of the Shrew* and to Mistress Ford in *Merry Wives*.

It may be that our assured conviction of Desdemona's blamelessness has obscured the affective changes that she undergoes in the course of the play,[50] or that tragic focus on the greater affective changes in Othello have drawn attention away from what goes on within Desdemona to effect radical change. In terms of psychophysiology, the language of the play is, as I suggest in chapter 1, very concerned to represent the material changes, the darkening of judgment, wrought by choler to the clear workings of Othello's spirits. Desdemona is not choleric, nor do we much observe her being wrought upon by strong passions until the strong onset of fear in the moments before she is murdered:

> And yet I fear you; for you're fatal then
> When your eyes roll so. Why I should fear I know not,
> Since guiltiness I know not; but yet I feel I fear.
>
> (5.2.37–39)

But as I noted earlier, the materialism of early modern thought means that embodiment is everywhere assumed in affective discourses, just as bodily references always assume an affective context or consequence. Thus, considering the narratives of melancholic virgins and the transformations wrought in them by desire, we ought to recognize strong affective change in Desdemona as she moves from being the reluctant virgin reported to us, in different ways, by both father and husband to being the bold and confident wife traduced by Iago and finally the fearful wife who shrinks before her husband's murderous anger and gives puzzlingly contradictory witness of a "guiltless death" whose doer she refuses to name: "Nobody; I myself" (5.2.122, 124).

For the early moderns, Othello's transformation from the self-contained man we meet confronting an outraged father and his armed supporters to the explosively angry one who believes himself cuckolded and decides to murder his wife writes a pathological narrative effected by such environmental factors as geohumoralism and the passions becoming increasingly associated with black skin.[51] Desdemona's sudden burst of confident agency, by contrast, reveals what the Elizabethans might have regarded as the ordinary workings of strong desire in young women—especially, perhaps (if we wish to follow Burton here), sheltered aristocratic ones moving out from their guardage to the wider social horizons of marriage. But we

50. On this point, see Korda, 149 and 245n100, where she argues that our forgetting "is likewise abetted by the displacement of Desdemona's shrewish attributes onto Bianca."

51. See Floyd-Wilson's discussion of *Othello* (132).

can recognize that ordinary change as more emphatic and meaningful, thanks to the complex allowances of the old fluid physiologies, wherein all the environmental factors of psychophysiological change are put into play. In these terms, Desdemona's marriage—even apart from its scandalousness—would itself have brought about a change in her capacity for agency, but the witness and scope of that agency are much enlarged by what Burton might see as the "torrent of inward humors" in her before marriage, by the change of scene that occurs so soon after her elopement, and by her change of status not just from maiden to wife but from maiden to wife of the governor of Cyprus. As I suggested above, Othello's narrative of his courtship of Desdemona seems to recognize her sense of powerlessness and desire for change as part of her capacity for desiring him:

> She wish'd she had not heard it, yet she wish'd
> That heaven had made her such a man.
>
> (1.3.162–63)

Changed by her translation in marriage to Othello in Cyprus, Desdemona is not rendered culpable by reason of her bold confidence and her vows to tame her husband, but she is made vulnerable by them.

Similar transformations, I would argue, occur in a number of Shakespeare heroines. In this section, I concentrate on the affective transformation that we see in Rosalind, because she is known more for merriment than for melancholy and because she inhabits a play not conspicuously attentive to the old fluid physiologies. I will argue that in Shakespeare's representation of Rosalind, as in his representation of Desdemona, we need to recognize traces of humoral discourse or its relation to the language of affect in order to recognize affective changes obscured for us by the post-Enlightenment dematerialization of embodied emotion.

In fact, it is the weight of Rosalind's sadness that immediately greets us in her first appearance onstage in *As You Like It*: "I pray thee, Rosalind, sweet my coz, be merry," Celia implores her (1.2.1–2). Rosalind's despondent reply—"I show more mirth than I am mistress of, and would you yet [I] were merrier?" (3–4)—is the first constitutive mark of her subjectivity. Like Hamlet, she insists upon a gap between "a socially visible exterior and an invisible personal interior," here between the effort of feigning mirth and the sudden flash of genuine melancholy.[52] And her sadness, like his, has

---

52. I am quoting here from Maus, 12. Valerie Traub has noted that Rosalind's silent denial of homoerotic bonds with Celia constitutes her power and sets the stage for the eradication of

the grief of parental loss and personal and political dispossession as external cause: "Unless you could teach me to forget a banish'd father, you *must*
not learn me how to remember any extraordinary pleasure" (5–6, emphasis
added). Such forgetting is impossible: her father's banishment is the sole
explanation for her current state of being, since it has reduced her from
being princess and heiress to a dukedom to being, in effect, her cousin's
waiting gentlewoman, handmaiden to Celia's destiny. Rosalind is unable to
take instruction in pleasure, to admit it into her mind, and she forbids Celia
to impose it on her. Disjunction between outer and inner states corresponds
to the social facts of her dispossession. She would be "mistress" of more
mirth were she mistress indeed, not Celia's social subordinate, a fact that
she marks grammatically in the pronouns of address. Though Celia
addresses her familiarly and affectionately as "thee," Rosalind replies with
the formal "you," here a grammar of sadness and self-loss. This grammatical
asymmetry of address is little noted by critics, because, as Margreta de
Grazia has noted apropos of *thou/you* address in the sonnets, the "highly
complex code" governing forms of address remains unbroken for us—
though "the unwritten rules governing second person usage in the
Renaissance were social and hierarchic."[53] Indeed, Rosalind's use of "you"
here could also work as a distancing device, with Celia asserting their identity and Rosalind asserting difference through their asymmetrical pronouns
of address.[54] The marked disparity in the two characters' moods tracked by
these pronoun changes corresponds to the inequality of their circumstances, the disparity in their terms of address, and to what Celia somewhat
accusingly names the gap in their affections: "Herein I see thou lov'st me
not with the full weight that I love thee. If my uncle, thy banish'd father,
had banish'd thy uncle, the Duke my father, so thou hadst been still with
me, I could have taught my love to take thy father for mine; so wouldst
thou, if the truth of thy love to me were so righteously temper'd as mine is
to thee" (8–14). Celia's implied rebuke—you do not take the "Duke my
father" as your father; I would love your father more than you do mine—
marks the truth of Rosalind's internal exile. Social difference thus elides
with a difference of temper, Rosalind's sense of powerlessness medicalized

homoerotic desire between women; see "The (In)significance of 'Lesbian' Desire in Early Modern
England," in *Erotic Politics: Desire on the Renaissance Stage*, ed. Susan Zimmerman (London:
Routledge, 1992), 157–58.

53. Margreta de Grazia, "The Scandal of Shakespeare's Sonnets," *Shakespeare Survey* 46
(1994): 43.

54. See Roger Brown and Albert Gilman, "The Pronouns of Power and Solidarity," in *Style in
Language*, ed. Thomas E. Sebeok (Cambridge, MA: MIT Press, 1960), 257.

and depoliticized by Celia as a distemper of affection, as coldness by comparison to Celia's warmth. Valerie Traub has argued that female homoerotic love such as that between Celia and Rosalind is primarily represented elegiacally, as "what *was* rather than what *is* or what *might be*."[55] Yet the self-interest in Celia's diagnosis, which is hard to miss, is also not uncharacteristic of humoral diagnosis generally, when social differences are naturalized or pathologized as humoral traits. It is Celia who will protest to her father that she and Rosalind, because inseparable, are indistinguishable:

> If she be a traitor,
> Why, so am I. We still have slept together,
> Rose at an instant, learn'd, play'd, eat together,
> And wheresoe'er we went, like Juno's swans,
> Still we went coupled and inseparable.
>
> (1.3.72–76)

Celia declares that her father's usurpation of Duke Senior took place years before, when she "was too young that time to value" Rosalind (71); perhaps we are to understand that her insistence on their indistinguishability and inseparability now is not merely self-interested, not merely the elegiac recollection of femme-femme love, but also the mark of a new difference in consciousness between them brought about by Rosalind's sudden or at least relatively new awareness of the extent of her deprivation—as she and her cousin move out of girlhood and approach the marital threshold with very different prospects.[56] Rosalind's melancholy—like the sudden sadness of Lange's Anna—could then be understood as brought on by a sense of dispossession that is indistinguishably political, dynastic, marital, and erotic. It is Celia whose version of emotional plenitude is a fantasy of permanent union with her cousin—"Rosalind lacks then the love which teacheth thee that thou and I am one" (1.3.96–97). After the Duke's abrupt decree of banishment against Rosalind, it is Celia who vows to take on Rosalind's sadness along with her expulsion, even as Rosalind keeps insisting on the differences and distances between them. To Celia's plea, "Be not thou more griev'd than I am," she curtly remarks, "I have more cause" (92–93).

---

55. Traub, *Renaissance of Lesbianism*, 172.

56. It is more usual for critics to accept Celia's language here as describing Rosalind's feelings about their youth as well as her own; see Mario DiGangi, "Queering the Shakespearean Family," *Shakespeare Quarterly* 47 (1996): 274–75. Valerie Traub does describe the power asymmetry between Celia and Rosalind, with Celia being disadvantaged by clinging to a homoerotic love for Rosalind while Rosalind abandons it. She does not, however, reflect on the effects of Rosalind's political circumstances; see Traub, "(In)significance of 'Lesbian' Desire," 158.

These marked temperamental and affective distinctions between the two cousins serve, among other things, to constitute Rosalind as the subject in question, to define Rosalind's sadness as performatively female insofar as femaleness connotes loss measured both objectively and subjectively. But Rosalind keeps insisting that her lack is objectively greater than Celia's— "I have more cause." Once Rosalind has fallen in love with Orlando—even before the decree of banishment later in the scene—her sadness and sense of dispossession deepen into hopelessness and inarticulateness. "Why, cousin, why Rosalind!" exclaims Celia after the wrestling match, "Cupid have mercy, not a word?" (1.3.1–2). As Mario DiGangi argues, the spectacle of male-male combat that the cousins watch spurs heteroerotic desire in Rosalind—indeed, a falling in love at first sight (275). But rather than moving her out of despair, falling in love intensifies Rosalind's sad mood with an augmented sense of self-absence and loss. A portion of her sadness now, Rosalind acknowledges, is reserved for her "child's father" (1.3.11). As the legitimate but dispossessed heir to a dukedom, recognized by her uncle as a political threat for the love the people bear her, Rosalind could not expect to have his permission to marry or bear a child—as Celia could and indeed must. Rosalind's dispossession is now political, marital, and reproductive, her chastity now doubly enforced. Even more than Burton's other idle and melancholy virgins, Rosalind has no social purpose—indeed has had a birthright social purpose taken away, apparently forever. Under such circumstances, to find an object of desire in Orlando can only mean what she says it does—grieving over the preemptive loss of her "child's father."

We should acknowledge these material grounds of Rosalind's sadness at her usurper uncle's court. Such deep causes of sadness would not be assuaged by the warmth of Celia's devotion, Celia's assertions (against the evidence) of their likeness, or Celia's promise to restore Rosalind's title upon Duke Frederick's death. Such a promise—clearly revocable, not enforceable—would, after all, turn Rosalind's lawful inheritance into Celia's gift. It is real hopelessness, I argue, that Rosalind dutifully tries to ward off for her cousin's sake—or at her cousin's urging. And if we do acknowledge this hopelessness, we can then see how the enforced removal to Arden could work a transforming magic on Rosalind's state of mind and body even apart from her adoption of male attire and the name of Ganymede. For, though she sets off to find her father upon her banishment, both that intention and her sadness disappear upon her arrival there with her impulsive decision as Ganymede to buy cottage and land and establish a tiny household with herself at its head. Not all of this difference in her can be chalked up to the cultural effects of male disguise or the presence of

Orlando in Arden. The sadness that belonged to the passive, dispossessed Rosalind does not inhere in the energetic, impulsive Ganymede because—I would argue, using Galen and Burton for technical support—a whole host of social, physical, and psychological circumstances collaborating to produce virgins' melancholy no longer obtains. Rosalind, thrust violently from a life of purposeless inactivity, no longer fits Burton's profile of the typical melancholic virgin with a life of enforced chastity and wrongful guardianship. Now tasked with the energizing responsibilities of heading a household, having assumed the body envelope of the male costume, we can imagine that she enjoys authority over the female cousin who has chosen to follow her as Aliena and that she revels in her freedom from the social and political oppression of an uncle whose last and least priority would have been to seek a husband for her, indeed whose political interests would have been served in finding Celia a mate but leaving Rosalind forever unmarried and dependent. If we should remember that "Rosalind is a princess, while Orlando is no more than a gentleman,"[57] we should also remember that at the beginning of the play Rosalind is a dispossessed princess looking forward to no independent future at all, barring the unexpected turn of events that sends her out to Arden. Only by remembering that Rosalind cannot have anticipated her banishment, only by not reading the play backward, can we fully appreciate the virgins' melancholy—the torrent of inward humors—that afflicts Rosalind at her uncle's court.

Rosalind's psychological and behavioral transformation has traditionally been understood as the performative effects of her adoption of male disguise, her exploration of the social and emotional privileges of maleness. What I am arguing here is intended to complicate rather than contradict that view, to suggest that the gender disguise is sign and symptom of a prior and more enveloping psychophysiological transformation. While the heroine's emotional transformation in this play does involve a culturally significant regendering in order to allow for the playful and transgressive homoerotics of the wooing scenes, the change from passive and withdrawn maidenly melancholy to the better-tempered activism of social and psychological maturity does not occur only by the adoption of male disguise but by the action tendencies of desire (of any stripe) with its enabling humoral heat. In my reading, the end of Rosalind's melancholy is only partly due to the fortuitous arrival of Orlando and the pleasures of vicarious courtship in Arden. That melancholy has already begun to dissipate before the courtship

57. Leo Salingar, *Shakespeare and the Traditions of Comedy* (Cambridge: Cambridge University Press, 1974), 297; quoted also in Louis Adrian Montrose, " 'The Place of a Brother' in *As You Like It*: Social Process and Comic Form," *Shakespeare Quarterly* 32 (1981): 28.

commences, the "torrent of inward humors" causing her distemper allevi-
ated by a change of scene, a reordering of her life, and relief from the
enforced inaction and overwhelming subjection imposed on her in Duke
Frederick's court. When, later in Arden, Celia teases her about the identity
of the swain writing verses in the forest, Rosalind's energetic, impatient
questioning of her is specifically described as performatively female: "Good
my complexion, dost thou think, though I am caparison'd like a man, I
have a doublet and hose in my disposition? One inch of delay more is a
South-sea of discovery" (3.2.194–97). We ought to note that Rosalind now
addresses Celia in the familiar second-person pronoun—indeed both characters move back and forth between *thou* and *you* constructions—even as
Rosalind asserts her inner femaleness.[58] And her statement of impatience is
itself the prelude to a series of rapid-fire questions that leave no space for
an answer.

In the mock-wooing scenes, Ganymede offers Orlando two contrasting
versions of what it is to be psychophysiologically female—both based upon
the familiar denigrations of early modern misogyny. One is a portrait of
emotional inconstancy that closely resembles the kind of lability Crooke
sees as constitutively female when he contrasts the sudden and brief flare-
ups of female wrath with the steady heat of male anger. Ganymede says
that, pretending to be a woman, he has thus cured one lovesick swain:
"would I, being but a moonish youth, grieve, be effeminate, changeable,
longing and liking, proud, fantastical, apish, shallow, inconstant, full of
tears, full of smiles; for every passion something, and for no passion truly
any thing, as boys and women are for the most part cattle of that color;
would now like him, now loathe him; then entertain him, then forswear
him; now weep for him, then spit at him" (3.2.409–17). Since she goes on to
describe the suitor as having gone from a "mad humor of love" to a "living
humor of madness" (418–19), it is clear that her description of female emotional volatility here is heavily inflected by humoral understanding and
conventional descriptions of maidenly lovesickness. It is just such a misogynistic portrait of female affectivity—for every passion something and for
no passion truly anything—that underlies Congreve's notion of female passions as preventing the formation of true individuality, for true individuality in this quasi-biological conception presupposes a greater degree of
affective stability than women were thought to possess. It is this same
volatility, shared by women and effeminate men, that in *Twelfth Night*

---

58. Brown and Gilman suggest that the *you/thou* changes would indicate mood and emotion in
very transient interactions; see 273–74.

underlies Maria's dismissive description of Sir Andrew as unable to maintain the emotional constancy to move from sudden anger to effective action: "he's a great quarreler; and but that he hath the gift of a coward to allay the gust he hath in quarreling, 'tis thought among the prudent he would quickly have the gift of a grave" (1.3.30–33).

Rosalind's second portrait—of women once they are wives—is premised on the fact of a dramatic change comparable to the change we have seen in Desdemona. Ganymede tells Orlando, "Maids are May when they are maids, but the sky changes when they are wives. I will be more jealous of thee than a Barbary cock-pigeon over his hen, more clamorous than a parrot against rain, more new-fangled than an ape, more giddy in my desires than a monkey. I will weep for nothing, like Diana in the fountain, and I will do that when you are dispos'd to be merry. I will laugh like a hyen, and that when thou art inclin'd to sleep" (4.1.148–56). Here, the similarity to Desdemona as wife lies less in the specific affects being promised than in the imagined degree of wifely boldness throughout, especially in the proclamation of wives' indifference to their husbands' moods. It is very much in this spirit that Desdemona promises Cassio, "I'll watch him tame and talk him out of patience." As we will see in chapter 4, the expectation of emotional subordination along hierarchical lines was one way that the social structure imposed itself on affective transactions. Here, what we need to pay attention to is less the misogynistic source material at work in Ganymede's portrait of women than the implied thermal transformation from the maiden's moody melancholy to the wife's emotional clamor—a transformation here deemed as inevitable as the calendar and as natural as the weather, to which mood changes were conventionally compared. The implied gender reversal—the wife as cock-pigeon, the husband as hen—resembles Desdemona's imagery of Othello as falcon, herself as tamer. Furthermore, like Desdemona's, Ganymede's is not a portrait of married life at court but of married life somewhat further down the social hierarchy, where either of the partners might be imagined as looking for one another in bed with a next-door neighbor.[59] So Rosalind is imagining not the socially privileged life she might have led without the usurpation, but a more ordinary life on an everyday scale of emotions where wives—with less penalty than Desdemona suffered—express themselves emotionally with remarkable heat and vigor.

It is, of course, the seriocomic specter of being married to a shrew that Ganymede offers to Orlando as the means of washing "your liver as clean as

59. DiGangi, 283.

a sound sheep's heart, that there shall not be one spot of love in't"
(3.2.422–24). The whole narrative is a forbidding, if playful, portrait of
female affective change from the excessive, cold passion of the maiden in
courtship to the hot clamorousness of the jealous wife. These passions are
represented as performatively, even generically female because, as Peter
Stallybrass has noted, misogyny generally is premised on a notion of
women as the same.[60] (Defenses of women are no less generic, of course, as
Celia indicates in scolding Rosalind for having "simply misus'd our sex in
your love-prate" [4.1.201–2]). In the love cure, itself premised on a kind of
behavioralism as a purge through theatrical rehearsal, Orlando is being
offered the option of escape from the obligation to manage and control
female affectivity—an option he does not choose in large part because he
(unlike Othello) refuses to buy into Ganymede's misogynistic representation of his beloved's likely behavior.

In *The Taming of the Shrew*, Shakespeare does actually create a shrewish
female protagonist, and the narrative of virginal diffidence because of
melancholy coldness is reversed. Here the cure targets not the lovesick
swain whose liver must be cleansed from spots of love but a choleric
maiden whose reluctance to marry—if that is what we may name it—mirrors the reluctance of her suitors to take on a choleric maiden: "She's too
rough for me," says Gremio, echoing the sentiments of the other wooers
onstage (1.1.55). In *Shrew*, the wooer-husband Petruchio's obligation
becomes one of reducing Kate's socially inappropriate and excessive female
heat to the more temperate thermal registers required of the properly
socialized wife. But in this harsh comedy, the lessons of emotional subordination are drawn in the contrasting experiments in Galenic humoralism
performed—in the frame and main plots—on Christopher Sly and
Katherine Minola. While the achievement of good temper involved a
manipulation of diet and other environmental factors theoretically available to all, in practice (as we have seen) humoral thinking and humoral tex-
tualization tended to reproduce—and thus to biologize—prevailing
narratives of social difference.[61] In vernacular medical texts, all the bodily
fluids of humoralism, but especially blood, are routinely classified in ethically and socially weighted language—a discourse of purity, clarity, differentiated worth. The sodden, lethargic tinker and the unruly choleric woman

60. Peter Stallybrass, "Patriarchal Territories: The Body Enclosed," in *Rewriting the Renaissance:
The Discourses of Sexual Difference in Early Modern Europe*, ed. Margaret W. Ferguson, Maureen
Quilligan, and Nancy Vickers (Chicago: University of Chicago Press, 1986), 133.

61. See Schoenfeldt, 11.

are represented humorally as opposites but socially as homologous in terms of their capacity for social disruption and unproductiveness. The play's actions present them both as subjects of behavioral experimentation through opposite means—pleasure therapy for Sly, aversion therapy for Kate. Together the two experiments in behavioral manipulation serve to question how far the mind's inclination really does follow the body's temperature, for they presume the possibility—though not the extent—of subjective transformation through environmental means.

The induction makes Sly a test case for human potentiality and productivity by constructing what I see as a set of humorally telling contrasts—with Sly in the middle between the lord's trained hunting dogs at one end of a localized scale of nature and the lord himself at the other. Such a contrast is implicitly a reminder (as we see in detail in chapter 3) that in this cosmology animals, too, were humoral creatures, their differences in flesh, blood, behavior, and temperament humorally determined and hierarchically ranked. Though the lord is not represented as a humoral subject himself (the question of his own temperament being mostly occluded), his trick on Sly does seem to be the result of lordly whim or caprice—humor in that sense of the term. And Sly's treatment is cast throughout as humoral therapy, both fictional (since Sly is not in fact a distracted lord) and real (since the means resemble actual practice on the insane). The lord comes upon Sly just after he and his huntsman have been discussing the care of his hounds and debating their merits. The dogs' traits identified as socially useful, pleasurable, and significant to the lord—their breeding; their individuality of voice and temperament; their responsiveness to training, management, and care; their economic value—are precisely at issue in Sly. Indeed his social progress in the two scenes is like an ascent up the scale of nature, since at first he seems barely to qualify as animate, to be more a feature of the landscape than of the human world: "What's here? One dead, or drunk? See, doth he breathe?" (induction, 1.31). Once established as alive, he looks to the lord like the wrong kind of animal: "O monstrous beast, how like a swine he lies" (34). Since in early modern cosmology to know a thing is to know what it resembles, the resemblance of man to pig is more disturbing to the conscious man at the top of the social order than to the barely conscious one at the bottom.[62] From this point of view, the lord's stated goal of seeing if he can make Sly "forget himself" (41) is paradoxical because it asks Sly to forget the self-forgetting already epitomized in his swinish drunken-

---

62. On the semiotics of the pig, see Peter Stallybrass and Allon White, *The Politics and Poetics of Transgression* (Ithaca, NY: Cornell University Press, 1986), 44–59.

ness. The higher form of self-forgetting that is supposed to occur by having him awaken suddenly as lord of an aristocratic household is a classic exercise in Galenic stimulation, designed to raise the slothful man's radical heat and moisture and clear the vapors of confusion from his sodden brain (here varied from the norm in that one form of confusion is being supplanted by another). The lord's tools range from the sensual enhancements of distilled waters, sweet smells, and music to the social enhancements of costly apparel, servants, a "lady wife," and the comic entertainment provided by the visiting players. Together these features constitute an almost complete transformation of the six nonnaturals and thus, within the terms of psychological materialism—of mind following the body's temperature—they signify analogously as the means of subjective overhaul. We can see, too, how the page Bartholomew's masquerade as Sly's wife is intended to function as a form of humoral subordination, to give to Sly what Malvolio imagined for himself as "the humor of state" in Olivia's household. "Such duty to the drunkard let him do," the lord instructs,

> With soft low tongue and lowly courtesy,
> And say, "What is't your honor will command,
> Wherein your lady, and your humble wife,
> May show her duty and make known her love?"

(ind., 114–17)

In effect, the lord's trick mimics the terms of Malvolio's gulling, offering up a dream of social elevation against the "humor" of lowness but in this case offering it to an unready object, one in whom the humoral ground is unprepared, one not already enamored of his own complexion. Returning to consciousness, Sly holds fast to the particularities of his identity—his name and social origins, his habits of drink and clothing, his series of lowly occupations. The lord pretends to find illness in this ordinary health, to find a disturbing continuity in Sly's residual lowness of nature:

> Heaven cease this idle humor in your honor!
> O that a mighty man of such descent,
> Of such possessions, and so high esteem,
> Should be infused with so foul a spirit.

(ind., 2.13–16)

The sensual inducements that Sly is then offered—the soft bed, the invitation to hunt, the visual stimulation of erotic scenes from Ovid—are intended

literally to warm him into activity from the lethargy associated with lowness
and drink. That metatheatrical reminder of the gender ideology of the
Elizabethan playhouses—the page's deferral "for a night or two" (ind., 2.119)
of Sly's sexual demands on him—also has a plausible medical explanation,
given that ejaculation was understood as a sometimes dangerous expenditure of spirit. As a well-known aphorism from Avicenna put it, the loss of
seed "harmeth a man more, then if hee should bleed forty times as much."[63]
Even the comedy that the visiting players provide for Sly's entertainment—
the comedy that becomes the main plot of Shakespeare's play—is presented
to him in humoral terms:

> your doctors hold it very meet,
> Seeing too much sadness hath congeal'd your blood,
> And melancholy is the nurse of frenzy.
> Therefore they thought it good you hear a play,
> And frame your mind to mirth and merriment,
> Which bars a thousand harms and lengthens life.
>
> (ind., 2.131–36)

The underlying medical thought here is analogous both to Maria's exhortation of Malvolio's blood and spirits and to Titania's promise of Bottom's
fleshly rarification through purging. The evidence of transformation in
Sly's case, however, is even more equivocal than in the others'. While the
tinker comes to accept that he is a lord on the basis of his new surroundings—"I smell sweet savors, and I feel soft things" (ind., 2.71)—he asks at
the same time for a "pot o'th' smallest ale" (75), the original signifier of his
swinish lowness and the means of his potential return to oblivion. Tellingly,
the lord's arousal of Sly's blood and spirits is more clearly successful in
phallic terms—the terms of nature, perhaps—than in social ones, since the
tinker grants his lady wife's demur only with reluctance: "it stands so that I
may hardly tarry so long. But I would be loath to fall into my dreams again.
I will therefore tarry in despite of the flesh and the blood" (125–28). The
comedy that he agrees to watch is thus a kind of erotic surrogate, a therapy
of gratification through deferral whose ultimate impact on Sly's transformation is left unresolved. Whatever threat to the meaning of hierarchy might
be embodied in Sly's transformation, it is fragmentary and imperfect—in
part because we know that Sly is the unconscious victim of lordly caprice,

---

63. Quoted in William Vaughan, *Approved Directions for Health, Both Naturall and Artificiall*
(London: T. S. for Roger Jackson, 1612), 70.

more a threat to himself than to others in his immediate world, and in part because the transformation is so equivocal and its final outcome left so unresolved by extant texts of the play.

While the induction leaves no doubt that any man would prefer to be a lord instead of a tinker, its antithetical presentations of lordliness in Sly and the lord himself only beg the question of what might constitute a true humoral reformation of this lowly subject once the unfolding of that reformation is displaced by the main play. Certainly, however, Shakespeare's strategic placement of Sly's gulling between the lord's discussion of his hunting dogs and Baptista Minola's introduction of Kate focuses attention on the play's underlying interest in social regulation of the natural and the appropriateness of the means for doing so. What complicates this question in the relation between Kate and Petruchio is that—unlike Sly and the lord—both protagonists of this plot are constructed as humoral subjects prone to the socially outrageous behaviors produced by chronic humoral imbalance.

Here I want to emphasize the contrast between the thermal expansion of agency that we have seen in Desdemona and Rosalind with the reduction of agency and the lowering of radical heat in Kate. What complicates this question is that both protagonists of this plot are constructed as choleric subjects prone to the socially outrageous behaviors produced by this chronic humoral imbalance. Both are given to violence throughout the play; both take delight in "crossing" others. The play does seem to offer an overall endorsement of Kate's taming and assigns Petruchio the task of undertaking it as the crux of his own masculinization. As Lyndal Roper has argued, "The real man was a household head, a little patriarch ruling over wife, children, servants, journeymen, and apprentices . . . What gave one access to the world of brothers was one's mastery of a woman which guaranteed one's sexual status."[64] The language of the play flirts with the possibility of defining Katherine as untamed nature—"intolerable curst / And shrowd and froward" (1.2.89–90)—and Petruchio as the self-motivated bearer of culture:

> Tell me her father's name, and 'tis enough;
> For I will board her, though she chide as loud
> As thunder when the clouds in autumn crack.

> (1.2.94–96)

---

64. Lyndal Roper, *Oedipus and the Devil: Witchcraft, Sexuality, and Religion in Early Modern Europe* (London: Routledge, 1994), 46.

Even the play's strong emphasis on Petruchio's economic motivation in the wooing serves to enhance the rationality of his motives and his control over appetite (however inappropriate such mercenary decisions seem in the context of romantic comedy). But his choleric nature is established independent of Kate's introduction onstage, his servant Grumio insisting not on Petruchio's rational self-control but rather on his excessive combativeness and imperviousness to persuasion. When Hortensio counsels Petruchio to think twice about courting Katherine, Grumio declares, "I pray you, sir, let him go while the humor lasts. A' my word, and she knew him as well as I do, she would think scolding would do little good upon him. She may perhaps call him half a score knaves or so. Why, that's nothing; and he begin once, he'll rail in his rope-tricks" (1.2.107–12). To see his courting Kate as a whim—while the humor lasts—is to make it equivalent to the lord's reforming Sly as a moment's caprice. But the play obscures the balance between humoral determinism and rational self-control in its representation of Petruchio by underscoring the strategic calculation and the deliberateness behind even his most outrageous behaviors, especially the sexual self-discipline signified by deferral of his marriage's consummation.

Typically, encouraging strategic calculation in the planning of long-range goals and discouraging impulsiveness are the goals of Renaissance conduct books, which represent self-management in elite men and women as the sign of clear thought and humors in balance. Elsewhere in Shakespeare, for example, we see the historical success of the strategic subject in the overdetermined contrast between the impulsive, choleric, and socially archaic Hotspur and that princely epitome of rational calculation, his rival Hal.[65] Here, it is not that Petruchio's combination of calculation and choleric impulsiveness balances itself out into good temper but that, in the project of taming the choleric woman, Petruchio finds a way to make his own choler socially productive by directing it against an even less socialized, even more disruptive object than himself. In this respect, *Taming of the Shrew* is a clear demonstration of the asymmetries of humorality and gender ideology working in tandem, because the choleric man could be tasked with taming the choleric woman, not the reverse.[66] Taming Kate offers Petruchio the opportunity to alter himself materially in two ways— the social alteration derived from marriage to a wealthy heiress and the physical alteration of expending choler against a socially sanctioned target.

---

65. Paster, "Nervous Tension," 121.

66. Fletcher's *The Tamer Tamed*—the sequel to *Taming of the Shrew*—is an obvious exception to this general rule.

I make this argument not in order to excuse what I regard as Petruchio's physical and psychological abuse of Kate but rather to note the ideological underpinnings of the play's humoral logic, in which both protagonists undergo humoral reformation, but only the woman's is called a taming. Most of the deprivations that Petruchio makes Kate undergo he also experiences himself, as when he explains the rationale of throwing out meat uneaten because, he says, it was overcooked:

> I tell thee, Kate, 'twas burnt and dried away,
> And I expressly am forbid to touch it;
> For it engenders choler, planteth anger,
> And better 'twere that both of us did fast,
> Since of ourselves, ourselves are choleric,
> Than feed it with such overroasted flesh
> Be patient, to-morrow't shall be mended,
> And for this night we'll fast for company.
>
>   (4.1.170–77)

His reference to the choleric humor they share is, of course, only a mock effort at consolation, since his emphatic, if ironic, pronouncement about what they are going to do—fast together companionably—underscores the obvious difference between voluntary and involuntary acceptance of a humoral regime. Similarly, Petruchio's attempts to rationally persuade her are only mock ones, brute exercises in physical and psychological intimidation, as when he is reported to deliver a "sermon of continency" in her chamber in a manner far from contained:

> And rails, and swears, and rates, that she, poor soul,
> Knows not which way to stand, to look, to speak,
> And sits as one new risen from a dream.
>
>   (4.1.184–86)

In the notorious analogy between taming a wife and taming a falcon, Petruchio presents his project as unrelenting, patient labor in the manipulation of Kate's environment: he must fling the bedcovers around the room and create disorder, he must stay awake to keep her from sleeping, and he must "rail and brawl" to unsettle her relation to her world and make her realize her powerlessness. Petruchio's question, only mock-rhetorical—"He that knows better how to tame a shrew, / Now let him speak; 'tis charity to shew" (4.1.210–11)—acknowledges the possible obnoxiousness of his methods and the sadistic thrust of the play's action to alter the inclinations of her soul by altering—here by lowering—the temperature of her body.

The play invites us to take much more pleasure in Petruchio's taming of Kate's humor than in the self-taming of his own and to accept that his dominion over her is socially more significant than any increase in his own self-dominion. Which members in early modern society were accorded a right to anger and to the impulsive, aggressive actions taken in anger was very much at issue in contemporary treatises on the passions (see chapter 4). In these terms, the violent behaviors manifest in both husband and wife, but especially in Petruchio, become humoral manifestations of the unruly bodiliness they both must contain in order to earn their places in the community. Even so, Petruchio's self-taming can only be partial, his boorishness incompletely refined, because he still needs a store of choler in order to maintain dominion over his wife. Within their own household, Petruchio's taming of Kate thus becomes a distinctive example of the privilege of humoral autonomy that must be claimed in order for princes to have sway over courtiers, masters over servants, and here—exaggerated and extended by the programmatic violence of its means—husbands over wives. This is why, from Petruchio's point of view, Kate cannot be returned to the paternal household that failed to contain her humorally until she subordinates her humor to his and thus ratifies gender norms. He complains, "Look what I speak, or do, or think to do"—here he covers the full range of his potential behaviors—"You are still crossing it" (4.3.192–93). Petruchio is willing to make the return journey only when she accepts his definitions of the phenomenal world as her own, when she agrees in effect to perceive the world through the spectacles of his humor even when that humor is willfully changeable. In the famous sun and moon scene, this involves not only relinquishing her independence of judgment but denying the evidence of her senses as well: "What you will have it nam'd"—she says of the sun standing metonymically here for all of reality—"even that is, / And so it shall be so for Katherine" (4.5.21–22).[67]

This moment is a famously dismaying one for feminist scholarship; in terms of humoral subordination, too, Kate's capitulation would seem to be complete. In order to underscore that dismay, but also by way of conclusion, I would like to emphasize the importance of this exchange to an understanding of humoralism's overall significance in the representation of

---

67. The sun and the moon were conventional emblems of the relation of husband to wife. See Frances E. Dolan, ed., "The Taming of the Shrew": Texts and Contexts (Boston: Bedford Books, 1996), 30.

the humoral life cycle in women. In its broadest application, the classical doctrine of the four humors is not a theory of personality at all but a discourse of nature and the human body's place within it. It is evidence of early modern phenomenology if we understand phenomenology—bodily self-experience—as a form of lived cosmology. In a universe constructed through what John Sutton calls the "nested systems of spirits in the cosmos, the environment, the human body, and in inanimate objects,"[68] the humors bring the natural world almost directly into the body and extend the body out to the natural world. As we have seen, the humors and the passions they release operate upon the body very much as strong movements of wind or water operate upon the natural world: they are the body's internal climate of mood and temper, inward motions carried to the sentient flesh by the animal spirits.

Petruchio requires Kate to symbolize her wifely submission through humoral subordination to his internal climate. At this moment, requiring her to accept his definition of time, place, and mood as equivalent to accepting a wholesale mediation of reality, Petruchio puts himself between Kate and the natural world, stands as if alone for the cultural mediation of her powers of sense perception. As the new principle of signification for a body that—even if female—is never simply the material unsignified, it is he who would be the means of bringing her body into the world, the world into her body. His apparently successful programmatic alteration of her humorality expands from being a crude caricature of customary socialization practices to being a fantasy of ownership of her bodily substance from the inside out. The goal is thus not to reform her humorality but virtually to erase it, to take away the independent ability to appraise and interact in characteristic fashion with her environment. Kate becomes, at least for the moment, a woman neither in nor out of her humor, but a woman without a distinctive humor at all. It is as if Petruchio has solved the problem Othello describes as the

> curse of marriage!
> That we can call these delicate creatures ours,
> And not their appetites.

> (3.3.268–70)

We may not believe Kate's private capitulation here—or later in her famous public pledge to place her hand beneath her husband's foot—to be

---

68. Sutton, *Philosophy and Memory Traces*, 36.

anything other than strategic, external compliance only for the sake of self-preservation. But in a cosmology governed by psychological materialism, where the psychological is not yet divorced from the physiological, Kate's soul is thus proved to have followed her body's temperature, whether the compliance is external or internal. In the reciprocities of humoralism, external compliance means internal alteration and internal alteration manifests itself in behavior. For Petruchio and Shakespeare's audience, watching the tamed Kate is humoral comedy, a ratification of male dominance, no matter how ironic we understand that ratification to be, given the emergence of Bianca as Padua's latest shrew. For Kate herself—having acquired a forbidding, new kind of mediation in bodily self-experience, having lost the humoral right of way—experience of the world has lost definition, and the result is more than tragicomic.

Except, perhaps, for *Taming of the Shrew*, there is nothing inevitable about humoral readings of the affective changes undergone by the female protagonists in the plays I have examined here. But to invoke the old fluid physiologies in the context provided by the kind of transformations I have tracked is to place female affectivity into the framework of an earlier way of inhabiting the world, a way in which passions, winds, waters, spirits, idle living, and hard-hearted guardians all work in dynamic and continuous interaction upon the impressionable humoral subject. "The history of the body is ultimately a history of ways of inhabiting the world," Shigehisa Kuriyama has written (237). The female characters who waken from sad passivity to vigorous and purposeful action suggest Shakespeare's recognition of an implied narrative of women's humors in which affective change occurs over time—sometimes with tragic results—but always to show how the mind's inclination may well be said to follow the body's temperature.

CHAPTER THREE

Melancholy Cats, Lugged Bears, and Other Passionate Animals

Reading Shakespeare's Psychological Materialism
across the Species Barrier

It is important to our historical understanding of the passions that they
belonged to a part of the natural order jointly occupied by humans and animals. As Thomas Wright pointed out, "Those actions [of the soul] then
which are common with vs, and beasts, we call Passions, and Affections, or
perturbations of the mind" (7). For the early moderns, the core intelligibility
of this commonplace observation depended upon three interrelated presuppositions of Renaissance cosmology. The first—as I point out in the introduction and in chapter 1—was that the hydraulic model governing early
modern psychology was based "on a clear localisation of psychological function by organ or system of organs."[1] The second was that the four humors
of yellow bile, black bile, phlegm, and blood were not confined to the
human body but were distributed differentially to all those creatures, more
and less perfect, possessing a heart and blood.[2] The different species of animals possessed humoral complexions that organized their behaviors and, as
we shall see, gave them characteristic ways of responding to their worlds.
Furthermore, since many of the body's organ systems, and hence the bodily
fluids produced by them, belonged not just to human beings but to animals
as well, it followed that humans and animals shared in the psychological

1. Park, "Organic Soul," 469.
2. On Aristotle's distinction between blooded and nonblooded creatures, see G. E. R. Lloyd,
Science, Folklore, and Ideology: Studies in the Life Sciences in Ancient Greece (Cambridge:
Cambridge University Press, 1983), 32–33.

consequences—the self-experience—of possessing them. The third, and perhaps most important, presupposition was the common possession of a sensitive soul. In its highest form, soul was defined by Aristotelian philosophers as "the life principle of the individual body—that which differentiated living from non-living things."[3] It was divided hierarchically into three parts. The lowest, the vegetative soul common to all plants and animals, was responsible for growth, nutrition, and generation; the highest, the intellective soul unique to human beings, governed intellect, will, and memory. In between came the sensitive soul, which controlled perceptual, motive, and appetitive faculties.[4] "It is of a certain fiery nature," argues Thomas Willis in 1683 of this corporeal soul in animals, "and its Act or Substance is either a Flame or a Breath, neer to, or a-Kin to Flame."[5] In this tripartite structure, the actions of the sensitive soul occupied a crucial middle ground between sense and reason—with sense defined as the purely external and material actions of the vegetable soul and reason as the purely internal and immaterial actions of the intellective soul.[6] The passions of this soul, according to Thomas Wright, were "certaine internall acts or operations of the soule, bordering vpon"—that is, intermediate between—"reason and sense, prosecuting some good thing, or flying some ill thing, causing therewithall some alteration in the body" (8). It is the last phrase in this formulation to which we need to attend. In the emotions, both human and animal beings had their earliest and most basic of survival skills, their fundamental orientations of aversion and desire, flight and attraction. Passions were the endowment of temperament—the temperaments of male and female animals no less than those of men and women.

The consequences of possessing a shared terrain of the affects are legible on those many occasions in early modern texts when characters express their feelings through references to animals. In this chapter I look at a few such moments, concentrating first on a thematically trivial but phenomenologically important exchange of similes between Hal and Falstaff in their opening conversation in *1 Henry IV* and, second, on that moment in *Antony*

---

3. Katharine Park, "The Concept of Psychology," in *The Cambridge History of Renaissance Philosophy*, ed. Charles B. Schmitt et al. (Cambridge: Cambridge University Press, 1988), 455.

4. On the faculties of the soul, see Park, "Organic Soul," 464–84; a helpful diagram appears on 466.

5. Thomas Willis, *Two Discourses concerning the Soul of Brutes*, trans. S. Pordage, with intro. by Solomon Diamond (1683; reprint, Gainesville, FL: Scholars' Facsimiles and Reprints, 1971), 5.

6. On the separation of human and animal by reason, see Bruce Boerher, *Shakespeare among the Animals: Nature and Society in the Drama of Early Modern England* (London: Palgrave, 2002), 8–13.

and Cleopatra when Cleopatra decides she might prefer to be not herself but rather the "happy horse" that bears "the weight of Antony" (1.5.21). Other dramatic references occur in later parts of the chapter. But these two moments, I will argue, demonstrate why it is not enough to recognize psychological materialism as located and expressed in the individual human subject; we must also interrogate the place of psychological materialism in the whole analogical network of early modern ontology. As Katharine Park has argued, because "there was no clear cut division between psychology and what we now call biology," Renaissance writing on the soul included "a good deal of plant and animal physiology."[7] Thus Thomas Wilson, when arguing for the heuristic importance of thinking in similes, refers to animals and other forms of creation: "oftentymes brute beasts, and thynges that have no life, minister greate matter in this behalfe. Therefore those that delite to prove thynges by similitudes, must learne to know the nature of diverse beastes, of metalles, of stones and al such, as have any vertue in them, and be applied to mannes life" (375).

But scholarship interested in the history of the humoral subject has thus far confined itself to the body's humoral contributions to the construction of individual subjectivity without describing how consciousness in the humoral body might actually function in relation to an analogously constructed universe of brute beasts and things that have no life.[8] To the picture of the human body as a "semipermeable, irrigated container in which humors moved sluggishly,"[9] we need to add a nuanced picture of humoral subjectivity in similar terms—as a form of consciousness that is open, penetrable, fluid, and extended outward to the higher animals with which it shared affective workings. The mental interior of the individual subject, so understood, begins to seem less bounded and contained than in prior accounts, less opposed to the world outside. To quote Shigehisa Kuriyama again, "the history of the body is ultimately a history of ways of inhabiting the world" (237). If so, then what is true of the history of the body must also be true of consciousness. Humoral subjectivity becomes recognizable as a fluid form of consciousness inhabited by, even as it inhabits, a universe composed of analogous elements.

---

7. Park, "Concept of Psychology," 455.

8. Schoenfeldt has begun such an investigation, but as I suggested in the introduction, his interests focus mainly on dietary regulation rather than the relations between humorality, consciousness, and the structure of the cosmos.

9. I am quoting from Paster, *Body Embarrassed*, 8.

Among the unsavory similes uttered by Prince Hal and Falstaff in their opening conversation in *1 Henry IV* is the following exchange. Hal has proposed that when he becomes king, he will give Falstaff the servile post of hangman, to which the old knight responds with the declaration that he is melancholy, indeed proverbially so:

> FALSTAFF. Well, Hal, well, and in some sort it jumps with my humor
>   as well as waiting in the court, I can tell you.
> PRINCE. For obtaining of suits?
> FALSTAFF. Yea, for obtaining of suits, whereof the hangman hath no
>   lean wardrobe. 'Sblood, I am as melancholy as a gib cat or a
>   lugg'd bear.
> PRINCE. Or an old lion, or a lover's lute.
> FALSTAFF. Yea, or the drone of a Lincolnshire bagpipe.
> PRINCE. What sayest thou to a hare, or the melancholy of Moor-
>   ditch?
> FALSTAFF. Thou hast the most unsavory [similes] and art indeed the
>   most comparative, rascalliest, sweet young prince.
>
>   (1.2.73–81)

Thanks to Harry Berger's pioneering work on the concealed and self-concealed motives complexly at work in the speech acts of these two characters, we find signs in this exchange of the intersubjective conspiracy between them as they begin to work their way toward the final rejection of Falstaff.[10] Each strives here to specify the quality of Falstaff's humor with a series of references to animals, sounds, and finally to urban topography—the wastewater of a city ditch. In Berger's terms, Falstaff makes a semi-serious, hence rhetorically and psychologically defended, bid for Hal's sympathetic attention to his needy state of mind and body by calling it melancholy and expanding its meaning through the implied narratives of pathetic similes.

In a sense, there should be nothing noteworthy about Falstaff's report of a low mood, either as predictable response to the prospect of such a degrading post as executioner (even with its benefit of hanged men's clothing) or as a prognostication of aging. In Galenic humoralism, old men were expected to be melancholy because the aging process lowered the body's

---

10. I have been influenced in my thinking about Hal and Falstaff's speech acts by Harry Berger Jr., "The Prince's Dog: Falstaff and the Perils of Speech-Prefixity," *Shakespeare Quarterly* 49 (1998): 40–73.

heat and evaporated its radical moisture, producing the coldness and dryness associated with the melancholic humor.[11] But Falstaff seeks notice by likening himself not just proverbially to a cat but to a (probably) gelded one, perhaps as a sign of sexual loss or injury.[12] He adds the baited bear, perhaps as a sign of anxiety about future persecution at the hands of authority, since the bear is being lugged—pulled—to the baiting ring with a predictable degree of unwillingness.[13] Hal initially accedes to Falstaff's attempt at pathos with his complementary additions of the old lion, the lover's lute, and the hare—all objects, editors suggest, conventionally associated with melancholy.[14] But the prince's final rhetorical turn to the undifference of excrement seems meant to be conclusively deflating—the first of many withering figurative references to the contents of Falstaff's mind and body ("that trunk of humors, that bolting-hutch of beastliness, that swoll'n parcel of dropsies, that huge bombard of sack, that stuff'd cloak-bag of guts, that roasted Manningtree ox with the pudding in his belly" [2.4.449–53]). Falstaff's refusal to continue the contest at this point and his move to complain instead about the unsavoriness of the prince's similes suggest that he accepts the analogy between his mood and city drainage—not necessarily as accurate, but as a way to organize and contain the other units in the series because, as Henri Lefebvre argues, social space "is not a thing among other things, nor a product among other products: rather, it subsumes things produced, and encompasses their interrelationships in their coexistence and simultaneity."[15] Hal's insult is thus on a par with the opening quarrel of Jonson's *Alchemist* when Face shames Subtle through deflating analogies with urban topography:

11. For an introduction to the early modern schema of human life, see Siraisi, 97–114.

12. On the proverbial melancholy of cats, see the entry for melancholy in *ODEP*, 524. The gib cat was not necessarily castrated, as Judith and Herbert Weil point out. See Shakespeare, *I Henry IV*, ed. Judith Weil and Herbert Weil, New Cambridge (Cambridge: Cambridge University Press, 1997), note to 1.2.58. The "hare is melancholy meat," according to the *ODEP*, 354. The association of hares and old, or more precisely dead, lions was also proverbial, says the *ODEP*: "Hares may pull dead lions by the beard" (354).

13. "As willingly as the bear goes to the stake," goes the proverb, as reported in the *ODEP*, 34. On the baiting of animals, see Stephen Dickey, "Shakespeare's Mastiff Comedy," *Shakespeare Quarterly* 42 (1991): 255–75, esp. 264–65; Erica Fudge, *Perceiving Animals: Humans and Beasts in Early Modern English Culture* (London: Macmillan; New York: St. Martin's, 2000), 13–18; and Jason Scott-Warren, "When Theaters Were Bear-Gardens; or, What's at Stake in the Comedy of Humors," *Shakespeare Quarterly* 54 (2003): 63–82. See also Keith Thomas's magisterial study, *Man and the Natural World: A History of the Modern Sensibility* (New York: Pantheon Books, 1983), 114.

14. In addition to the Weils' edition, see David Bevington's edition: *Henry IV, Part I* (Oxford: Clarendon Press, 1987), notes to 1.2.69–78.

15. Henri Lefebvre, *The Production of Space*, trans. Donald Nicholson-Smith (Oxford: Blackwell, 1991), 73.

> But I shall put you in mind, sir, at Pie Corner,
> Taking your meal of steam in, from cooks' stalls,
> Where, like the father of hunger, you did walk
> Piteously costive, with your pinch'd-horn nose,
> And your complexion, of the Roman wash,
> Stuck full of black and melancholic worms,
> Like powder corns, shot, at th'artillery yard.
>
> $(1.1.25–31)^{16}$

In such an attack, Subtle's blackheads become part of the rhetoric of shame, evidence of his melancholy. The self-presence and social specificity of urban space work to fix and limit the human subject caught, inferentially, in its network of shame.

Even for Harry Berger, there *might* be nothing more to say about this exchange in *1 Henry IV* as part of the conspiratorial performances of Falstaff as self-dramatizing seducer and Hal as his victim. For my purposes, however, the phenomenological linkages in this series provide an unusual form of access to early modern self-experience. Rather than a proverbial set of loose associations, the simile contest constructs an epistemic set, a natural class, that (like Face's attack on Subtle) places Falstaff's aging body in a particular analogical relation to its physical environment—one composed of animals, sounds, and elemental liquids, all of which would be accepted by an early modern audience as literally (if maybe laughably) describable in terms of melancholy. This exchange, I propose, reveals a difference between modern and premodern ways of knowing about and feeling oneself related to the physical world. In order to appreciate this difference, we need to remember the building blocks of the ancient macrocosm, still durable in early modern Europe: the elements of earth, water, fire, and air and the qualities of cold, wet, hot, and dry with which they were linked. The elements and the qualities combined in various ways and degrees to constitute the particular, objectively real properties of all matter, animate and inanimate alike.[17] In these correspondences, as we have endlessly been told, lower forms of life were expressed and contained in the higher forms. As Bacon noted, "there is no nature which can be regarded as simple; every one seeming to participate and be compounded of two. Man has something of the brute; the brute has something of the vegetable; the vegetable

---

16. I quote here from Ben Jonson, *The Alchemist*, ed. F. H. Mares, Revels Plays (Cambridge, MA: Harvard University Press, 1967).

17. There is a succinct discussion of the qualities in Lester S. King, "The Transformation of Galenism," in Debus, *Medicine in Seventeenth Century England*, 17–24.

something of the inanimate body; and so all things are in truth biformed and made up of a higher species and a lower."[18] The cosmic chain reached its highest earthly expression in man, the paragon of animals, "the Epitome or Abstract of the whole world, in whom something of every thing (to speak Platonically and yet truly) is placed and inserted."[19] But the lower levels were expressive too: the humor melancholy to be found in human and other living bodies was analogically linked to the earth through their shared properties of cold and dry.[20] Old men such as Falstaff, losing radical heat and moisture and thus becoming subject to an increase of melancholy in their bodies, approached earth qualitatively even as they approached the deaths that would return them to it. As Hamlet explains to Horatio, "Alexander died, Alexander was buried, Alexander returneth to dust, the dust is earth, of earth we make loam, and why of that loam whereto he was converted might they not stop a beer-barrel?" (5.1.208–12). But melancholy, as well as signaling the cold, dry retentive behavior of old age (retentiveness being perhaps another reason for Hal to depict Falstaff proleptically as a hangman coveting the clothing of the condemned), could also be a by-product of the body's processes of internal combustion—yellow bile burned to become black bile. This "melancholy adust" represented the cold, dry ashes—the soot—of a body's excessive heat, consumed by the expenditure of choleric humors and the agitation of the body's spirits.[21] Melancholy adust explains the after-effects of spent rage, the melancholy of warriors or men younger and more active than sedentary Falstaff. Melancholy in this form especially was bodily waste, ominously darkening the color of the body's other fluids and spirits and clogging their flow. The passage from Thomas Nashe's *The Terrors of the Night*, quoted in chapter 1 with reference to Othello's loathing of the toads lurking in cisterns, is equally relevant here. Nashe likens "the thick steaming fenny vapours" of bodily melancholy to wastewater: "even as slime and dirt in a standing puddle engender toads and frogs and many other unsightly creatures, so this slimy melancholy humor, still still [*sic*] thickening as it stands still, engendreth many mis-shapen objects in our imaginations" (217). This analogy explains the force

18. Francis Bacon, "Of the Wisdom of the Ancients" (De sapientia veterum), in *Works*, 6:710–11.

19. I am quoting from Thomas Moffett, *Health's Improvement* (London, 1655), 264, but the thought is a commonplace.

20. For a diagrammatic representation of these linkages, see Londa Schiebinger, *The Mind Has No Sex? Women in the Origins of Modern Science* (Cambridge, MA: Harvard University Press, 1989), 162.

21. The classic treatment of melancholy remains Klibansky, Panofsky, and Saxl; but see also Schiesari.

of the prince's deflating comparison of Falstaff's mood—understood not in post-Enlightenment terms as a disembodied mental event but rather as the feelings residing in congealed bodily liquid stored in heart and mind—to what Edward Sugden calls "the depository for all kinds of filth and rubbish."[22]

The doctrine of natural correspondences adds epistemic significance to the other references in this series, especially perhaps Falstaff's self-comparison to the melancholy of the gib cat. As editors suggest, cats' howling and nocturnal habits would have associated them with melancholy; but here, as elsewhere in this affective schema, the analogies multiply and deepen. In naturalist Edward Topsell's entry on the cat in his *Historie of Foure-Footed Beastes*, for example, feline melancholy explains the animal's coloration: "Cats are of diuers colours, but for the most part gryseld, like to congealed yse, which commeth from the condition of her meate."[23] Using inductive reasoning born of the thermal classifications of Aristotelian biology, Topsell describes melancholy as a physical attribute reciprocal with the extreme coldness of the cat's flesh.[24] This coldness, which constitutes, saturates, and explains feline being, expresses itself in what Topsell sees as icelike in the streaks and patterns of its parti-color fur (see fig. 9). Fur, being bodily excrement, was necessarily characteristic of the flesh from which it grew. For Topsell, a cat's vocalizations, being its natural language, were also biologically based, but nonetheless affecting, its voice "hauing as many tunes as turnes." He writes of the wildness "in the time of their lust" of male cats, which "at that time (except they be gelded) will not keepe the house: at which time they haue a peculiar direfull voice" (105). As with the melancholy of Falstaff, a cat's melancholy is a humor—hence a temperature, a temperament, a disposition, and a liquid of specific consistency organizing a cat's relations with the world. Melancholy produces a cat's way of being no less than—and by virtue of—the temperature of its flesh.[25] The rutting

22. See Edward H. Sugden, *A Topographical Dictionary to the Works of Shakespeare and His Fellow Dramatists* (Manchester: Manchester University Press, 1925), 352. Apparently the fetid waters of Moorditch did not usually move at all, since in *Lenten Stuffe* Nashe mentions the wonder of the "common people about London, some few years since . . . at the bubbling of Moorditch"; see *Unfortunate Traveller*, 442. Sugden speculates that this led in 1592 to the cleansing and broadening of the ditch (352), but John Stow complains that it was "neuer the better"; see *The Survey of London*, with intro. and notes by Charles Lethbridge Kingsford, 2 vols. (1908; reprint, Oxford: Clarendon Press, 1971), 2:20.

23. Edward Topsell, *The Historie of Foure-Footed Beastes* (London: William Jaggard, 1607), 103 (all citations of Topsell in this chapter refer to this work unless otherwise indicated).

24. On the relation of heat to blood in Aristotle, see Lloyd, 32–33.

25. For a related argument on the ramifications of temperature, see Paster, "Unbearable Coldness."

Of the Cat.   103

Figure 9. A melancholic cat, from Edward Topsell, *Historie of Foure-Footed Beastes* (London, 1607). By permission of the Folger Shakespeare Library.

cat's direful sounds and nocturnal habits link it to the nighttime sounds of the doleful lover playing his lute, while—in a self-deprecating move on Falstaff's part—comparison to the Lincolnshire bagpipe may link both cat and knight to the vanity and verbal flatulence that bagpipes shared, figuratively, with "an inflated and senseless talker, a windbag."[26]

<hr />

26. See the *OED* entry (4a) for *bagpipe*, quoting Henry Crosse, *Vertues Commonwealth* (London, 1603): "The Seruingman, the Image of sloath, the bagge-pipe of vanitie, like a windie Instrument, soundeth nothing but prophanenesse." Interestingly, Falstaff asks Hal to "trouble me no more with vanity" (1.2.81–82).

The latter moralistic association, moreover, suggests how easily ostensibly neutral biological discourse mixes with the overdeterminations of Aesopian moral discourse.[27] Thus in the poetic fable of Adamic creation in the Third Eclogues of Sir Philip Sidney's *Arcadia*, the cat joins in with the other animals that must donate an attribute toward God's shaping of the human ruler they all think they desire. These faculties seem variously physical, behavioral, and affective: the lion gives heart, the sparrow "lust to play"; the bear offers climbing, the elephant "a perfect memory; / And parrot, ready tongue." The stag "did give the harm-eschewing fear," and the cat "his melancholy."[28] Behaviorally, the cat's donation of a useful part of its character would seem more ethical than physical, on a par with the stag's contribution of fear, rather than with the physical or mental capacities donated by bear, parrot, or elephant. But classification here is conceptually more elusive than that, and more telling of the analogical thought underlying Hal and Falstaff's similes. Cat melancholy, Sidney's fable suggests, is both originary and exemplary, a physical part of the natural order, a property the cat in its splenetic abundance may decide to bequeath. Melancholy locates the cat metonymically, just as it locates Falstaff, in a determinate place in relation to a host of other things, animate and inanimate, natural and human.

It is cosmological fixing, then, that gives the series of similes its epistemic weight in the construction of humoral subjectivity. Hal and Falstaff have begun their dialogue postulating a periphrastic ability to rename—and in so doing, to remake—the nature of reality:[29] "Marry, then, sweet wag, when thou art king, let not us that are squires of the night's body be call'd thieves of the day's beauty" (1.2.23–25). Their turn to the proverbs of melancholy, however, offers a limit to the world-making capacities of the motivated word, for simile fixes both participants in analogical relationships founded in a theoretically immutable, emblematic order. To quote William Ashworth again, "to know the peacock, you must know its associations—its affinities, similitudes, and sympathies with the rest of the created

27. Discussion of animals' characters is to be found in Aristotle's *Historia animalium*, in *The Complete Works of Aristotle: The Revised Oxford Translation*, ed. Jonathan Barnes (Princeton, NJ: Princeton University Press, 1984); see Lloyd, 18–26.

28. Philip Sidney, *The Countess of Pembroke's Arcadia (The Old Arcadia)*, ed. Katherine Duncan-Jones (Oxford: Oxford University Press, 1985), 223. Annabel M. Patterson offers a political reading of this fable in *Fables of Power: Aesopian Writing and Political History* (Durham, NC: Duke University Press, 1991), 67–75.

29. The point of origin for this critical commonplace is probably C. L. Barber, *Shakespeare's Festive Comedy: A Study of Dramatic Form and Its Relation to Social Custom* (Princeton, NJ: Princeton University Press, 1959), 197.

order" (306). As with peacocks, so with cats; and so too with Falstaff and the bagpipe—which is precisely why the final move to Moorditch is felt to be so contaminating. For these associations, like the associations we noticed in chapter 1 between Pyrrhus's blackness of purpose and the fires burning in Troy, are grounded in the premodern doctrine of sympathies and correspondences. Natural sympathy and antipathy, those bonds of likeness and unlikeness that drew like things together in forces of mutual attraction and pulled unlike things apart, explained, for example, the soul's receptivity to music and to sounds generally, as Thomas Moffett points out: "the very noise of bells, guns, Trumpets, breaketh the clouds . . . yea Musick it self, cureth the brain of madness, and the heart of melancholy" (22). What I want to draw attention to, then, are the historical possibilities lodged in the analogy between the cat's melancholy and Falstaff's. Not only does the elemental nature of cat melancholy support the elemental embodiment of Falstaff's, but the playful spinning out of melancholy's forms into animals, musical instruments, and sewage ditches emphasizes how broadly the passions were thought to be distributed sensible features of a natural world traversed by a host of sympathies and antipathies. In this sense, Falstaff's comparison of his mood to a cat's may be self-interested, but it is not sentimental. It serves less to project and objectify human melancholy outward through the familiar procedures of anthropomorphism than to introject the natural, God-given self-sameness of cat melancholy—expressed in flesh and fur and howling—into an emotionally justified, ethically naturalized, and humorally subjectified Falstaff.[30] Sidney's archetypal cat has donated its natural store of melancholy to that representative of fallen man, that offending Adam—Sir John Falstaff.

A similar movement of self-justification through reference to animal affect occurs in *Macbeth* when the beleaguered usurper, his castle surrounded by his enemies, likens himself to a baited bear: "They have tied me to a stake," Macbeth says to himself, "I cannot fly, / But bear-like I must fight the course" (5.7.1–2).[31] Earlier he berated a fearful servant for his birdlike pallor—"The devil damn thee black, thou cream-fac'd loon! / Where got'st

30. In this, I wish to counter the argument put forward by Erica Fudge, 1–10, that virtually all early modern thinking about animals is anthropomorphic at bottom. The issue is not, as anthropologist Richard Tapper has pointed out in a more general context, that ways of categorizing animals simply derive from human social classifications. Rather, a society's ways of classifying the natural order inform categories describing the relation of the individual to the group; see "Animality, Humanity, Morality, Society," in *What Is an Animal?* ed. Tim Ingold (London: Unwin Hyman, 1988), 50–51.

31. In *King Lear*, Gloucester has virtually the same comment: "I am tied to th'stake, and I must stand the course" (3.7.54).

thou that goose-look?" (5.3.11–12)—in contrast to his own (increasingly desperate) claims to fearlessness born of the witches' prophecies: "The mind I sway by, and the heart I bear, / Shall never sag with doubt, nor shake with fear" (5.3.9–10). Here, Macbeth's reference to the bear begins with a likeness in physical circumstance at the hands of persecuting humans—"they have tied me to a stake"—and moves metatheatrically toward more complex trajectories of identification and fantasy, underwritten by Elizabethan habits of thought. Baited bears, for example, were always known by the surnames of their keepers.[32] Macbeth may be likening his own property of courage in battle to the bear's known fierceness of disposition: "Great is the fiercenes of a beare," says Topsell, "as appeareth by holie scripture *Osee* 13. *I will meet them as a beare robbed of her whelpes* (saith the Lorde) *and will teare in pieces their froward heart*" (43). John Taylor praises the arena bear for its courage:

> For whoso'ere comes thither, most and least,
> May see and learne some courage from a Beast.[33]

Like the bear in the baiting arena met by waves of attacking mastiffs, Macbeth enters onstage alone to meet the first encounter with his human attackers (see fig. 10). Here it is Young Siward, whom he easily defeats before facing more ferocious onslaughts. One effect of Macbeth's bear simile is oddly distancing—to make Macbeth's defeat, though predictable, not certain (bears customarily survived the dogs' attacks and were baited again).[34] But because it is spoken by Macbeth about himself in relation to an environment made up of surrounding humans, the simile's larger effects draw us into his state of mind—serving not to bestialize him but rather, as phenomenological figuration, to convey the heightened texture of his self-experience, his determination to quell panic and "fight the course." Note the reversal of customary identifications: in its sense of beleaguerment and compulsion, its objectification of the human opponent as animal-Other to

---

32. On the complexity of attitudes toward the bears and other blood-sport animals, see David Wiles, *Shakespeare's Clown: Actor and Text in the Elizabethan Playhouse* (Cambridge: Cambridge University Press, 1987), 168–72, especially on the interchangeability of actors and bears and other Shakespearean references.

33. John Taylor, *Bull, Beare, and Horse* (1638), in *Works of John Taylor, the Water Poet. Third Collection* (London: Spenser Society, 1876; reprint, New York: Burt Franklin, 1967), 59; also quoted in Wiles, 169.

34. Dickey comments: "this simile registers Macbeth's bitter awareness that he has become a beast whose sole function is to perform in the spectacle of his own execution" (264–65).

Figure 10. Dogs attacking a baited bear, from William Lily, *Antibossicon* (London, 1521), title page verso. By permission of the Folger Shakespeare Library.

the bear as fantasy-Self, the simile insists upon Macbeth's identification with the bear as the subject of its own heroic drama—desiring flight but unable to attain it, constrained to conduct its battle for self-preservation within the limits posed by the length of its chain and the spectatorial circuits of the arena. In *The Unfortunate Traveller*, Thomas Nashe includes a similar cross-current of feeling between bear and human victims as he describes the slaughter of rebellious Anabaptists in Münster: "Pitiful and lamentable was their unpitied and well-performed slaughter. To see even a bear, which is the most cruellest of all beasts, too too bloodily overmatched and deformedly rent in pieces by an unconscionable number of curs, it would move compassion against kind, and make those that, beholding him at the stake yet uncoped with, wished him a suitable death to his ugly shape, now to re-call their hard-hearted wishes and moan him suffering as a mild beast, in comparison of the foul-mouthed mastiffs, his butchers" (285). Here, like Macbeth, Nashe reverses the human and animal fields, though not on his own behalf as a matter of self-reference. His narrator Jack Wilton has displayed hostility toward the rebellious Anabaptists, describing them as ones who only follow God to upbraid him, daring him to punish them. They run "headlong," he says, "on their well-deserved confusion." But when the slaughter begins, the cruelty of the persecutors is so extreme that it overrides the customary loyalty of species, moves "compassion against kind." Just as sympathetic spectators at a bear-baiting revise their placement of the bear on an axis of cruelty, displacing cruelty from the bear to the dogs, so the narrator revises his judgment of the Anabaptists: "Even such comparison did those overmatched ungracious Münsterians obtain of many indifferent eyes, who now thought them, suffering, to be sheep brought innocent to the shambles, whenas before they deemed them as a number of wolves up in arms against the shepherds" (285).

A bear's conscious experience of terror, moreover, would have been understood as entailing a transformation in its flesh. As Thomas Moffett notes, animals' flesh was thought to change with their experiences and the character of their affects: "*Patrocles* affirmed, that a Lion being shewed to a strong Bull three or four hours before he be killed; causeth his flesh to be as tender as the flesh of a Steer: fear dissolving his hardest parts and making his very heart to become pulpy. Perhaps upon the like reason we use to bait our Bulls before we kill them: for their blood is otherwise so hard, that none can digest it in the flesh, but afterwards . . . it becometh tender and nourishing food" (44–45).[35] Similar thinking, we should remember, underlies Lear's anguish about how the practices of cruelty might have transformed the flesh of his daughters: "Is there any cause in nature that make these hard hearts?" (3.6.77–78).

It is thus important to recognize the bear's experience, in seventeenth-century terms, as exemplary of the passions, human and animal, insofar as the passions were understood as a primary instrument of self-preservation comparable to what elsewhere in the natural order promoted the stable self-sameness of inanimate objects. As Thomas Wright explains, "God, the

---

35. Patricia Fumerton has discussed this practice and similar cooking practices as torturing animals: "torture is the tasty seasoning that flavors the otherwise plain meat." See "Introduction: A New New Historicism," in *Renaissance Culture and the Everyday*, ed. Patricia Fumerton and Simon Hunt (Philadelphia: University of Pennsylvania Press, 1999), 1–3, esp. 2. The analogy between human and animal flesh allows us to think differently about the meaning of this enforced tenderization while not denying the reality of the animals' suffering.

author of nature, and imparter of all goodnesse hath printed in euery creature ... an inclination, faculty, or power to conserue it selfe, procure what it
needeth, to resist and impugne whatsoeuer hindereth it of that appertaineth unto his good and conseruation. So we see fire continually ascendeth vpward, because the coldnesse of the water, earth, and ayre much
impeacheth the vertue of his heate: ... the Hare flieth from the Hounds: the
Partridge hideth her selfe from the talon of the Hawke" (12–13). The bear's
passion for self-preservation justifies and naturalizes Macbeth's; the bear's
passion is subsumed into and equated with Macbeth's own: "bear-like I
must fight the course."

Stephen Dickey has argued that Elizabethan spectators were amused by
animal-baiting spectacles, citing contemporary testimony of "great amuse-
ment," "good contentment," and unspeakable "pleasure."[36] But Nashe's
revised judgment against the bear and recognition of the deep transformations wrought by fear on the flesh of bull, bear, or human in the passage
from Moffett cited above complicate this too-simple picture of callousness.
Insofar as Macbeth's simile works to draw us into identification with his
terror and defiance, we are also drawn into a fantasy-projection of animal
selfhood—led imaginatively beyond the boundaries of isolate human subjectivity into the wilder territory of an animal's suffering and its desire for
mere survival. Here, as with Pyrrhus and Pyrochles in chapter 1, we are in
affective terrain very like what Deleuze and Guattari label the "Body without Organs"—a *"field of immanence* of desire, the *plane of consistency* specific to desire" (154). In their conception of a Body without Organs, the
body's desires are neither localized nor named. The human body—organized by Western epistemologies into a sex, a morphology, a subjectivity, a
surface, a depth, and a central place in the natural order—is replaced by a
dynamic entity of intensities and flows, a body conceived simply as a unit
of matter in time, a body desiring its own continuance and the satisfaction
of its appetites (153). For the early moderns, as we have repeatedly seen in
humoral discourse, desire necessarily occurred in a body *with* organs—
organs understood in the highly specific terms of psychophysiological functioning associated with the production and expression of melancholy,
choler, and so forth. Furthermore, the functions of those organs, as I have

36. Quotations from contemporary documents appear in Dickey, 257; in contrast to Dickey's
implication that Elizabethans could not imagine or care about animal suffering, there is Thomas
Moffett's comment in *Health's Improvement* about sympathy for beasts going to slaughter. Moffett
describes the pain and suffering of beasts about to be slaughtered—a sight he says only hard-
hearted butchers can see—"the hearing of heavy sighs, sobs, and grones, the passionate struling
and panting for life" (30). Also see Wiles, 168–69.

been insisting, necessarily make sense in relation to the early modern doctrine of correspondences. But early modern thinking does resemble that of
Deleuze and Guattari in that the fluids emanating from heart, liver, spleen,
and gall bladder to produce affects were delivered by the bloodstream and
saturated animate flesh, flooding and altering its character. We shall see
below that disposition, behavior, and action—while produced by the action
of the affectively motivated heart—emanated from an intention of the
whole body, and that body's deepest affections were what located it most
strongly in the natural order.

As Falstaff's and Macbeth's self-comparisons to animals suggest, identification across the species barrier was compelling for the early moderns
because it seemed both to reinforce affective self-experience and to offer an
escape from it into the imagined self-sameness of animal passion. For my
purposes, such similes have particular significance in offering evidence for
the early modern conception of the sensitive soul as governing a subject's
appetites and emotions. Joint possession of it, as I noted earlier, constituted
the essential similarity between humans and animals.[37] The passions,
located between "reason and sense," were not identical to the bodily
humors, but the two were closely allied in their workings, teleological function, and significance. As Thomas Wright explains, "me thinkes the passions of our minde, are not vnlike the foure humours of our bodies, . . . for if
blood, flegme, choller, or melancholy exceed the due proportion required to
the constitution and health of our bodies, presently we fall into some disease: euen so, if the passions of the Minde be not moderated according to
reason (and that temperature vertue requireth) immediatly the soule is
molested with some maladie" (16–17). This similarity explains not only
how passions could originate within the body and then express themselves
externally but also how a body's reaction, whether to an external stimulus
acting upon the senses or to an internal prompting of memory or imagination, necessarily entailed the humors:

> First then, to our imagination commeth by sense or memorie, some obiect
> to be knowne, . . . the which being knowne . . . in the imagination which
> resideth in the former part of the braine, (as we proue) when we imagine
> any thing, presently the purer spirits, flocke from the brayne, by certaine
> secret channels to the heart, where they pitch at the dore, signifying what
> an obiect was presented, conuenient or disconuenient for it. The heart

37. Park, "Organic Soul," 469.

immediatly bendeth, either to prosecute it, or to eschew it: and the better to
effect that affection, draweth other humours to helpe him, and so in pleasure concurre great store of pure spirits; in paine and sadnesse, much melancholy blood; in ire, blood and choller. (45)

Though Wright does not say so, this description of how human passions
worked in relation to the recognition of external sense objects would also
have applied, necessarily, to the workings of animal passion—and to the
changes in animal fluids and flesh that such passions brought about. It was
obvious to him that animals, like humans, recognized and remembered
what was good or bad for them; both kinds were animate creatures
endowed with a heart, the passions' seat: "al passions may be distinguished
by the dilatation, enlargement, or diffusion of the heart: and the contraction, collection, or compression of the same" (24). Common possession of
the heart guaranteed that "men and beasts with one appetite procure the
good they desire and with another they flie the euill they abhor" (12).[38] That
is, men and beasts share in their possession of the concupiscible appetite
that identifies and pursues a good thing and the irascible appetite that identifies and seeks to avoid a bad one.

But in the comparative workings of hearts and emotions, the differences
between human and animal become almost as meaningful as the similari-
ties. In Renaissance natural philosophy, animals played a key role heuristically in the early modern production of practical knowledge about the
passions. In beings lacking the constraint of reason—it was thought—the
passions were at their purest, most intense, and most visible. "Wee may best
discouer [them] in children," says Wright, "because they lack the vse of reason and are guided by an internall imagination, following nothing else but
that pleaseth their senses, euen after the same maner as bruit beasts doe:
for, as we see beasts hate, loue, feare and hope, so doe children" (7).[39] Thus,
while Falstaff in a calculated bid for sympathy might report feeling melancholy without actually being so and might even imitate the bodily dejection
associated with that self-report, his feline counterpart could not. Cat melancholy might express itself by howling or the color of fur, but it could not be
falsified or used promotionally to deceive. Cat melancholy—being incapable either of sincerity or insincerity—is for the same reason self-present,
self-identical, a form of animal plenitude, a feature of the flesh. This is also
why cat melancholy is more generic than individualizing: in the discourse

---

38. On the heart as the receptacle of feelings, see Erickson, 11–15.
39. On children and animals, see Boerher, 133–37.

of proverbs and natural history alike, animal traits such as humors and passions tend to belong to the species rather than being unique expressions of and by an individual member. Indeed, it is precisely this tendency away from the individual and toward the generic that marks a paradoxical tension in the conversation between Hal and Falstaff. Even as they seek to particularize the facts or fictions about Falstaff's melancholy, they extend that melancholy outward to its likenesses in the world and move it closer to the fecal undifference of Moorditch.

Where Falstaff and Macbeth most closely approximate the early modern philosophical discussions of animal emotions is in their desire to understand their emotions as like animals' in being exemplary and thereby emblematically meaningful. Early modern taxonomies of the passions are virtually unthinkable without the examples for both animal and human cognition provided by the physiology of animal emotion and its behavioral effects. As Claude Lévi-Strauss famously remarked, animals are important to human classifications not so much because they are good to eat as because they are good to think with.[40] In English moral philosophy, the locus classicus of animal exemplarity is probably to be found in Thomas Wright's discussion of the eleven primary emotions experienced by the wolf and the sheep as they recognize each other as objects of fear and desire: "First, the Wolfe loueth the flesh of the Sheep; then he desireth to haue it; thirdly, he reioyceth in his prey when he hath gotten it: Contrariwise, the Sheepe hateth the Wolfe, as an euill thing in himselfe, and thereupon detesteth him, as hurtfull to herselfe; and finally, if the Wolf seaze vpon her, she paineth and grieueth to become his prey: thus we haue loue, desire, delight, hatred, abhomination, griefe, or heauinesse, the six passions of our coueting appetite" (23). But Wright is less interested in the uncomplicated emotions of the fearful sheep than in what he represents as the complex emotional texture of the wolf's experience as it confronts obstacles to the fulfillment of its desire in the shepherd and his dogs:

> then the Wolfe fearing the difficulty of purchasing his prey, yet thinking the
> euent, though doubtfull, not impossible, then he erecteth himselfe with the
> passion of Hope, perswading him the sheepe shall be his future spoyle after
> the conquest: and thereupon contemning the dogges, despising the shep-
> heard, . . . with a bold and audacious courage, not regarding any daunger; he
> setteth vpon the flocke; where, in the first assault, presently a mastife
> pincheth him by the legge; the iniurie he imagineth ought not to be toller-

40. As paraphrased by Tapper, 50.

ated: but inmediatly inflamed with the passion of Ire, procureth by all meanes possible to reuenge it: the Shepheard protecteth his dog, and basteth the Wolfe ... The Wolfe perceiuing himself weaker than he imagined, & his enemies stronger than he conceiued, falleth sodainly into the passion of Feare, (as braggers doe, who vaunt much at the beginning, but quaile commonly in the midle of the fray) yet not abandoned of all hope of the victory; therefore he stirreth vp himselfe, and proceedth forward; but in fine, receiuing more blowes of the shepheard, more woundes of the dogges, awearied with fighting, fearing his life, thinking the enterprise impossible, oppressed with the passion of Desperation, resolueth himself that his heeles are a surer defence, than his teeth, and so runneth away. By this example we may collect the other fiue passions of the inuading appetite, hope, boldnesse or presumption, anger or ire, feare, and Desperation. (23–24)

In this mock-heroic agon, Wright throws himself without a trace of anthropomorphic embarrassment into the wolf's drama. He underscores the animal's emotional progression from hope to defeat by infusing it with a full-blown stylistic apparatus—the extended syntactic parallelisms of the verb forms as the wolf circles his prey; the elevated heroic diction of spite, contempt, audacity, and revenge; the exaggerated trajectory of the rise to combat and the fall into retreat. The result is to produce a dynamic subject position for the wolf and to make the subject positions of the shepherd and his dogs almost entirely inadmissible. Immersion into the wolf's point of view produces a set of clearly cognitive, even metacognitive activities activated by and activating changes in the wolf's emotions as he appraises, reappraises, and decides how he feels about developments in his *Umwelt*.[41] Even more important, this account of lupine emotions is less the result of anthropomorphic thinking than it is an example of early modern fluid physiology at work in the behavior of animals and humans alike. In physiological terms, what animates the wolf's recognition of its environment, dictates its assessment of opportunity and peril, and governs its responses to what it desires or fears are the spirits that move along the neural pathways from the wolf's brain out to its body and back; these are the "purer spirits" that, according to Wright, "flocke from the brayne, by certaine secret channels to the heart" (45). What this account does not do (perhaps cannot do) is

41. For a summary of environmental appraisal by animals as part of what anthropologists call ecological psychology, see Edward S. Reed, "The Affordances of the Animate Environment: Social Science from the Ecological Point of View," in Ingold, *What Is an Animal?* 110–26.

to separate the wolf's affective responses from his cognitive appraisals, because for Wright, as for other early modern thinkers on the passions, affects are by definition bodily states—psychophysiological responses to perceived changes in the environment.[42] The wolf weighs the pros and cons of the attack, persuades himself to go forward, thinks the event not impossible, regards not his danger, imagines his injury intolerable, perceives "himself weaker than he imagined, & his enemies stronger than he conceiued." In wolf consciousness (as in human, this account implies), affects produce cognitive changes and cognitive changes produce affective responses. Thus, as the event approaches its climax and denouement, the signifiers of emotional and cognitive experience—"awearied with fighting, fearing his life, thinking the enterprise impossible"—thicken and superpose themselves.

Clearly Wright's overall investment in Aquinas's taxonomy of the eleven primary passions determines his hyperbolic portrayal of lupine affect. But it owes less to anthropomorphism per se than to the doctrine of correspondences and sympathies, itself, of course, a doctrine decidedly anthropocentric by design. This is why his account of the affects has much in common with the animal affects described elsewhere in early modern behavioral thought. In Topsell's *Historie of Foure-Footed Beastes*, there is not only significant continuity between human and animal emotions but also, as in Wright, a descriptive vocabulary in which ethical, physical, and psychophysiological discourses intermix. The result is a taxonomy of animals thoroughly moralized not in terms of their relations to men but in terms of their relations to each other, thanks to their own position on the analogical chain of sympathies, antipathies, and correspondences and the various qualities that their bodies and minds possess. For Topsell, as for other early modern thinkers, it was not just that the qualities of animals resembled those of human beings, but that those qualities were directly transferable from animal to human as humans applied and incorporated animal flesh into their own. He quotes Conrad Gesner as writing, "many beastes are vsed for meate, nourishment, and medicine, and for that cause are not only applied outwardly, but inwardly to the body of man . . . for because of the similitude they carry with mankind in body and affections, they suffer many diseases in common with vs" (sig. ¶1v).

---

42. In this respect, as in others, the early modern account of cognitive function is remarkably like that of some current cognitive science; see Antonio Damasio, *The Feeling of What Happens: Body and Emotion in the Making of Consciousness* (New York: Harcourt Brace, 1999), 35–38 and passim; and Sutton, *Philosophy and Memory Traces*, 13–20.

What is important to recognize, in terms of an early modern history of the passions, is that Thomas Wright's account of the emotional origins of the wolf's behaviors is necessarily little different from his accounts of the emotional behaviors of a human being caught up in similar conflict between pursuit of an object of desire and avoidance of the obstacles to it. Insofar as Wright endows the wolf with self-in-the-act-of-knowing, he attributes to him what Antonio Damasio has called a core self, a "transient protagonist of consciousness," continuously generated in pulses by interactions with objects in the environment. And he also endows him with elements of what Damasio calls an autobiographical self, insofar as that involves the activation of memory.[43] For Wright, what seems to make the wolf's emotions expressively animal rather than characteristically human is the nature and, in a sense, the ethical neutrality of the object of its desire—sheep on the hoof, meat raw rather than cooked.[44] Even the suddenness of the wolf's emotional progression from hope to rage to defeat is paralleled in Wright's account (quoted earlier) of the suddenness with which the human heart responds—"immediatly bendeth"—to a stimulus from the "purer spirits."[45] The static melancholy of the proverbial cat has been superseded by the dynamic experience of an emotionally conflicted wolf caught between the affective poles of desire and aversion, hope and fear. The cat as humoral object, or perhaps as subject manqué, has been succeeded by the wolf as humoral subject full-fledged.

Indeed the overlap between animal and human affect is critical to at least two of Wright's larger arguments in *Passions of the Minde in Generall*: first, that the Aquinian taxonomy of eleven basic emotions is rooted in the natural order and governs the workings of the sensitive soul in all those creatures endowed with one; and second, that the commonality between human and animal in the possession of the sensitive soul proves how hard it is for the rational soul to control the unruly passions when they fix on an object of desire and—in the space of a moment—inflame, dilate, or contract the heart with their contrariety, their insatiability, their importunity, their impossibility: "There is no man in this life, which followeth the streame of

43. Damasio, 168–94; see Damasio's tables 6.1 and 6.2 on 174–75 for a diagram of the differences.

44. Wright's neutrality may be a function of his own distance from the rural life or the fact that no wolves remained in England. Tapper, 51, argues that animal behavior serves as a natural basis for human morality because animals can be seen to act like humans but do so without the imposition of rules, here against the theft and devouring of another's property.

45. Suddenness is, for Paul Ekman, a defining attribute of the onset of emotion; see "Biological and Cultural Contributions to Body and Facial Movement in the Expression of Emotions," in Rorty, *Explaining Emotions*, 81.

his passions, but expecteth, and verily beleeueth to get at last a firme rest, contentation & full satiety of all his appetites: the which is as possible, as to quench fire with fuell, extinguish a burning Ague with hot wines, drowne an Eele with water" (74). Wright's wolf is not, therefore, a surrogate human being of the kind familiar in Aesopian fable but a "real," if hypothetical, animal, whose rhetorical function here is to show what life in the stream of one's passions is like in a life-critical event, even one lasting only a few minutes.

As anthropologists tell us, this way of thinking about animal behavior as driven "as if continually in a passion" is not unusual in itself.[46] What distinguishes Wright's wolf is that the workings of his passions are exemplary of our own. Because he has passions and a body, because he has a complex physiological apparatus for successfully appraising and reappraising the challenges of his environment, because his interaction with shepherd and dogs is profoundly social in its communication of moves and counter-moves, Wright's wolf is indeed a humoral subject. The workings of his passions, by means of the spirits animating his neural pathways, give proof from the other side of the species barrier of what John Sutton has proposed of mind-body relations in the early modern human subject: "the body theorised by early modern neuro-philosophers was never just an inert house for a ghostly soul. The body's fluids and spirits, and the traces it conceals, were always active, always escaping notice, always exceeding the domain of the will, always giving shape and flavour to the soul's plans."[47]

Perhaps it is the wolf's capacity for vivid emotions—here considered under the benignly comic aspect of a narrative that ends without much bloodshed on either side—that recommends him to Wright as an affective exemplar. But when that emotionalism is considered more negatively—as it is, for example, in Topsell's account of the wolf in *The Historie of Foure-Footed Beastes*—the wolf changes from being a creature given to complex cognitive assessments of risk and reward to being a helpless coward with a distinct affective resemblance to woman, whose emotions were known for being "most vehement and mutable," as Wright puts it (3). Topsell's wolf is in general a treacherous, subtle, ravening creature who eats all the sheep in a flock "not because hee feareth the ouer-livers [i.e., survivors] wil tel tales, but for that his insatiable mind thinketh he can neuer bee satisfied, and then when al are slaine, he falleth to eat one of them" (739). But in peril, Topsell argues, wolves become "extreamely fearefull, astonished, and

46. I am quoting Tim Ingold, introduction to Ingold, *What Is an Animal?* 6.
47. Sutton, *Philosophy and Memory Traces*, 16–17.

affraide" and especially vulnerable to surprise. As proof, he cites two stories "as they were related to *Gesner* by *Michaell Herus,* and *Iustinius Goblerus,"* both of which involve terrorized women. In one, a woman alone in her house with her children runs out and shuts the door behind her when a wolf enters by accident. Her children remain trapped inside until the husband returns home and rushes in, "longing to saue and deliuer his poore infants," only to find the wolf "in worse case, astonished, amazed, daunted, and standing like a stocke without sence, not able to run awaie, but as it were offering himselfe to be destroyed" (747). In the "more admirable" (more amazing) second story, a woman falls into a pit dug as a trap by a lord addicted to hunting and is followed therein by a fox and shortly afterward a wolf. Topsell renders the woman's anguish with all the detail that Wright lavished on the wolf:

> then she lost her hope, and in lamentable maner thinking of husband and children, how little they conceiued of her extremity, resolued to to [*sic*] forsake the world, and commended her soule to God, making no other reckoning but that her distressed leane lims should now be a supper and breakefast to the Wolfe ... while thus she mused, she saw the wolfe lie downe, she sitting in the one corner, and the Fox resting in another, and the wolf apaled as much as either of boeth, so the woman had no harme but an ill nightes lodging, with the feare whereof she was almost out of her wits. (748)

The comic interest in both stories is the paralysis to which both wolf and woman succumb when they find themselves suddenly in danger by being precisely in the wrong place, even perhaps in the other's place—the wolf trapped in the house in the first instance, the woman trapped like an animal of prey in the second. (Indeed the stories work for us, if at all, only by suppressing their own implausibility and our interest in how wolf and woman came to be there.) We should note the second woman's interior drama over the long night of entrapment, "striuing betwixt hope, feare, and griefe" (748), worrying about her husband and children, commending her soul to God, and even ironically anticipating the wolf's probable disappointment at having to make two meals, supper and breakfast, from a poor woman's "distressed leane lims"—*distressed* (*OED,* 1a) meaning not only afflicted with pain or trouble, but pain or trouble peculiarly applied to the poor. In the event, of course, the woman's intensity of emotion is implicitly ridiculed—rendered causeless and purposeless—by the story's comic outcome. But the moral that Topsell will acknowledge finding here—"that a

Wolfe dareth doe nothing when hee is in feare himself" (748)—works by
pretending that the stories make only the animals abject, rather than engaging in a parallel or even reversible abjection of women and wolf. The wolf's
shame inheres in his affective resemblance to the women, whose cowardice
and ineffectuality would otherwise go without saying. The women's
shame—and I do think we should read them as shamed—is subtler, more
particular, and redoubled. Topsell suggests a resemblance between women
and wolves only when the latter experience danger; hence the women's
comic slide from human to animal derives from the wolf's gender demo-
tion—from implicitly male to symbolically female—when women are
caught in a kind of mimetic regression, resembling him resembling them.
In the perverse logic of these stories, the women cannot aspire to manly
passions, or even to normative beastly passions; they can aspire only to the
vehement and mutable passions of women.

What is striking here, in Topsell as in Wright, is that the wolf functions
to represent powerful emotions strikingly different from those more conventionally associated with the animal. What Thomas Wright depicts as the
transparency of his wolf's cognitive and affective behavior is key to its
exemplarity as animal nature and sensitive soul. But Wright cannot have
chosen this exemplar unaware of the wolf's more usual demonization in
mythological, juridical, and medical contexts, ranging from Ovid's description of Lykaon's transformation in book 1 of the *Metamorphoses* to the
werewolf trials of men accused of mass murder in early modern France.[48]
As Leslie Dunton-Downer has pointed out, the wolf man "is a malevolent
figure whose unforeseeably rapacious activities and irrational destructive-
ness have been understood . . . to capture the animal aspect of the human
being, the capacity each of us bears to act without humanity or reason."[49] It
is precisely against the force of such conventional meanings, I would argue,
that Wright rewrites the wolf-man figure into a nondemonic creature in
order to represent the affectivity shared by humans and animals as functional, natural, and sympathetic. But the wolf-man literature—though it
seems to have little in common with the preoccupations either of natural
philosophy or of early modern humoralism—is in fact allied to both and
does offer its own, slightly off-center contribution to the affective cosmology of the sensitive soul. This contribution is directly related to the wolf

48. See Caroline Oates, "Metamorphosis and Lycanthropy in Franche-Comté, 1521–1643," in
Fragments for a History of the Human Body, Part One, ed. Michel Feher (New York: Zone Books,
1989), 305–63.

49. Leslie Dunton-Downer, "Wolf Man," in *Becoming Male in the Middle Ages*, ed. Jeffrey Jerome
Cohen and Bonnie Wheeler (New York: Garland, 1997), 205.

man's episodic bestiality—as he moves back and forth between ordinary social life within a human community and the rapacious behaviors associated with a solitary life in the forest. By his spectacular departures from human society, the wolf man—particularly in his medicalized form as the lycanthrope, the man deluded into thinking he is a wolf—demonstrates by antithesis the regulatory, self-preserving, and even socializing functions of the embodied passions. The werewolf has lost his human shape; the lycanthrope has lost the ordinary social behaviors that make him recognizable as human. In this sense, again as Dunton-Downer argues, the werewolf functions semiotically as a test case of the tensions between being male (werewolves are normatively male) and being human (205). But within early modern humoralism, to lose human shape or characteristically human behaviors is of necessity to lose ordinary human humorality—the bodily basis for the proper functioning of the passions—and vice versa. "The manners," says Burton, repeating the Galenic commonplace we examined in chapter 2, "doe follow the temperature of the body" (1:372). In physical terms, it is to lose the proper balance of radical heat and moisture peculiar to the overall humoral requirements—universally considered—of human beings and to take on the alien humorality of other creatures, metonymically here that of the wolf. Clinical descriptions of lycanthropy classify it as a disease of unnatural melancholy and conventionally emphasize the sufferer's excessive thirst and dryness. As Tommaso Garzoni describes it,

> Among these humours of melancholy, the Phisitions place a kinde of madnes by the Greeks called *Lycanthropia*, termed by the Latines *Insania Lupina*; or wolues furie: which bringeth a man to this point ... that in Februarie he will goe out of the house in the night like a wolfe, hunting about the graues of the dead with great howling, and plucke the dead mens bones out of the sepulchers, carrying them about the streetes, to the great feare and astonishment of all them that meete him: And the foresaide author affirmeth, that melancholike persons of this kinde, haue pale faces, soaked and hollow eies, with a weake sight, neuer shedding one teare to the view of the worlde, a drie toong, extreme thirst, and they want spittle and moisture exceedingly.[50]

---

50. Tommaso Garzoni, *The Hospitall of Incurable Fooles* (London, 1600), 19. But the description is frequently repeated and derives ultimately from Aëtius, *De melancholia* (sixth century), as Lynn Enterline points out in *The Tears of Narcissus: Melancholia and Masculinity in Early Modern Writing* (Stanford, CA: Stanford University Press, 1995), 396n37.

The lycanthrope's thirst and dryness point to the aftereffects of spent rage; indeed he bears a striking resemblance to a warrior figure such as Pyrrhus with his carbuncle eyes and hardened, wrath-roasted disposition. All the other details, environmental and behavioral, conform to the cold, dry residue of unnatural melancholy in such a man—the nighttime wanderings, the wintry time of year, the sympathetic attraction to graveyards and the bodies of the dead, and the howling, which (as we have seen above with Falstaff's cat) is a sound associated with melancholy beasts. But the lycanthrope's ghoulish behaviors should not distract us from recognizing the greater significance of the paradoxes of his bodily loss. To have such a surfeit of black bile in its worst, pathological form necessarily meant losing the radical heat and moisture proper to the disposition of any ordinarily healthy human being and essential—as we have seen in Hamlet and Othello in chapter 1—for the workings of reason.[51] It is to lack what Wright describes as "that temperature vertue requireth" (17). Or, as Burton exclaims about unnatural melancholy, "How should a man choose but be cholericke and angry, that hath his body so clogged with abundance of grosse humours?" (1:373). In the circular logic of early modern humoralism, the wolf man's thirst and dryness may be stimulated either by some external event or by some internal motion of the soul. But in either case, the deficits, as Burton suggests, are both affective and bodily in nature. This means that, for all his monstrous depredation against others, the wolf man's disease should first be understood humorally as a failure of self-love, because self-love is the name for those God-given natural appetites that allow any thing to remain itself. To quote Thomas Wright again: "So we see fire continually ascendeth vpward, because the coldnesse of the water, earth, and ayre much impeacheth the vertue of his heate . . . the Hare flieth from the Hounds: the Partridge hideth her selfe from the talon of the Hawke" (12). As we have seen, what occurs without internal conflict in inanimate creatures requires the joint operation of two appetites—the irascible and the concupiscible—in those endowed with sensitive souls: "Men and beasts w[ith] one appetite prosecute the good they desire and with an other they flie the euill they abhor" (12). But the wolf man is humorally no longer himself, no longer able in that most basic form of self-love to identify with (and love) his own body. As the doctor reports of Duke Ferdinand in Webster's *The Duchess of Malfi*:

---

51. On the pathology of melancholy, see the classic discussion in Babb, 21–23, 33–37.

> he howled fearfully;
> Said he was a wolf, only the difference
> Was, a wolf's skin was hairy on the outside,
> His on the inside; bade them take their swords,
> Rip up his flesh, and try.
>
> (5.2.15–19)

In her powerful reading of this play, Lynn Enterline explains the Duke's "descent into a quasi-human form with sore eyes" as a trope for the dissolution of masculinity, for a corruption both political and bodily that spreads from the Duke to other male members of his court, and for Webster's critique of the impossible desire—which theater is implicitly accused of fostering—to know and hence control others by attaining scopic mastery of the visual field (242–303, esp. 266). What I am proposing here is meant not to displace her argument but to ground it in a prior discourse, in the early modern logic of the passions and the biological facts that sustain them. According to Aristotle, what maintained the life of living creatures was native heat and radical moisture. Thomas Walkington describes the interactions of heat and moisture using the simile of a lamp and its oil: "our heate is like the flame of a burning lampe; the moisture like the foieson or oyle of the lampe, wherewith it continues burning. As in the lampe, if there bee not a symmetrie and a just measure of the one with the other, they will in a short time, the one of them destroy the other" (64–65). In humoralism, a store of radical heat and moisture—what the wolf man with his dry tongue and sore eyes lacks—is necessary for humoral creatures not only to love and remain themselves, but to love others as well. Heat and moisture signal an inclination to love others—as when Othello complains that Desdemona's "hot, hot, and moist" hand "argues fruitfulness and liberal heart" (3.4.38–39) or when Venus seizes on Adonis's

> sweating palm,
> The president of pith and livelihood,
> And trembling in her passion, calls it balm.
>
> (*Venus and Adonis*, 25–27)

But the rage that consumes Ferdinand's heat and moisture shrivels up such capacity altogether, causes him to draw back into himself only to find a disturbing unfamiliarity there, a wolf hairy "on the inside." (Since hair was known to be the driest of the body's parts and completely indigestible, for Ferdinand to feel himself to be hairy on the inside is the psychophysiological evidence of his total self-alienation.)[52] Since the signs of that rage are present from the beginning of the play, lycanthropy functions as the signifier of an extreme but not altogether unpredictable outcome. As Timothy Bright explains, if the melancholy disease "rise of choler, then rage playeth her part, and furie ioyned with madnesse, putteth all out of frame" (111).

It is important to underscore that Webster uses humoralism less to explain the cause of Ferdinand's horrible descent into wolfish fury than to naturalize and theatricalize its symptomatology. Webster associates both Aragonian brothers, early in the play, with corrupt bodily humors; Antonio describes them as "like plum trees that grow crooked over standing pools" (1.1.48–49)—the stagnant water that, as we have seen tragically in Othello's "puddled spirit" and comically in Hal's comparison of Falstaff and Moorditch, is conventionally associated with melancholy. Melancholic rage seems involved in Ferdinand's denial of independent emotions in others as he rebukes his courtiers in implicitly humoral language for daring to laugh without his doing so first: "Why do you laugh? Methinks you that are courtiers should be my touchwood, take fire when I give fire; that is, laugh when I laugh, were the subject never so witty" (1.1.122–25).[53] But he does not "give fire" to them—in what might be thought of as a companionable emanation of bodily warmth—and he does not laugh. "What appears in him mirth," explains Antonio to Delio, "is merely outside" (1.1.170). He burns instead with a "wildfire" choler against his sister, which he calls desperately "for rhubarb / To purge" (2.5.12–13). In this respect, the cultural role of melancholy adust dries up what might once have been Ferdinand's own normative appetites and desires and causes the death of his desire for self-continuance in his own humanly humoral flesh. In doing so, it provides a humoral logic for his more fundamental inability to recognize the Duchess's own appetites and desires—for sexual fulfillment, for domestic companionship, for the happiness of offspring—as a ordinary form of bodily well-being, an ordinary expression of bodily health and the social purposiveness that, as we saw in chapter 2, belongs to temperamental warmth. He becomes a wolf, in other words, losing the humoral benefit of his own sensitive human soul, because he cannot identify with his sister *and her desires* as natural—which is indeed the usual explanation of Ferdinand's insanity put humorally in reverse. Indeed, Ferdinand's lycanthropy offers

52. See *Problems of Aristotle*, sig. A3v: "no beast can digest feathers or haire, but do voide them vndigested."

53. For a fuller discussion of this moment, see Gail Kern Paster, "The Humor of It: Bodies, Fluids, and Social Discipline in Shakespearean Comedy," in *A Companion to Shakespeare's Works*, ed. Richard Dutton and Jean E. Howard, vol. 3, *The Comedies* (Malden, MA: Blackwell, 2003), 55.

another reason for Webster to make the siblings twins. Their shared maternal origin becomes the ontological sign not of their common place at the
top of the play's social order (which would be a function of shared paternal
origin) but more fundamentally of their common humanness. Ferdinand's
shame at the Duchess's desires for a companionate marriage—perhaps
especially a morganatic one—also make this clear, as when she protests to
him:

> Why might I not marry?
> I have not gone about, in this, to create
> Any new world, or custom.
>
> (3.2.109–11)

Since it cannot be on the basis of their shared paternal origin, his denial of
her humanness must therefore be on the basis of her sexual alterity alone—
as if sexual difference were equivalent to the human-animal divide, as if
woman were an anomalous third term in the human-animal binary and
women's passions were by their very nature pathological and excessive as
those of man and animal are not.[54] Denying differences between women, as
Peter Stallybrass has argued (133), is fundamental to misogyny; as we shall
see in more detail below, denying individual difference among animals
within the same species in order to fix it exclusively in human beings is
fundamental to humanist praises of the dignity of man. In Ferdinand, virulent misogyny collapses into the "extreme ontological states" of lycanthropy.[55] By linking the two sociopathologies—more properly, by finding
such links between them—Webster hints at the emotional impoverishment
characteristic of both. Since this impoverishment emerges directly from a
profound failure to identify with a victimized other, Webster allows us to
see again, as Wright and his wolf did earlier, that enhancing and legitimat-
ing objects and modes of identification is, cosmologically speaking, the sensitive soul's raison d'être. Ferdinand's willful destruction of his sensitive
soul and insane embrace of the outwardly bestial reveal Webster's play as in
some sense the tragic antithesis of Topsell's comic stories—trapping
the woman and her animal counterpart, the wolf, in the same social and

---

54. Frank Whigham sees the brothers' obsessive attention to their sister's sexuality as a
displacement for aristocratic anxieties about class stability; see "Sexual and Social Mobility in *The
Duchess of Malfi*," *PMLA* 100 (1985): 167–86. My argument would not displace this one either, but
only ground it in anxiety about an ontological divide in which women can come between men and
animals. On the relation of women and animals, see Boehrer, 57–64.

55. The quoted phrase belongs to Dunton-Downer, 213.

theatrical space and allowing them, by the force and nature of their disjunctive appetites, to destroy each other.

The wolf, as we have seen the animal in Wright, Topsell, and Webster, seems to function as a limit-case of the sensitive soul—in this respect, as in others, the very opposite of the melancholy cat as Falstaff presents it or even the subjectified bear in Macbeth's embattled analogy. In Wright's representation of the wolf especially, the extraordinary sequence of cognitive and affective operations is notable less in terms of early modern understandings of animal emotions—with which it is mostly cognate—than as a deeply sympathetic and ethically neutral identification with the subjectivity of an animal widely demonized by centuries of European mythological, medical, and juridical narratives. As I have tried to make clear, what is important about Wright's account is that it owes less to anthropomorphism per se than to the doctrine of correspondences and sympathies, itself, of course, a doctrine decidedly anthropocentric by design.[56] What I argue below, by turning to Cleopatra's extraordinary manipulations of the species barrier, is how the early modern idea of humans and animals as linked by their shared subjection to the passions works to produce a form of bodily self-experience epistemically prior to and other than our own. Early modern interest in animal passions, once it is understood as cosmological in motivation, then becomes legible not only as a discourse of redemptive self-criticism—as we might expect and as we will see below in *Antony and Cleopatra*—but also as the basis of a skeptical deconstruction of humanist man.

This deconstruction begins, early in the play, when Cleopatra imagines that it would better to be a horse than queen of Egypt: "O happy horse, to bear the weight of Antony!" (1.5.21). Her melodramatic exclamation is funny and fanciful—a moment of bawdy sublime. But more than bawdy goes on here: for if Cleopatra's hailing of the horse reminds us of Falstaff's self-comparison to a cat, it does so more for its contrast in mood and motive than for comparison. Unlike that of man and cat, the image of horse and rider is close to the emotional and ideological center of heroic iconography. As Sidney famously recalls in the beginning of *The Defence of Poesy*, the Italian horseman John Pietro Pugliano claimed that "soldiers were the noblest estate of mankind, and horsemen the noblest of soldiers." Sidney was much impressed with Pugliano's praise of the horse as "the only serviceable courtier without flattery, the beast of most beauty, faithfulness,

---

56. See Boerher's discussion (13–27) of relative and absolute anthropocentrism.

courage, and such more"; he writes, "I think he would have persuaded me to have wished myself a horse."[57] But it is one thing for a chivalric icon such as Sidney to switch places with a horse. The intrusion of an unruly woman such as Cleopatra into that tightly unified, necessarily intersubjective assemblage of warfare, conquest, and aristocratic male identity holds more transgressive possibility.[58] Indeed, from her exclamation a number of histories spin out, including the tropological history of women *as* horses with the attendant scenarios of breaking, taming, and bridling; the history of domestic property relations in which women and horses participate; and the scandalous history of sexual relations with animals, in which the equine as sexual partner has both mythological and juridical legacies.[59] One thinks here of Titania's monstrous desire for Bottom or even John Aubrey's notorious reports about Mary Herbert, Countess of Pembroke, looking through a secret peephole at her stallions rutting before receiving her own lovers.[60] But the scandals of these histories seem to stand entirely apart from Cleopatra's momentary envy of animal affect—however comically expressed—in ways that our earlier explorations of the shared terrain of human-animal affect may help to construe.

As we will see, the play's opposition of Egypt and Rome has the effect of highlighting the role of the passions in humanistic descriptions of human nature, because the passions—predictably—are forces of indeterminacy that challenge not only Rome's geopolitical order but its intellectual order as well, imperiling the great interlocking binaries of difference in gender and species. *Antony and Cleopatra* manipulates the terms of shared human-animal affectivity because, even as the play levies boldly upon this early modern notion of the sensitive soul, it also deploys the fundamental binaries on which humanist constructions of man's dignity rest.[61] In this respect, Cleopatra's hailing of the horse as a fellow subject united by desire for Antony adds to the intellectual and ethical burden that the play places

57. Philip Sidney, *The Defence of Poesy*, in *Sir Philip Sidney*, ed. Katherine Duncan-Jones (Oxford: Oxford University Press, 1989), 212.

58. For this picture of horse and rider, see Jeffrey Jerome Cohen, *Medieval Identity Machines* (Minneapolis: University of Minnesota Press, 2003), 45–71.

59. On women and horses, see Jeanne Addison Roberts, *The Shakespearean Wild: Geography, Genus, and Gender* (Lincoln: University of Nebraska Press, 1991), 64–67.

60. This is according to John Aubrey, *Aubrey's Brief Lives*, ed. Oliver Lawson Dick (London: Secker and Warburg, 1949), 138. I owe this reference to Dympna Callaghan.

61. For a groundbreaking feminist analysis of these constructions, see Marilyn Migiel, "The Dignity of Man: A Feminist Perspective," in *Refiguring Woman: Perspectives on Gender and the Italian Renaissance*, ed. Marilyn Migiel and Juliana Schiesari (Ithaca, NY: Cornell University Press, 1991), 211–32.

on Antony as paradigmatic man. He is the biographical subject in whom
Rome's massive investment in human dignity has come into question.
Precisely because the heroic accomplishments of the younger Antony
seemed to secure the binaries of gender and species, the older Antony's
infatuation in Egypt dismantles them. Thus Caesar remembers the young
Antony's stoical triumph over disgust as the sign of his strong difference
from beasts and ordinary men. He alone among the Roman soldiers could
eat raw food like a beast and drink the puddled wastewater that even beasts
refused:

> Thou didst drink
> The stale of horses and the gilded puddle
> Which beasts would cough at; thy palate then did deign
> The roughest berry on the rudest hedge;
> Yea, like the stag, when snow the pasture sheets,
> The barks of trees thou brows'd. On the Alps
> It is reported that thou didst eat strange flesh,
> Which some did die to look on.
>
> (1.4.61–68)

Caesar invokes the human-animal divide here in order to identify a superior
form of manliness—Stoic patience, with which he can identify the younger
Antony. He marks this hypermanliness not only by its rational suppression
of the disgust common to animal and human alike, but, paradoxically, by
Antony's imitation of animal eating and even—in the oddly indeterminate
phrase "strange flesh"—by the hint of perverse eating.[62] Antony is manlier
than other men, that is, by willing himself to be more animal-like than the
animals, even to his adopting the habits of a stag or the omnivorous
appetites of a wolf or a wolf man. By subsuming both ordinary humanness
and ordinary animalness, Antony's hypertrophied will produces humanness
in a new form, identifiable mostly by the suppression of disgust.[63] Indeed
Antony here is imagined as being so able to overcome appetite that self-
love—which among passion theorists such as Thomas Wright is nearly synonymous with appetite and the key to self-continuance—becomes wholly a

---

62. Plutarch comments: "they did eat the barcks of trees, and such beasts, as never man tasted
their flesh before." See "The Life of Marcus Antonius," in *Plutarch's Lives of the Noble Grecians and
Romans*, trans. Thomas North (1579), reprinted in *Narrative and Dramatic Sources of Shakespeare*,
ed. Geoffrey Bullough (London: Routledge and Kegan Paul, 1964), 5:267–68.

63. William Ian Miller, *The Anatomy of Disgust* (Cambridge, MA: Harvard University Press,
1997).

function of will. Others "die to look on" what he wills himself to eat. In the process, Antony ends up doing things that are admirable because they are disgusting—placing himself all alone in a rude heroic mold that other, perhaps too-civilized, Roman soldiers can envy but not emulate. Thus one irony here is the unalloyed disgust and dismay that Antony's current behavior in eating and drinking now provokes in Caesar:

> he fishes, drinks, and wastes
> The lamps of night in revel.

> (1.4.4–5)

Far from judging Antony's surrender to the exquisite pleasures of Egypt as a civilized man's reward for extreme self-denial, Caesar reproves Antony now for removing the difference in himself between human and animal and, by extension, removing it from them all. His appetites now bring them all closer to a specter of bestial undifference reaching to the very top of the social hierarchy. Antony

> is not more manlike
> Than Cleopatra; nor the queen of Ptolomy
> More womanly than he.

> (1.4.5–7)

As we will see below, differences between the sexes were thought to be fewer and less significant in animals than in human beings—so the blurring of that difference in their behaviors becomes another sign of Antony's decline. And Antony's passions reverse the generational hierarchy, moving the younger Caesar to wish he could command a disciplinary pedagogy over an older man betrayed back into ungendered, appetitive boyhood:

> 'tis to be chid—
> As we rate boys who, being mature in knowledge,
> Pawn their experience to their present pleasure,
> And so rebel to judgment.

> (1.4.30–33)

Antony's regression toward gender undifference is thus reciprocal with his surrender of the willpower that once separated him from beasts, boys, and women.

It is Rome's investment in the opposition of man to beast that gives importance to Cleopatra's hailing of Antony's horse. If we understand her identification with the horse as expressing a simple womanly longing to be mastered sexually, then her exclamation upholds those structures of domination in which women and animals are alike in subjection and man's dignity is staked out through difference from them both. Indeed this would be true even if masculine self-mastery would then seem frighteningly to follow from, rather than produce, mastery of others. Cleopatra's identification with the horse would serve to ratify Antony's recall to Rome as a resecuring of masculine difference and of the Roman heroism that, for her, he continues to represent. "Do bravely, horse," she exhorts it,

> for wot'st thou whom thou mov'st?
> The demi-Atlas of this earth, the arm
> And burgonet of men.
>
> (1.5.22–24)

But her fantasy here is not a simple one of female subjection through identification with the horse; rather, her equine imaginings have the power to disrupt the fixity of gender and species. In this hailing of the horse, she becomes a Circe-like figure who, rather than enacting a shameful transformation of species, finds in the physical and psychological fellowship of desire a reason for denying essential differences between human and animal. And she finds in that denial a principle of opposition to Rome. In this mini-address to the offstage horse and in her address, later, to the asp she takes to her bosom, Cleopatra allows us to glimpse the possibility of an unhumanistic interrogation of the dignity of "man" in terms not entirely foreign to our own cyborgian speculations.

In being hailed across the species barrier, then, Antony's horse is Cleopatra's surrogate in Rome, doing the work of her desire by other means, achieving the physical and psychological unity with Antony that she longs for. Cleopatra's implicit acknowledgment of Antony's physical or ceremonial dependence on the horse ("Do bravely, horse") pales before her interest in imagining a pride within the horse that derives vicariously from its recognition of its rider's political supremacy. The horse thus becomes part of an emotional hierarchy that, as we shall see in chapter 4, is an integral part of the social consequences of humoralism. In fact, Cleopatra's hint of belief in the horse's potential to identify itself with imperial politics may not be far-fetched, for the early modern classification of horses is fully cognate with the complex hierarchical classifications of people. Thus Gervase

Markham begins his discussion of the temperament of horses rather grandly by placing the horse within the natural order—almost as if it were human or some other thing apart: "A Horse is compounded of seauen naturall thinges, that is Elements, Temperatures, Humors, Members, powers, Operations and Spirits."[64] All animals, including humans, were by definition composed of the seven naturals, of course, but it is hard to imagine Markham using the same rhetorical flourish to introduce any other animal species except for man. He devotes an entire chapter in the fifth book of *Cavelarice* to *"the passions which are in horses, and the loue which keepers should beare vnto them"* and argues that "it is most certaine, that eueire [*sic*] horse is possest with these passions, *loue, ioy, hate, sorrow,* and *feare*" (5:45). Other animals, as we have seen, were thought to possess a range of emotions—even, if we are to believe Wright, the wolf. But unlike other animals that were thought to manifest only a single temperament common to their species, horses were further distinguished by the five humoral temperaments known to exist in people. In horses as in human beings, an "indifferent" or equal mixture of the elements produces the best temperament—a horse that is light, swift, long-lived, and, best of all, combining in itself boldness and tractability (7:3). But, again as in people, more often one of the four qualities predominated in a horse's disposition to produce horses that were hot (furious, mad, desperate), moist (apish, fantastical, and forgetful), cold (fearful, skittish, and subject to tiring), or dry (dull, slothful, rebellious, and malicious). The way for men to predict which element predominated in a given horse was through skin color, as we might expect, so that the many chromatic variations in horses were organized—like the many skin colors in people—into the four shades of humoralism: horses of red or coal-black hues tended toward choler, bright bays and roans were sanguine, milk-white and yellow dun horses were phlegmatic, and iron gray or mouse-dun horses were melancholic. But as Markham takes care to point out, the temperamental differences of horses were themselves affected by age and by differences in climate—the same differences of time and space, in other words, that affected human temperaments: "Now these tempers do alter, as the powers of a horse either increase or diminish, as thus, a Foale is said to haue his temper from the Fire and Ayre, a horse of middle age from the Fire and Earth, and a horse of old age from the Earth and Water." And he goes on: "Horses likewise take their temperatures from the Clymbes where they are bredde, as commonly those which are neerest the Sunne, are euer of

64. Gervase Markham, *Cavelarice; or, The English Horseman* (London, 1607), 7.2. Since each book division in Markham's treatise is paginated separately, I cite book and page number.

purest spirits & longest liues, and those which are farthest of, are more dull, and of lesse continuance" (7:3). In *Henry V* the Dauphin boasts that his nutmeg-colored warhorse is "pure air and fire; and the dull elements of earth and water never appear in him, but only in patient stillness while his rider mounts him" (3.7.21–23). A similar association with air marks the temperamentally lively stallion of Adonis:

> Anon he starts at stirring of a feather;
> To bid the wind a base he now prepares,
> And whe'er he run, or fly, they know not whether;
> > For through his mane and tail the high wind sings,
> > Fanning the hairs, who wave like feath'red wings.
>
> (*Venus and Adonis*, 302–6)

This young horse's moods and behaviors—no less affected by wind than people's were—express the "pneumatic character of life" in the poem, while the horse's volatility and sensitivity to the wind bring the reader closer phenomenologically to his experience of sexual desire.[65] Shakespeare's point in the poem seems to be precisely to contrast the ultimately tragic complexity of human sexual desire as represented by Venus and Adonis with the horse's relatively simple capacity for sexual pleasure.[66]

As aristocrats of the animal world, horses were especially vulnerable—according to Topsell—to the emotions ranged along the shame-pride axis, and especially sensitive to beauty. He describes the mutual admiration of the great Median horses and their masters, which begins with the masters being "bewitched" by the size of these beasts and "with the rich attire and shape of their bodies" and ends with the horses' reciprocal attraction: "the horses take delight in their maisters, both in greatnes and in fairenes of body, and such costly furniture vpon their backes, that they seeme to perceiue their owne stature and comeliness" (290). The mirroring of delight here brings the horse-master relation into emotional circuits very like those of male homosociality, engaging horse and man across the species barrier in a mutual narcissistic reinforcement that seems more like the equal terms of idealized male friendship than the hierarchical opposition of man and

---

65. I am quoting here from Kuriyama, 240.

66. On this theme, see John Doebler, "*Venus and Adonis*: Shakespeare's Horses," in *Images of Shakespeare: Proceedings of the Third Congress of the International Shakespeare Association, 1986*, ed. Werner Habicht, D. J. Palmer, and Roger Pringle (Newark: University of Delaware Press, 1988), 64–72.

animal.[67] This works only because the horses here are implicitly gendered male, the mutual admiration of horse and master seemingly untouched by negative suggestions of vanity. In this respect, Topsell's treatment of the warhorse is conspicuously less satirical than that in *Henry V*, where the French noblemen compete in celebrations of their horses—and their mistresses. His companions recognize the Dauphin's exaggerated praise of his mount as a form of self-flattery and belittle his claims both to superior horsemanship and sexual prowess: "your horse," the Constable tells him, "would trot as well, were some of your brags dismounted" (3.7.76–78). But human manipulations of the equine pride-shame axis work inversely when the horses are female and destined for sexual subjection to their masters' breeding programs, no matter what resistance the mares might offer. Do not shave off horses' manes, Topsell writes, since horses are naturally proud of them, as may be seen in the refusal of mares to engender with "snaueling and short haired" asses. The keepers respond by shaving the mares and leading them to see their reflections in water, "wherein while the Mares behold their owne deformity, they grow so shamed, deiected, and discouraged, that euer after they admit with quietnesse the Asses to couer them" (283).

Both emotional circuits—of interspecies pride and subjection—come into play in Richard II's bitterly nostalgic memories of glory on horseback when a groom of the stable reports a favorite steed's change of rider:

> O how it ern'd my heart when I beheld
> In London streets, that coronation-day,
> When Bullingbrook rode on roan Barbary,
> That horse that thou so often hast bestrid,
> That horse that I so carefully have dress'd!

$$(5.5.76-80)$$

Although Richard first reacts to this news by invoking horse-man reciprocal sociality—"This hand hath made him proud with clapping him" (86)—he pulls back from such a painful identification with reminders of the hierarchical scale of nature:

---

67. On friendship, see Jeffrey Masten, *Textual Intercourse: Collaboration, Authorship, and Sexualities in Renaissance Drama* (Cambridge: Cambridge University Press, 1997), 28–37.

why do I rail on thee,
Since thou, created to be aw'd by man,
Wast born to bear?

(90–92)

But the emotional logic of horse-man interactions and his own new status as subject carry him into further and more painful identifications as his sense of abjection demotes him from king to human to horse to ass:

I was not made a horse,
And yet I bear the burthen like an ass,
Spurr'd, gall'd, and tir'd by jauncing Bullingbrook.

(92–94)

Here, like the shorn mares bred to asses, Richard discovers the high cost of interspecies pride, because the distinction that he and Barbary once gave exclusively to each other not only is transferable but also, when denied to him, becomes metaphorically an extrusion either from active maleness—in being "spurr'd, gall'd, and tir'd" by Bolingbroke—or from the ranks of humanity altogether. Perhaps equally important, though only implied here, is that Bolingbroke might have used the occasion of riding Richard's Barbary roan as a further ceremonial demonstration of his complete physical and symbolic replacement of the king. In this sense, when the horse is seen going proudly under Bolingbroke "as if he disdain'd the ground" (83), the event becomes metonymic of the usurper king's attempt to claim a natural mastery over all his subjects, including his animal ones.[68]

The close relationship between horse and human hierarchies, the sexual analogy of masculinity as ridership, and the human sympathy attributed to horses charge these tropes with an intensity foreign to other references to domesticated animals. Indeed, like Sidney's Italian horse-master Pugliano, Topsell finds horses so extraordinary in their beauty, spirit, usefulness, and emotional complexity that he is almost willing to make them an exception to what otherwise he finds the defining trait of "perfect beasts"—that beasts "do promiscuously couer one another; the father the Daughter, the Sonne the mother, the Brother the Sister." He relates the story (found in Pliny, Oppianus, Aelianus, and Aristotle) about the mare and her offspring—the

68. It is important here to understand the differences between ambling horses, used for long distances because of their easy pace, and the impressively high-stepping gait of the great trotting or footcloth horse, used for ceremonial entrances like this one; see D. H. Madden, *The Diary of Master William Silence* (London: Longmans, Green, 1907), 260–62.

last of a "generous breed of Horsse destroyed by a pestilence"—refusing to mate because "the Horsse refused copulation with his own parents." Only when both animals are covered with artificial skins does the mating take place, but once the horses are revealed to one another, they become so "guiltye in themselues of incestious commixtion" (299) that they run together to the top of a rock and throw themselves off. Tales of other suicidal animals are to be found in Renaissance animal lore, especially tales of dogs doing themselves in out of grief for a departed master.[69] This is why Topsell's skepticism about the story is not directed at the two horses' capacity for extreme and self-destructive emotions but only at their exceptional recognition of the incest taboo: "the stories before recited may be true, yet are they extraordinary: otherwise the common rule of *Ouid* remaineth true. That it is not a filthy thing for beasts to obserue no degrees of nature" (299).

As for Cleopatra, she creates a subject position for the horse imagined as happier and more fortunate than she is in order to make the quality of its projected happiness a simulacrum of her own. The horse serves human desire as a prosthetic agent not for its rider (as was the case for Richard and for Bolingbroke) but for herself as animal—a royal subject whose restless desires override the paltry containment of species. Antony's horse, endowed like other horses—like Richard's Barbary—with longings for the ontologically elevated Other, gives Cleopatra a means for exteriorizing and expanding her own desire. Identification with the horse allows her desire to connect her human body to its animal one and conquers the distance between Egypt and Rome. Cleopatra's relation to the horse—I am suggesting—is one neither of anthropocentric appropriation nor of incorporation but rather of a narcissistic fantasy of omnipotence, imagining extension beyond the frustrations of single and particular being, locked as a human being is into one place, one body, one sex, and one overarching historical design.

In the play, Cleopatra's intersubjective travel across the species barrier reconciles her momentarily to her lover's absence and, perhaps, by troping riding as a form of intercourse, to the Roman imperatives that have caused it. Having constructed a desire in Antony's horse indivisible from her own, Cleopatra is then able to enter intimately into Antony's desire, fashioning a contemporaneous longing—again through animal reference—in him:

> He's speaking now,
> Or murmuring, "Where's my serpent of old Nile?"
>
> (1.5.24–25)

69. For one of these stories, see Thomas Lupton, *A Thousand Notable Things* (London, 1579), 11.

The erotic triangle of woman-horse-man suddenly metamorphoses into horse-man-serpent. Her ventriloquism pushes hard against the constraints of time and space, not only looking forward to what the audience knows will be the serpent-instrument of her death but perhaps also celebrating the self-presence that Antony's image of her as serpent would represent. In the barge scene, he tells the drunken Lepidus—who is curious about Egyptian crocodiles and queens—that the crocodile "is shap'd, sir, like itself and it is as broad as it hath breadth. It is just so high as it is, and moves with it own organs ... Of it own color too ... and the tears of it are wet" (2.7.42–49).[70] (One almost expects to hear Antony underline the crocodile's utter self-presence with a Corporal Nym–like refrain, "And that's the humor of it.") But for Cleopatra at this moment of longing, the undivided passions of animals fuel the appetites of her soul as food does her body. This imagining is self-nourishment of a sophisticated aversiveness, the pursuit of pleasurable pain:

> Now I feed myself
> With most delicious poison.
>
> (1.5.26–27)

Like Hamlet's proverbial chameleon, Cleopatra eats the air that she has crammed with thoughts of horse and Antony.

As references here to serpents and poison suggest, this moment also anticipates the more theatricalized instance of desire crossing the species barrier at the end of the play when Cleopatra puts the asp to her breast. In the later moment, Cleopatra welcomes death as the means of union with her lover, whose absence now comes through death. She does not speculate any longer as to the relative happiness of human and animal, nor does she pretend that the "pretty worm of Nilus" (5.2.243) has any notion of service or intersubjectivity, or any of the ability to take discipline that the higher animals possess. Its only impulse is the self-protective bite that, in the event, she must encourage it to perform:

> Poor venomous fool,
> Be angry and dispatch.
>
> (5.2.305–6)

---

70. Topsell defines serpents broadly to include "all venomous Beasts," whether those without legs, such as adders and snakes, or those with legs, such as crocodiles and lizards; see *Historie of Serpents*, 10.

But her use of the asp to challenge Rome is even more insistent than her deployment of Antony's horse was. The horse, however indispensable for imperial practices, is a near-impossibility in theatrical practice.[71] At the moment of its invocation, Antony's horse remained a figure for her analogical imagination and our sympathetic one; its ability to move her across time and space toward Antony in Rome was merely notional. But the clown's onstage delivery of the asp—presumably in response to her bidding—is accompanied by Cleopatra's interview with him about the creature's behavioral properties, properties comically invested (like the crocodile's) with the self-sameness of tautology: "his biting is immortal," says the country fellow; "those that do die of it do seldom or never recover" (5.2.246–48). But Cleopatra still needs reassurance that the animal will follow its nature: "You must think this, look you, that the worm will do his kind" (262–63). "Look you," says the country fellow, "the worm is not to be trusted but in the keeping of wise people; for indeed, there is no goodness in the worm . . . it is not worth the feeding" (5.2.265–67, 270).

I have argued elsewhere that Cleopatra's troping of the asp as a suckling child here is Shakespeare's specific inversion of wet-nursing practices familiar to his audience. Instead of the upper-class baby sent out to the home of a lower-class woman, the play offers us the remarkable spectacle of a queen embracing the poisonous snake-baby in a monument that becomes at that moment an image of the hermetically sealed birthing chamber.[72] Here the baby weans its nurse from human nourishment, helps its nurse to make the journey from life to death: "Now no more / The juice of Egypt's grape shall moist this lip," Cleopatra declares (5.2.281–82). Once it is troped as an angry suckling biting the breast that feeds it, the asp cannot escape being endowed with the full weight of desire that Cleopatra projected onto the horse. And it too becomes a vehicle of transport, taking her beyond bodily contingency and Roman capture. "Husband, I come!" she exclaims (287).

> I am fire and air; my other elements
> I give to baser life.
>
> (289–90)

71. For a discussion of horses appearing on stage, see Alan C. Dessen and Leslie Thomson, *A Dictionary of Stage Directions in English Drama, 1580–1642* (Cambridge: Cambridge University Press, 1999), 117.

72. See Paster, *Body Embarrassed*, 239–43.

Engaging the asp in a mock dialogue of instruction, Cleopatra arms it metaphorically with a powerful arsenal of oedipal emotions and the discourse of the unconscious:

> O, couldst thou speak,
> That I might hear thee call great Caesar ass
> Unpolicied!
>
> (5.2.306–8)

She imagines so complete a reversal that this sharp-toothed baby's immunity from the Roman emperor has the effect of transforming Caesar into a beast of metaphorical burden—here bearing the heavy burden of shame at the twin escapes of the asp-baby and its royal nurse. Perhaps Antony's horse, having served its metonymic turn, has here been demoted and metamorphosed into the great Roman ass.

That Antony's happy horse and the "pretty worm of Nilus" serve Cleopatra as the displacements of her desire is as obvious to her as it is to us. But in the case of these animals—as in the case of Falstaff's cat, Macbeth's bear, and Wright's wolf—simple anthropomorphic projection based on physical analogies between sex and riding or between a serpent's biting and a baby's suckling does not account for the emotional character of what we find. Early modern theories of the passions, however, do help to explain why Cleopatra's strategies of displacement should cross the species barrier and how they affect the play's implied representation of man's dignity and cosmological makeup. As Julie Solomon has suggested, praises such as Pico della Mirandola's famous "Oration on the Dignity of Man" define man as the uniquely composite animal, "the being who is literally not himself, whose body is essentially other."[73] Cleopatra's willed, knowing use of the animals is passion's challenge to such humanistic representations of man as a self-alienated rational animal alone in a universe of passionate, animal low Others. For what really enables such identifications, as we have seen, is neither the possibility of animal-human sexual relations—even in fantasy—nor that of cross-species suckling, but ontological facts about the passions as the common property of all animate life acting predictably on the body. "Al passions," writes Thomas Wright, "may be distinguished by the dilatation,

73. Julie R. Solomon, "From Species to Speculation: Naming the Animals with Calvin and Bacon," in *Women and Reason*, ed. Elizabeth D. Harvey and Kathleen Okruhlik (Ann Arbor: University of Michigan Press, 1992), 92.

enlargement, or diffusion of the heart: and the contraction, collection, or compression of the same: for (as afterward shall be declared in all Passions) the hart is dilated or coarcted more or lesse" (24). This holds true for the queen, the horse, the snake—creatures capable of experiencing passion, if not of communicating it effectively across the species barrier, thanks to the possession of a heart and the action of the sensitive soul upon it.

Cleopatra herself recognizes the effects of the passions in collapsing Roman structures of difference and categories of experience. She sees the collapse of such differences as liberation from the social and psychophysiological imprisonment of human subjectivity. Near the end of the play, having fainted in response to Antony's death, she wakes to hear Iras and Charmian rousing her:

> Royal Egypt!
> Empress!
>
> (4.15.70–71)

But such hailing by her women seems to Cleopatra irrelevant in the face of a grief so intense that it abrogates petty distinctions of social kind:

> No more but [e'en] a woman, and commanded
> By such poor passion as the maid that milks
> And does the meanest chares.
>
> (4.15.73–75)

But as we have seen, Cleopatra's tropological deployments of horse and asp reach well beyond this identification with another woman. Because the horse and the asp are metonymies for embodied passions that are, by definition in this period, not specific to humankind, they can reflect human desire in an uncompromised, more knowable form (as Wright says, "for, as we see beasts hate, loue, feare, and hope, so doe children"). Thus Cleopatra uses the passions attributed to all animal life to gesture toward a horizon of desire beyond single subjectivity, to strive for something like the Deleuzian "Body without Organs" that I discussed earlier with reference to the baited bear, Macbeth's fellow subject in terror. In a body extended outward to become "a *field of immanence* of desire, the *plane of consistency* specific to desire," the body, whether human or animal, resembles an egg before the development of organs; its desires are neither localized nor named. Deleuze and Guattari do not ask what such a body is, but rather what it can do. The human body organized by Western epistemologies is replaced by a dynamic entity of intensities and flows, a body conceived simply as a unit of matter in time: "Flows of intensity, their fluids, their fibers, their continuums and conjunctions of actions of affects, the wind, fine segmentation, microperceptions, have replaced the world of the subject" (162). When Cleopatra and Antony's horse become mutually incorporate in desire, when Cleopatra absorbs "delicious poison" from the bite of the asp, human and animal bodies are transformed into proximate fields of desire: the two bodies, animal and human, are "in no way the same thing, but Being expresses them both in a single meaning in a language that is no longer that of words, in a matter that is no longer that of forms," and—most important—"in an affectability that is no longer that of subjects."[74] As prepsychoanalytic subjects, the early moderns—with their yearning palm trees, pneumatic spirits, the "melancholy of Moor-ditch," and a universe filled with the strivings of desire—are in a better position than we may be epistemologically to understand an affectability no longer that of subjects.

A thoroughgoing Deleuzian reading of *Antony and Cleopatra* is a contradiction in terms, since the Body without Organs exceeds interpretation ("there is nothing to interpret") just as it exceeds hierarchy.[75] Nor is a full-fledged reading of the play, in any case, my intention here. But I do think it is possible to use the Body without Organs as a historically productive way of understanding the cross-species identifications of Cleopatra here, as of Falstaff and Macbeth earlier, and of applying that understanding to the passions of other characters in early modern texts. As we have seen, animals function heuristically as received instantiations of the passions because the bodies of animals and men form those passions out of the same physical stuff and physiological procedures and because the sensitive souls of animals and men use them to the same end of preservation through the appetites of self-love. Thus, although man, the paragon of animals, was sometimes required discursively to oppose the rest of creation in order to secure hierarchical structures of difference, the more fluid economy of attributes suggested by Thomas Wright's definition of the passions and Cleopatra's deployment of horse and asp was no less requisite in other discourses, such as humoralism.[76] It makes sense within Galenic humoralism, for example, that the elaborate purgative regimes that maintained human health and psychological well-being applied in veterinary contexts as well. Thus Topsell summarizes the protocols for equine phlebotomy, including a

74. Deleuze and Guattari, 258.
75. Ibid., 153.
76. For an overview of these contexts, see Thomas, 121–36.

warning about the danger of bleeding stallions prior to their duties of inter-course: "it is no good part of husbandry to let them bleed that yeare, wherein they admit copulation, for the vacuation of blood and seede, is a dubble charge to nature" (284).[77] Such advice was familiar to male readers of medical self-help treatises that cautioned against the dangers of combin-ing sex and phlebotomy. As a much-quoted aphorism from Avicenna put it, a loss of seed "harmeth a man more, then if hee should bleed forty times as much."[78] Springtime bleedings were intended to relieve the body of its excess blood and humors, built up over a long inactive winter when the body's natural evacuations slowed. What was good physically for the man was good for the horse, and vice versa. But given the full significance of affectivity in horses, their exquisite capacity to suffer shame and pride, it is also fair to wonder if horses were thought to experience the psychological benefits in bloodletting that many human patients reported.[79]

This understanding of early modern emotions as especially visible and knowable in animals—produced physiologically by the same means but without the inhibiting filters and self-appraisals imposed by the civilizing process—suggests why Cleopatra would use imaginative transcendence of the species barrier as a means of denying the social imprisonment of gen-der differences. Cleopatra willfully tropes the asp, as poisoner of a suicidal queen, as having a natural capacity to commit lèse majesté against Caesar. The move is itself representative of a tendency in early modern skepticism to use animal faculties in order to question the scope of human difference from animals—and its meanings. The probable source of such interroga-tions comes from Plutarch, whose two essays devoted to animals supply most of the topoi later used by writers on the subject.[80] The most famous of such arguments is Montaigne's in *The Apology of Raymond Sebond*. On the ground that "there is a greater equality and a more uniform relationship in the organization of the world" than is commonly understood,[81] he praises

---

77. It may be worth noting that such protocols were not universally accepted. Markham, for example, objects to the common practice of quarterly bleedings and would allow it only upon "vrgent necessitie, and apparent reasons" (7.2:9–10).

78. Vaughan, 70. Vaughan paraphrases Avicenna's *De animalibus*.

79. See Paster, *Body Embarrassed*, 83–84.

80. In Philemon Holland's translation, these essays are entitled "That Brute Beastes Have Use of Reason" and "Whether Creatvres be more wise, they of the land, or those of the water"; see *The Philosophie, Commonlie Called the Morals . . . of Plutarch* (London, 1603).

81. Michel de Montaigne, *The Apology for Raymond Sebond*, in *The Complete Essays*, ed. and trans. Donald M. Frame (Stanford, CA: Stanford University Press, 1958), 334.

the emotional intelligence of animals and denies mankind's sole possession
of reason and the knowledge of God: "Is it possible to imagine anything so
ridiculous as that this miserable and puny creature, who is not even master
of himself, exposed to the attacks of all things, should call himself master
and emperor of the universe, the least part of which it is not in his power to
know, much less to command?" (329). For Montaigne, the species barrier is
man's self-deluding fiction, a denial contrary to sensory evidence that animals communicate with each other and intersubjectively with us:

> It is by the vanity of this same imagination that he equals himself to God,
> attributes to himself divine characteristics, picks himself out and separates
> himself from the horde of other creatures, carves out their shares to his fel-
> lows and companions the animals, and distributes among them such por-
> tions of faculties and powers as he sees fit. How does he know, by the force
> of his intelligence, the secret internal stirrings of animals? By what compar-
> ison between them and us does he infer the stupidity that he attributes to
> them? . . . When I play with my cat, who knows but if I am not a pastime to
> her more than she is to me? (331)

The 1595 edition adds, charmingly: "We entertain each other with reciprocal monkey tricks. If I have my time to begin or to refuse, so has she hers"
(331n). Montaigne's rhetorical vehemence here gives us reason to suspect
the motivation for his account of the practical consciousness of animals; his
praise for them is fueled by a ferocious contempt, bred at least in part of
the French civil wars, for human pretension and claims to uniqueness.
Montaigne is even more specific than Wright was in his assessments of cognitive activity in animals, both perfect and imperfect, warm-blooded or not:
thus he finds "reason and foresight" (332) in the cooperative activities of
honey bees; judgment and discrimination in swallows' choice of nesting
places; reflection and inference in spiders' nest-building. He sees only
human self-interest in the notion of animal instinct—what he calls "natural
and servile inclination"—as the explanation for "works which surpass all
that we can do by nature and by art" (333). And lest he seem to be overly
praising animals, he argues that animals are as capable as we are of the
"affectionate leanings" called sympathy and are not "exempt from our jeal-
ousies, or from extreme and irreconcilable envy" (346). In such assessments,
Montaigne is less interested in the exercise of commending animals in
order to merely derogate human beings than he is in praising Nature for the
adequacy of her order in giving every creature "all powers necessary for
the preservation of its being" (333). It is human reason, not Caesar, that

Montaigne wishes to decenter by an extended and often idiosyncratic likening of human and animal capacities, as for example his comparison of
"changes of color in fear, anger, shame, and other passions" in humans to
the changes in color perfected by chameleons and octopuses: "Now these
effects which we recognize in the other animals, greater than our own, tes-
tify to some more excellent faculty in them which is concealed from us, as
are in all likelihood many others of their properties and powers of which no
signs come through to us" (344). And when Montaigne surveys and general-
izes the whole of animal existence in comparison to that of humans, it is
the similarity of the two that impresses him most of all: "Since animals are
born, beget, feed, act, move, live, and die in a manner so close to our own,
all that we detract from their motive powers, and all that we add to ours to
raise our state above theirs, can in no way proceed from the judgment of
our reason" (345). He speculates about the possibility of religious feeling in
elephants because they keep "their eyes fixed toward the rising sun" and
"stand still a long time in meditation and contemplation" (343); he hypothe-
sizes death rituals in ants, which, according to the philosopher Cleanthes,
negotiate the return of the body of a fallen comrade from a rival anthill.
Thus, says Montaigne, if we do not see signs of religion in other animals
such as those we infer in elephants when their behavior resembles our own,
this is because we "cannot grasp any part of what is hidden from us" (343).

Montaigne does not explicitly award individual subjectivity as such to
animals anywhere in the *Apology*—except possibly to the cat that conde-
scends to play as his equal—but this is a result of his tendency, cat notwith-
standing, to treat animals in terms of their species (the ant, the elephant,
the chameleon) rather than as individuals. But if Montaigne seems to break
down the species barrier at one place, he reerects it in another: "They have
many qualities that are related to ours; from these by comparison we can
draw some conjecture; but as for what is peculiar to them, what do we
know about it?" (343). Nonetheless, by celebrating animals' adequacy to the
myriad challenges of life and insisting that we cannot know "what is peculiar to them," Montaigne would seem to acknowledge the possibility of animals' subjective experience of the object-world and to admit it as parallel to
but not necessarily cognate with our own. In such acknowledgment, human
reason becomes noticeably partial, and its claims to knowledge about the
world shrink.

Skeptic, or Speculation, a work attributed to Raleigh and published
posthumously, goes even further in positing the possible incommensurability between human and animal sense perception, beginning with the observable fact of the great variety in species and the contrary temperaments that

the different humoral compositions of animals produce: "These great differences cannot but cause a divers and contrary temperament, and qualitie in
those creatures, and consequently a great diversitie in their phantasie and
conceit; so that they apprehend one and the same object, yet they must do it
after a divers manner."[82] Creatures with eyes differing in color, shape, and
size, he speculates, must see the world differently: the slanting pupils of
goats, cats, foxes "do convey the fashion of that which they behold under
another form to the imagination" than round pupils do (3). As with sight,
Raleigh argues, so with the other senses: animals with hard shells experience
the world differently than furry or smooth-skinned ones; animals with narrow or wide ear openings hear differently from one another, and so on
through the other senses. The argument is conducted analogically, beginning
with received assumptions about human humorality and other knowledge
of the world: for example, a man with a cold—"abounding with Fleagm"—
smells otherwise than if his head "be full of bloud" (8). Thus differently
humored animals differ in smelling, and animals with tongues of different
qualities taste differently, as when the hand in striking the harp sounds a
high or a low note "according to the qualitie of the string that is stricken"
(8–9). But what is important about this remarkable train of thought, for my
purposes here, is that it relies upon the weight of differences conceptually
basic to humoral psychophysiology. It is not possible, says Raleigh, to imagine "that creatures differ so much in temperature, and yet agree in conceit
concerning one and the same object" (3). Difference in imagination and perception of the world follows logically from differences in humoral constitution—between animals and humans, among human beings, and by
implication within a human being as he changes humorally from moment to
moment. Here is early modern phenomenology: human perception of the
world becomes body-based and almost arbitrary, a function of the physical
traits that human bodies—generically and individually—happen to have.
Although the challenge here is directed, as it was in Montaigne, against the
truth claims of human reason, my interest is in noting how basic apprehension of the world is thought to be, at least in part, humorally determined—
with creatures that differ in temperature therefore experiencing everything
differently. As Thomas Wright says, apropos of how strong passions organize one's view of the world: "the Passions, not vnfitly may be compared to
greene spectacles, which make all things resemble the colour of greene; euen
so, he that loueth, hateth, or by any other passion is vehemently possessed,
iudgeth all things that occur in favour of that passion" (49).

82. Walter Raleigh, *Skeptick, or Speculations* (London, 1651), 3.

While Raleigh's argument, as Katharine Maus has pointed out, "argues against the authority of sense perception" (7), his interest lies strongly in imagining how those different sense perceptions in effect constitute, for each perceiver, a different world and a different experience of it. The effect is not only to erode confidence in the accuracy of sense perception—the treatise's avowed aim—but also to decenter human sense perception itself in favor of a perspectivism that we must define broadly enough to include not only what a fox or a cat sees but how it experiences and thus feels about what it sees. Skepticism in this form recognizes the phenomenological role of the passions in constituting the world and thus takes us back to the cosmological network of sympathies and antipathies in which Wright's wolf takes its place beside Falstaff's melancholy cat.

But it is in *La Circe*, a relatively little-known text by the Florentine shoemaker-humanist Giovan Battista Gelli, that Cleopatra's imaginative crossing of the species barrier is most strikingly anticipated. The text, a set of ten dialogues deeply indebted to Plutarch, between Ulysses and a variety of animal speakers, was translated into English by Henry Iden in 1557. In Gelli's work, the shipwrecked Ulysses, bored with his Circean idyll, asks Circe to give him Greek companions for his journey home. She agrees to do so if any of her animals will agree to reassume human form. In dialogue after dialogue, however, Ulysses' animal interlocutors describe their lives in Edenic terms, as containing material and emotional plenitude, freedom from human social and gender hierarchies, and release from the burdens of selfhood. The oyster, formerly a fisherman, cherishes the safety of his portable home; the mole, formerly a plowman, appreciates getting food without labor; the hare and the doe praise animal society for abjuring servitude, indignities of gender difference, and private property. Among them, only the elephant, a Greek named Aglaphemus, finally agrees to a retransformation. His decision to do so is immediately rewarded by a reawakened knowledge of the Creator: "as sone as I was become man againe," says Aglaphemus, "I felt it spring in my mind, almost as my *naturall propertie*."[83] This knowledge becomes the unique possession of mankind.

Robert Adams, *La Circe*'s modern editor, insists that the text's intention is to ratify the unique and lonely burdens of human consciousness.[84] I find Gelli's text more remarkable for the extent to which it is willing to particularize points of view constructed as nonhuman in order to ask if reason is

---

83. [Giovan Battista Gelli], *Circes of Iohn Baptista Gello*, trans. Henry Iden (London, 1557), sig. T4r. Quotations from *La Circe* are from this edition.

84. [Giovan Battista Gelli], *The Circe*, trans. Thomas Brown (1702), ed. Robert M. Adams; rev. ed. (Ithaca, NY: Cornell University Press, 1963), xxix.

really the foundation of human difference not only from animals but between one human and another as well. As Marilyn Migiel has suggested, "Gelli's dialogue is progressive inasmuch as it permits various animals to voice certain kinds of dissatisfactions, but conservative inasmuch as it quickly muffles any social critique that addresses the really crucial issues" (225). For the most part, the dissatisfactions refracted ironically in the animals' praise of their lives as beasts are those peculiar to human society—the burdens of social difference, the wretchedness of poverty and labor, the subjection of women, and the terrors theoretically unique to a complex being aware of the riskiness of life and the certainty of death. Such a critique is this text's overriding interest. But what Gelli does use the animals to articulate—even if fleetingly—is a vision of meaningful social being without gender or bodily difference, being founded in the paradox of immanent desire as desirelessness and skillfully defended by its possessors against human challenge. Ulysses rationalizes his failure to recruit the lowly animals for human return on the ground that such creatures could not rationally understand their own good. The presumption of massive difference in the possession of reason founds the uniquely complex hierarchy of human beings, a hierarchy that of course contains and naturalizes the structure of gender difference as well. But Circe denies that this ground of difference plays a part in the animals' refusal to reassume human form, affirming instead, in tones very like those of Montaigne, the sufficiency of embodied knowing in every creature and the efficacy of the passions to furnish creatures with knowledge of their own good: "Yf the good and the euylles that chaunce vnto a man in that state wherin he liueth, coulde onelye be knowen by witte, and vnderstanding, I wold then thinke thou saydest truth. But they are knowen by profe: and experience . . . (as thou knowest) causeth eche man to knowe thynges as they are" (sig. C5r).

Unlike Montaigne, who wishes to reduce human-animal difference in order to promote the sufficiency of man in nature, Gelli's animal speakers insist that all species other than man experience the natural order as comfortable and convenient, perfectly suited to their needs. Oyster asks belligerently, "what care hath [Nature] shewed to haue of you, syns she causeth you to be borne naked? Wher contrary she hath shewed to esteme vs muche, causing vs to come into the world clothed, . . . some with one thing, and some with an other, the which is a manifest token that she hath greatly in her harte mynded our conseruation" (sig. B2r). This physical contentment in self-plenitude constitutes the basis for the animals' sustained critique of private property and human striving. Hare argues that human envy comes about because "he who can do most, wyll take most. Wher as amongest vs it is not so: because none desyreth, or can possesse any thinge that nature hath made for vs, more then an other" (sigs. F1r–v). More crucially in terms of comparative passions, the dialogues offer a portrait of animal desire in eating, drinking, smelling, tasting, and sexual pleasure as so naturally tempered that animals never desire what will not content them or will do them harm. As Snake claims, "we haue desyre onelye to those thinges that are good for vs, and so much as our nature requireth, and we will not one morsell aboue thys, nor we can not vary, or mingle our metes in such sorte, that they may enforce our appetyte with the pleasing vs" (sig. C8r).

Snake goes on to offer a lesson in comparative anatomy and physiology in which the humanistic celebration of the complexity of man in body, brain, and complexion is answered once again by the natural temperance of animal being. Snake justifies his refusal to reassume human form by pointing out "the weakenes of the complexcion, that nature hath geuen to you, by the whiche you are subiecte to so many kindes of infirmities" (sig. C6v). But, Ulysses replies, the complexity of the human constitution is a function of reason, which requires a diet more varied than that of animals: "She hathe done this for that we had nede of greter quantitie of braine, to the proportion of other bests, the which is naturally cold for the operations of the inner sences" (sig. C8r). And if the possession of reason carries along with it a superfluity of humors and hence a superfluity of diseases, "we haue meanes to remedie it" (sigs. C8v–D1r). Snake, unpersuaded, reminds Ulysses, as this text's paradigmatic man, of the self-adequacy of animal nature, the self-regulated, healthy plenitude of animal desire: "She hath fyrste geuen vnto vs a complexion so stronge, and a desyer so well ruled, that it neuer prouoketh vs to do anye thinge that is agaynst our nature" (sig. D4v). Ulysses counters this vision of ideally regulated animal desire and health by pointing out the directionlessness of animal existence: "you haue a confused fantasie, and such a remembraunce as the flye also hath, wherby you determine no more vnto one place, then vnto an other but are guided by chaunce" (sig. C2r). In the existential choice of destination lies the core of human reasoning. But Ulysses' celebrations of human motivation do not cause Snake any nostalgia for the mode of being he has left behind, and the ambiguous closure of this dialogue—like that of the others—sustains desire's plenitude as the quintessential ground of animal well-being.

Clearly Gelli's representation of animal contentment and self-sameness is powerfully overdetermined and highly selective. His animals do experience the darker emotions: Oyster asks Ulysses to watch out for crabs coming to eat him; Hare knows by the voice when any of his kind experiences grief; as soon as he hears himself speaking in human language, Snake worries that he will be returned to human shape against his will. All of the animals have strong memories of the passions and fears that ruled their lives as men. As Marilyn Migiel points out, the animals deride as unnatural the power struggles endemic in human society even as they accept the naturalness of power struggles between animals of different species (218). More important for my purposes here is how hard it is to recognize the perfectly realized temperance of Gelli's animals as part of a cosmology otherwise filled with warring elements, with urgent and endless desires. And it is even harder to recognize the physical and emotional contentment of Gelli's animals as true to what contemporary philosophers such as Roger Caillois, Alphonso Lingis, and Elizabeth Grosz have identified as the "structural, anatomical, or behavioral superabundance . . . the very superfluity of life over and above the survival needs of the organism."[85] Because animal desire far exceeds a species's reproductive requirements, what it expresses instead may well be a fact about the universe, what opens up bodies and the world "for redistribution, dis-organization, transformation . . . something incapable of being determined in advance."[86] In this respect, the desirelessness of Gelli's animals and their refusal to undergo another metamorphosis clearly reflect Gelli's polemical purposes first to sabotage and then to reaffirm the dignity of man rather than the elemental appetitiveness and fundamental playfulness characteristic of early modern nature. But Gelli's text is faithful to the essential structures of early modern cosmology and to what we have seen expressed powerfully in Wright and Montaigne in its recognition—affirmed in his dialogue most strongly by Circe herself—that emotions in animals are central to their experience of the world and their ability to function effectively within it. For despite Gelli's anthropocentric bias, his dialogues express a persuasive understanding of animal experience as complex, knowing, and full of independent authority, even if we can only imagine that authority by allowing the animals to speak of it in the voice of humans.

At the end of *Antony and Cleopatra*, Cleopatra's asp disappears from view, not needing—any more than Circe's snake does—to know where it might be going next. But Cleopatra's deployment of the snake's irascible appetite to bite as the means for her desire to achieve a painless death and escape Roman capture allows us to see the limits of Roman knowing in terms that

85. Elizabeth Grosz, "Animal Sex," in *Space, Time, and Perversion: Essays on the Politics of Bodies* (New York: Routledge, 1995), 190.

86. Ibid., 200.

link woman and animal in the praxes of desire. Just as her momentary pang of envy of Antony's horse gave her erotic pleasure despite her lover's absence, so her final connection with the body of the asp gives Cleopatra a pleasurable transport from life to death. In the cold eye of Roman forensics, the asp's behavior and the means of Cleopatra's suicide are equally opaque: "Here, on her breast," says Dolabella, "there is a vent of blood, and something blown; / The like is on her arm" (5.2.348–50). The drop of Cleopatra's blood, leaving her body, has followed the trail of the departing animal. In this final tableau, Cleopatra has become the human animal itself, the embodiment of passionate being that is other than and more than merely human.

That the passions shared by humans and animals were elemental in their nature makes affective regulation an early modern aspect of basic bodily management in ways that we may find difficult to recognize. I have tried to suggest that what looks like a relatively simple form of anthropomorphism—the attribution of complex emotional states and cognitive operations to animals—is more properly understood as a significant aspect of the period's deepest habits of thought, which involve a specific placing of self within a universe understood to be filled with desire and moved by the strivings of appetite. Within such an epistemology, to identify with the melancholy of cats or to envy the pride of a hero's horse was not a simple sentimental error of projecting human desire outward and seeing it reflected where it could not occur. Rather, cross-species identification meant drawing into oneself the world's panoply of desires in a particular, close, and knowable form even at the risk of having one's very own melancholy compared, finally, to the fetid fluids of Moorditch. We come full circle, then, from Gelli's recalcitrant animals to the melancholy of gib cats and lugged bears, but with a more eclectic appreciation of early modern psychological materialism. As I have tried to suggest, recognizing the humoral constitution of animals along with its affective entailments serves to widen the active scope of the passions well beyond the species barrier, extending the passions' salience out to the universe at large and underscoring the passions' ontological status in nature. Thus to embed humoral affectivity in the world is not to take it out of the body; rather, it is to deterritorialize it, to remap it, to extend it. It is to understand humorality in Deleuzian terms as a means and mechanism of bodily desire.

How would it feel to experience one's own passions as part of the natural order, and how would one speak that experience? While answering such questions would forever be beyond the scope of this or any other critical essay, traces of that phenomenological experience—I have been arguing—may be captured from time to time in Shakespearean and other contemporary texts. For such an enterprise, it is helpful to remember Linda Charnes's useful distinction between identity and subjectivity—identity being a relatively fixed and objective feature of social (and/or textual) being and subjectivity being the moment-to-moment experience of that identity.[87] In these terms, early modern identity contains a cosmological component that, as we have seen in Falstaff, fixes the individual through simile and makes that person knowable in his or her affinities, sympathies, and linkages. And in this model of humoral subjectivity, the early modern subject's passionate experience of self turns out to be a feelingly intimate transaction with the world as well.

87. Linda Charnes, *Notorious Identity: Materializing the Subject in Shakespeare* (Cambridge, MA: Harvard University Press, 1993), 75.

CHAPTER FOUR

BELCHING QUARRELS

Male Passions and the Problem of Individuation

General interest in the passions as natural phenomena and perturbations of the soul, as we have seen, ran high in early modern English thought and writing.[1] But in such a hierarchical society, more specific and more urgent questions concerned whose passions counted most and whose passions most required the twin disciplines of scrutiny and regulation—by self and others. Thomas Wright begins his influential 1604 treatise *The Passions of the Minde in Generall* by explaining his topic's "goodly and faire glosse of profit and commodity" (2) for many sorts of Englishmen. The passions as "speciall causes" (2) of sin and "extrinsecall causes of diseases" (4), he writes, are of keen professional interest to preachers and physicians, the healers of bodies and souls. For the good wayfaring Christian, whose passions take away his quiet, threaten his prosperity, and deject him in adversity, knowledge of the passions allows him the better to view his "domesticall enemie" (5). But Wright's recommendation of his subject to preacher, physician, and Christian seems to me perfunctory in tone by comparison to the strong interest he demonstrates in attracting the attention of the English gentleman. Wright's main goal lies in promoting secular knowledge of the passions as the master key to social conduct for the "ciuill Gentleman and prudent Politician" (5–6), who, by restraining his inordinate emotions,

---

1. The philosophical value of the topic has "darkened with time and grown opaque," remarks Susan James (1), by way of reminding readers of the passions' centrality in early modern thought generally.

"winneth a gratious carriage of himselfe, and rendreth his conuersation most gratefull to men" (6).[2]

So far, so good, one might say: who would not wish to have a gracious carriage and grateful (i.e., pleasing) conversation? But Wright's apparently unexceptionable phrasing points to a more contested early modern project involving codes of conduct, urbanization, and individuation, a project contested because it enlisted a discourse of passions and humors in a critique of gentlemanly behavior. Thus, in his preface, Wright compares Englishmen to Italians or Spaniards and faults his countrymen for a lack of "wit, policy, and prudence" and a "defect of conversation" (lx), which he attributes to worldly inexperience derived from living in the country or smaller cities. With a rhetorical authority derived from years of living among Italians, Wright implies that Englishmen do not know how to behave themselves when possessed by extraordinary passions and lack the civilized arts of "gentlemanlike conversation" (lxii). Even allowing for the inflated rhetoric characteristic of prefaces to the reader, Wright's remarks about the passionateness of the English gentleman seem pointed and direct. "I thought good," he writes, "to trie if a little direction would helpe our Countriemen to counterpoise their native warinesse, and open the way . . . to discover other mens passions, and how to behave our selves when such affections extraordinarily possess vs, the which is the chiefest poynt of prudence, and fittest mean to attayne vnto religious, civil, & gentlemanlike conversation, which is vertuous" (lxii). As this emphasis suggests, it is less the knowledge of others than the control of oneself when "extraordinarily" possessed by passion that constitutes for Wright a gentleman's "chiefest poynt" of prudence.

Wright's concerns for Englishmen's behavior reflect the tensions of a particular moment in the history of manners, one that Anna Bryson has described as the replacement of modes of lordship with modes of urbanity. In the first mode, male elites enjoy a commanding position in relatively isolated country households organized by hierarchies of service, kinship, and allegiance. In the second mode, members of elites centered in courts and cities express their social identity through a shared culture and more or less socially equal relations with one other (113). The transition from one mode of conduct to another was both slow and tentative, as Bryson suggests—and as Wright's treatise also implies. Among lordly men asked to give up commanding positions in a household for the more equivocal pleasures of

---

2. On the importance of conversation to regulation of the passions, see Lorna Hutson, "Civility and Virility in Ben Jonson," *Representations* 78 (2002): 11–15.

being a courtier, the transition cannot have been an easy one—especially
among courtiers under a powerful and capricious female monarch.[3] Indeed,
it is precisely Norbert Elias's point that, compared to isolated households
with their relative unconstraint in personal demeanor, court society
required a more exigent degree of autoscopic self-control not just in bodily
matters such as nose-wiping or evacuation but in the whole terrain of emotional control.[4] As a result, the very terms of homosocial relationships, once
securely hierarchized through kin and allegiance networks, would seem to
need fundamental rethinking in new, more egalitarian settings—as would
the emotions supporting them.[5] That Wright has such social anxieties in
mind is clear when he reports to "haue seen some, Gentlemen by blood, and
Noblemen by birth" who were "so appassionate in affections, that their company was to most men intolerable" (6). Wright's language here hints
broadly at a social crux that he says he has witnessed—that of the intemperate birthright gentleman or, worse, the intolerable nobleman who must
nevertheless be tolerated, even indulged, by those beneath him. Indeed, the
phenomenon of a socially intolerable nobleman in a society as hierarchical
as early modern England would have been no small matter, as Wright goes
on to imply, especially in the dense copresence of courts and cities: "how
vngratefull must his company seeme, whose passions ouer-rule him? and a
man had need of an Astrolabe alwayes, to see in what height or eleuation
his affections are, lest, by casting forth a sparke of fire, his gun-powdred
minde of a sudden bee inflamed" (6). *Ungrateful* here means unpleasing,
disagreeable, what we might call ungracious. But it is the odd ambiguity in
Wright's syntax and male pronouns and the solecism of his mixed
metaphor that indicate the real delicacy of the problem, for astrolabical
inspection of the height and elevation of one's own passions—though
grammatically if not anatomically possible—is only secondarily at issue.
There are two men imagined in this passage: one man encounters
another—identified obliquely as the referent for "his affections" and "his
gun-powdred mind"—and must use an astrolabe to check the state of the
other's passions, lest an unintended word or gesture ignite an outburst. If
the two men are equals in rank and age, the obligation of one anxiously to

3. On Elizabeth's cultural power, see Louis A. Montrose, *The Purpose of Playing: Shakespeare
and the Cultural Politics of the Elizabethan Theatre* (Chicago: University of Chicago Press, 1996),
152–59; also Steven Mullaney, "Mourning and Misogyny: *Hamlet, The Revenger's Tragedy*, and the
Final Progress of Elizabeth I: 1600–1607," *Shakespeare Quarterly* 45 (1996): 139–62.

4. See Elias, *The Civilizing Process*; but see also Chartier, 74.

5. On a similar point, see Daniel Juan Gil, "At the Limits of the Social World: Fear and Pride in
Troilus and Cressida," *Shakespeare Quarterly* 52 (2001): 338–39.

inspect the other's emotional state is disagreeable enough. But a larger danger would belong to the lower-status man in this vaguely imagined but
nevertheless threatening scenario, navigating his way through socially
dangerous waters, carefully measuring the mood of his superior, lest an ill-
timed or ill-phrased remark cause an explosion that—in the rhetorical logic
of the figure if not in the hierarchical logic of early modern social life—will
destroy them both.

The tension in Wright's language here may, of course, reflect the insecu-
rity of his own position, as a Jesuit living in England on sufferance of the
great men holding his life and freedom in their hands.[6] But his tropes seem
meant to generalize beyond the autobiographical, because Wright's
metaphorical reference to an astrolabe for the passions implies, even as it
exaggerates, the scale and generality of the matter—the unknowable distance between the little man on the ground and the remote but powerful
heavenly object whose unstable affections are a cosmological given in his
universe. Indeed, if we take the liberty of pushing the astrolabe metaphor
further than Wright does, the passionate nobleman as planet or star
becomes an astrological influence, raining down invisible forces—benign
and malign—on all those who live, planet-struck, below. The mixed
metaphor relies on what Frank Whigham has called "Mystification of the
Contingent as Absolute," which he defines as "the presentation of difference
of degree as difference in kind, of contingent difference as absolute."[7] Here
the effect is to magnify the destructive power of the nobleman, not so much
because of his greatness per se as because of his catastrophic explosiveness.
But despite Wright's focus on the nameless great man, the real cause of
such explosiveness, as Mervyn James has suggested, was not individual but
structural. Aggressivity was always latent in the relations of "men of honour" and, by extension, among aspirants to that place in the social order.
Among equals, each gentleman was expected to assert preeminence, a
"requirement which imparted a note of tension even to ordinary social
intercourse and conversation."[8] Vincentio Saviolo cautions that "he that is a
Gentleman and conuerseth with men of honorable quality, must aboue all
others haue a great regard to frame his speech and answeres with such

---

6. On Wright's biography generally and the political delicacy of his tenure in England, see the
introduction to Thomas Wright, *The Passions of the Mind in General*, ed. William Webster Newbold
(1604; New York: Garland, 1986), 3–10.

7. Frank Whigham, *Ambition and Privilege: The Social Tropes of Elizabethan Courtesy Theory*
(Berkeley and Los Angeles: University of California Press, 1984), 67.

8. Mervyn James, *English Politics and the Concept of Honour, 1485–1642* (Oxford: Past and
Present Society, 1978), 5.

respectiue reuerence, that there neuer growe against him anie quarrell vpon a foolish worde or a froward answere."[9] The tendency to resolve quarrels with swords, according to Bacon, bore the potential for general social upheaval in the state. He describes the consequence in humoral analogies: "so that the state by this means shall be like to a distempered and unperfect body, continually subject to inflammations and convulsions."[10] This tension in everyday intercourse—what we might think of as a propensity to quarrelsomeness leading to violence—is why Stefano Guazzo recommends that the gentleman should relax only in the company of his inferiors: "he shal be the chiefe man ... and rule the company as he list; neither shall he be forced to favor or do anything contrary to his mind: which libertie is seldom allowed him amongst his equals," for "they will look for as much preheminence every way as himselfe."[11] Notice the dream of personal liberty here—the possibility of emotional and psychological unconstraint, the fantasy of emotional sway, the lure of autonomy.

However, as Wright's mixed metaphor of the heavenly object with a gunpowdered mind suggests, the great man is not really an unapproachably distant or mystified object on the social horizon but a more proximate source of danger. The exact content of his disposition at any given moment is an object of critical scrutiny for those in his immediate orbit who might cast forth the "spark" of an unthinking word or gesture. Later in his treatise, Wright again resorts to the gunpowder analogy in a similar context to describe how the same passion works differently on different persons depending on their disposition: "for, as we see fire applied to drie wood, to yron, to flaxe and gunpowder, worketh diuers wayes; for in wood it kindleth with some difficultie, and with some difficultie is quenched; but in flaxe soone it kindleth, and quencheth; in yron with great difficultie it is kindled, & with as great extinguished; but in gunpowder it is kindled in a moment, and neuer can bee quenched till the powder be consumed" (37). Choleric men, he goes on to explain, "are all fiery, and in a moment, at euery trifle they are inflamed, and, till their hearts be consumed (almost) with choller, they neuer cease, except they be reuenged" (37). His reference to revenge here calls to mind threatened aristocrats such as Lorenzo in *The Spanish Tragedy*, whose exquisitely vengeful acts of hypertrophied will

9. Vincentio Saviolo, *His Practice: In Two Books*, in *Three Elizabethan Fencing Manuals*, ed. James L. Jackson (London, 1595; reprint, Delmar, NY: Scholars' Facsimiles and Reprints, 1972), 194.

10. Francis Bacon, "The Charge Touching Duelling," in *Francis Bacon: Selections*, ed. Brian Vickers (Oxford: Oxford University Press, 1996), 305.

11. Stefano Guazzo, *The Civile Conversation of M. Steeven Guazzo*, trans. George Pettie (London, 1581), bk. 2, fol. 44b; also quoted in Mervyn James, 5.

against the vulnerable lower orders who dare to infringe on his sense of
absolute social mastery have been examined with scrupulous attention by
Frank Whigham.[12] More specifically, Wright's reference to flammable materials recalls the exchange between Duke Ferdinand and his courtiers at the
opening of *The Duchess of Malfi*, also quoted in chapter 3, when Ferdinand
excoriates one of his courtiers for daring to laugh without his permission:
"Why do you laugh? Methinks you that are courtiers should be my touchwood, take fire when I give fire; that is, laugh when I laugh, were the subject never so witty" (1.1.122–25). Only a carefully willed subjection of body
and mood would protect against the social danger represented here, as
when, in Jonson's *Sejanus*, flatterers are described as men who

> laugh, when their patron laughs; sweat, when he sweats;
> Be hot, and cold with him; change every mood,
> Habit and garb, as often as he varies.
>
> $$(1.33-35)^{13}$$

If a nobleman chooses inferior company in order to achieve a relaxation
understood to require this kind of social mirroring and responsiveness, the
members of that company have no such option, this passage suggests,
because each must be ready to alter body, mood, and behavior in response
to the patron's.

What I wish to emphasize is how Wright's use of thermal imagery to
express the passionate unrestraint characteristic of some birthright gentlemen, like the imagery in the passages quoted above, calls attention to the
role that Galenic humoralism plays in the master social tropes of early modern urbanization and elite socialization. I have argued elsewhere that the
language of the bodily spirits coursing through the veins, arteries, and neural pathways of the (normatively) male body enacts a highly differentiated
narrative of social privilege and stratification that values the energetic faculties—the "spirits"—making a body move and feel, but it wishes at the same
time to regulate impulsivity and bodily force.[14] These qualities can be beau-
tiful, even awesome, as Bacon suggests when he explains the forcefulness
contained and expressed in human movements by comparing it to the com-
bustible properties of various minerals: "*Flame* and *Aire* do not Mingle,

12. Whigham, *Seizures of the Will*, 31–36.

13. Ben Jonson, *Sejanus*, in *The Complete Plays of Ben Jonson*, ed. G. A. Wilkes, vol. 2 (Oxford:
Clarendon Press, 1981).

14. See Paster, "Nervous Tension," 116–21.

except it be in an *Instant*; Or in *vitall Spirits* of *vegetables* and *liuing Creatures.*" He goes on to compare explosion in such materials as "*Brimstone, Pitch, Camphire, Wilde-Fire,* and diuers other Inflammable Matters" and sudden exertions of physical force in the human body: "It is no maruaile therfore, that a small *Quantity* of *Spiritts,* in the Cells of the Braine, and Canales of the Sinewes [i.e., the nerve pathways in the tendons and ligaments] are able to moue the whole Body, (which is of so great Masse,) both with so great Force, as in Wrestling, Leaping; And with so great Swiftnes, As in playing Diuision vpon the *Lute.* Such is the force of these two Natures, *Aire* and *Flame,* when they incorporate."[15] What is dazzling here is that Bacon travels with air and fire up the scale of nature from gunpowder to the hands of the lutenist, from mining saltpeter to wrestling and making music. The beauty of human movement is seen as part of the structure of the cosmos. We ought to notice here what kinds of activities Bacon singles out as examples of human forcefulness. Though he writes enthusiastically about the animal spirits to be found in the neural pathways of all human bodies, his praise of the explosive force of the spirits acting on muscle uses physical skills associated with the athletic, and implicitly gentlemanly, body as the human equivalent of gunpowder and quicksilver. In the larger narrative implied here, high cultural value is assigned to aristocratic spiritedness, courage, and impulsivity. Thus a character such as Hotspur in *1 Henry IV* is conspicuously marked by traits of high spiritedness—by vigorous strength, athleticism, spontaneity, and all the other behavioral products of hot-bloodedness. His aristocratic vivacity is directly opposed to Prince Hal's initial languor and forms the core of what the beleaguered King Henry IV finds to praise when he describes Hotspur as

> a son who is the theme of honor's tongue,
> Amongst a grove the very straightest plant.
>
> (1.1.81–82)

And the king himself acknowledges having lacked the appropriate heat to respond to Hotspur's defiant hot-bloodedness:

> My blood hath been too cold and temperate,
> Unapt to stir at these indignities.
>
> (1.3.1–2)

---

15. Francis Bacon, *Sylva Sylvarum; or, A Naturall Historie in Ten Centuries* (London, 1626), 10.

But high-spiritedness in Hotspur is valued only so long as that spirit can be managed by and accommodated to the long-range interests of the centralized state; once it escapes such management and escalates into political rebellion, impulsivity is recoded as rusticity, social backwardness, or archaism. "You are altogether govern'd by humors," Hotspur's wife tells him reprovingly (3.1.233) when the restless warrior is unable to lie quietly, his head in his wife's lap, long enough to listen to Lady Mortimer's Welsh singing: "I had rather hear Lady, my brach, howl in Irish" (235–36), he complains. The moment is part of the play's careful revaluation of Hotspur from the valued warrior, "amongst a grove the very straightest plant," to a version of Wright's intolerable aristocrat with the gunpowdered mind, unable or unwilling to calibrate his behavior to time, place, and civilized company. Hal throws off idleness and "unyok'd humor" (1.2.196)—that is, throws off bodily faculties uninformed by discipline and not harnessed to any larger enterprise. Thus it is he who responds to royal and paternal injunction with a sudden explosion of heated activity, a timely show of youthful aristocratic spirit. He and his comrades-in-arms, says Vernon, are

> as full of spirit as the month of May,
> And gorgeous as the sun at midsummer.
>
> (4.1.101–2)

In many early modern texts, such ethical oppositions as those between Hotspur and Hal work to reveal the historically specific regulatory reforms of the civilizing process and to display the kind of moderated, emotionally continuous, and socially distinct subject those reforms were meant to produce. Characters, whether male or female, represented in fictions as impulsive, inconsistent, or unable to sustain a mood or an action are also likely—like Hotspur—to bear an imprint of social backwardness, rusticity, or offensiveness. The humors, as the fluids most directly associated with impulsiveness, are thus a key part of the narrative of social reform that texts such as Wright's moral treatise on the passions are meant to promote. In this chapter, I want to expand on the problematic relationship between the social and the emotional hierarchies of early modern England, with particular attention to the key issue of male humors and passions—and especially the social privileges both required by and often assumed in the expression of male anger. First, though, it is important to suggest how contemporary rhetoric of the passions and the humors functions in two discourses that work together to express, manage, and adjudicate among claims to emotional privilege. One, the biological discourse we have seen

earlier, describes the humors as a psychophysiological determinant of gentlemanliness, in a more or less socially recognized system classification; the
other, a discourse of literary satire, describes the humors as an agreed-upon
social fiction by which men describe and claim individuality.[16] The first discourse borrows heavily from Galenic theory and carries with it the semantic
authority of literal meaning. In the second discourse, the bodily humors are
recognized as part of a self-interested claim to emotional privilege and
peremptory interiority—a way of demanding the humoral right of way in
order to have something of the emotional unconstraint that Guazzo saw as
possible only for a man secure in his preeminence among inferiors. In this
discourse, the usefulness and meaningfulness of the concept of the
humors—hence a traditional way of appraising the behavior of others—is
represented as at issue. In the induction to *Every Man out of His Humour*,
the two choric characters Cordatus and Asper lament how the "poor innocent word" (83) *humor* "Is racked and tortured" (84) through misuse when it
refers properly to a set of biological givens:

> we thus define it
> To be a quality of air or water,
> And in itself it holds these two properties,
> Moisture and fluxure;
>
> .   .   .   .
>
> And hence we do conclude
> That whatso'er hath fluxure and humidity,
> As wanting power to contain itself,
> Is humour. So in every human body
> The choler, melancholy, phlegm, and blood,
> By reason that they flow continually
> In some one part, and are not continent
> Receive the name of humours.
>
> (induction, 88–91, 95–102)

Here Jonson introduces humor in its largest sense—as the name for the two
liquid elements helping to compose all things—and then applies it to the
more complex liquids in the human body. He is even willing to acknowledge that the word *humor* may extend to characterize the "general disposition" of a person "by metaphor" (104, 103). A metaphorical transfer of terms

---

16. See Shapin, 42–64.

is required here in that a disposition is not a liquid itself but is rather the
result, Jonson says, of a "peculiar" quality's power to

> draw
> All his affects, his spirits, and his powers,
> In their confluctions, all to run one way.
>
> (106–8)

But even though disposition may not literally be liquid, Jonson does con-
ceptualize affects, spirits, and powers to flow—sometimes in a single direction, as in the behavior of one ruled by a single affect, but more often (he
implies) in the changeable currents of feeling characteristic of most individuals. But Jonson's spokesman Asper is unwilling to extend the proper meanings of humor to include such behavioral signs as transient social
affectations of dress and adornment:

> But that a rook, in wearing a pied feather,
> The cable hatband, or the three-piled ruff,
> A yard of shoetie, or the Switzers' knot
> On his French garters, should affect a humour!
>
> (110–13)

Asper's rapid rhetorical descent from the overarching dignity of the elements to a "yard of shoetie" or "three-piled ruff" suggests Jonson's overall
line of attack on contemporary forms of masculine desire. In this contemptuous (and ultimately circular) formulation, the rook borrows from the
order of things as if it were available to him as an additional resource in the
process of self-adornment, as if the cosmological framework were his for
the taking or could be demonstrable in clothes, feathers, and other forms of
decoration. Such affectation is not merely narcissism in a socially conspicuous form—indeed narcissism *for the sake of* conspicuous form—but colos-
sal misrecognition of one's place in the world. For Jonson, there is nothing
humanly voluntary, nothing chosen about the cosmological framework or
the human frame that reproduces it in little. Presumably that is why he
begins by defining *humor* as a function of the cosmos first and the human
body later. Thus Jonson seeks to distinguish between the universal givens
and the arbitrary range of human social practices, to place human passions
within their proper cosmological framework. The signs of the order of
things are not subject to human manipulation or to the vagaries of fashion;
they cannot be lodged in ruffs, feathers, or shoelaces. It is true that the

human being whose affects, spirits, and powers all run in one direction might have some small power of self-regulation over his disposition, except that Jonson-Asper describes him as "possessed" by a quality—possessed, that is, by something itself unquestionably part of the fabric of things. Such a person has no real choice about how or who to be. But there is nothing similarly inevitable or cosmically demonstrable, Jonson wants to insist, in one's petty range of choice in what to wear, or eat, or take as medicine, especially when that choice is itself preceded by an exaggerated insistence on its importance as signifier of one's peremptory humorality. The offense is, among other things, one of proportion and scale. Jonson's sense of the alarming downward mobility or diminution of the term *humor* is clear in the prologue to *The Alchemist* when he introduces his topic as "manners, now call'd humours" (9)—as if the universal were now being subsumed by the particular, interiority by exteriority, the timeless by the ephemeral.

For Jonson, the fashionable discourse of the humors thus arises as an offense to the order of things, as when, in *Every Man in His Humour*, Cash seeks to inform the water-carrier Cob of what it means to have a humor: "I'll tell thee, Cob; it is a gentleman-like monster, bred in the special gallantry of our time by affectation; and fed by folly" (3.4.18–20).[17] Humorality in this sense is monstrous, as Peter Womack has explained, because it represents "incompleteness and difference" as opposed to the self-sameness of the universal order.[18] Although as a liquid, any humor wants "power to contain itself,"[19] its status as an "incontinent" part requiring containment is not in itself problematic except when self-containment fails, as it does for humorous gentlemen who, like the prototypical gull in Dekker's *Gull's Hornbook*, "desires to pour himself into all fashions" and abandons the quest for identity as self-sameness.[20] Humors can be yoked to accomplishment—as Hal's specification of his own humor early in *1 Henry IV* as "unyok'd" implies. So it is lack of containment, lack of manly fixity and yoking to worthy activity, that produces the "gentleman-like monster," that emblem of uncontainment and Bakhtinian grotesqueness.

---

17. Unless otherwise noted, I quote from the 1616 Folio version of *Every Man in His Humour* reprinted in *The Complete Plays of Ben Jonson*, ed. G. A. Wilkes, vol. 1 (Oxford: Clarendon Press, 1981). But I am interested in Jonson's humoral language in both the Folio and the earlier 1601 quarto text, with its Italian setting and characters, and I quote from the quarto when its language provides interesting evidence of Jonsonian humoralism. For the quarto, I follow *Every Man in His Humour*, ed. Robert S. Miola (Manchester: Manchester University Press, 2000).

18. Peter Womack, *Ben Jonson* (Oxford: Basil Blackwell, 1986), 48.

19. *Every Man out of His Humour*, induction, 97.

20. Thomas Dekker, *The Gull's Hornbook*, in *Thomas Dekker*, ed. E. D. Pendry (Cambridge, MA: Harvard University Press, 1968), 88.

In social practice as it is embodied in play texts, the two senses of *humor* as denoting the psychophysiological and the social become deeply inter-mingled, since (as we shall see) characters in plays tend to use their humorality—or their claim to humorality—as an unstable but necessary instrumentation of complex social performances, especially performances undertaken to forward what Guazzo calls preeminence. While this rhetoric of the humors is worked out most systematically in Jonsonian humors com-edy, where the two senses of the term are easier to disentangle, it also hov-ers around Shakespeare's figures of comic aspiration such as Malvolio or that figure of wildly comic disintegration, the irregular humorist Nym. My intention is to follow the trail of male humors in and out of several play texts, Shakespearean and not, in order to rescue the humors from their crit-ical relegation as an annoying and psychologically archaic feature of early city comedy and argue for their importance, instead, as a key heuristic in the troubled representations of male individuation.

It has been easy for historical criticism to dismiss Jonsonian and other forms of humors comedy as long as the Galenic humoralism on which it rested was reductively linked to a rigid typology of the four tempera-ments—sanguine, choleric, phlegmatic, and melancholic. But Jonson, as we just saw, regards that application of the term as hardly its major semantic function: "it may, by metaphor, apply itself / Unto the general disposition." Once humoralism is seen properly as "a vibrantly inconsistent but bril-liantly supple discourse of selfhood and agency,"[21] the specific function of characters associated with or representative of the humors takes on a new interest. As a case in point, I would like first to offer Shakespeare's irascible Corporal Nym of *Henry V* and *The Merry Wives of Windsor*, since of all Shakespearean characters he most relies on the term *humor*, defending his actions by citing his humor as that force within him that simply and unan-swerably moves him to feel and do: "I have an humor to knock you indiffer-ently well," he tells Pistol early in *Henry V*. "I would prick your guts a little in good terms, as I may, and that's the humor of it" (2.1.55, 58–59). As Keir Elam writes, Nym uses the word "as a substitute for virtually any existing lexeme (noun, verb, modifier, and all), or simply as a hopefully prestigious filler in place of nothing at all."[22] As the choric presenter Mitis says in *Every Man out of His Humour*, "this fellow's discourse were nothing, but for the

---

21. I am quoting here from Schoenfeldt, 11.

22. Keir Elam, *Shakespeare's Universe of Discourse: Language-Games in the Comedies* (Cambridge: Cambridge University Press, 1984), 274.

word humour" (2.1.50–51). But for Nym, the possibility of verbal recourse to *humor* as a word that substitutes for his lack of ideas and normative vocabulary makes his world full of self-evidence. Nym's speech habits are thus worth examining with some care. Humor is the force Nym recognizes not only in himself but in all other things as well; no wonder that it can do duty for any part of speech. It is synonymous with, or metonymic for, things as they are, which explains why tautology and pleonasm function so frequently in Nym's fatalistic phraseology: "Faith," he tells Bardolph, "I will live so long as I may, that's the certain of it; and when I cannot live any longer, I will do as I may: that is my rest, that is the rendezvous of it" (*Henry V*, 2.1.14–16). The verbal form of Nym's self-interest, humor is also the badge of his self-acceptance and the source of his resistance to alteration. He is marked no less for what he will say and do as for what he will not or cannot do—kiss Mrs. Quickly, fight at Harfleur, pay for what he takes, or explain himself. This obsessively reiterated language of interiority in Nym points to its own primitiveness and rigidity. Nym tries to use self-reference to compel his social world's acknowledgment of his peremptory moodiness, yet his ferocity in doing so instead breeds doubt that meaningful interiority exists in him at all. The deictics of feeling in him are untouched by the subtleties of personal expression and self-reference that language allows us to construct. In this sense Nym is the humoral opposite of Hamlet and his famous inexpressibility, because Nym insists on his own psychophysiological promptings as always the same, always articulable as uninflected humor. He would deny Nietzsche's declaration on the limits of physical self-knowledge that "however far a man may go in self-knowledge, nothing however can be more incomplete than his image of the totality of drives which constitute his being. He can scarcely name even the cruder ones."[23] Nym always names the cruder ones, and names them with variations on the theme of humors, because in effect they constitute the only drives that he has.

In *Merry Wives*, Nym's reliance on the term is even more pronounced than in *Henry V*, perhaps, as Patricia Parker has suggested, because of the play's preoccupation with the vagaries of language generally and English variations of it in particular.[24] The word *humor* in that play is deliberately evacuated of denotative meaning, I think, in order that we may ponder the nature of its usefulness not as a description of the world or self but as a

---

23. Friedrich Nietzsche, *Daybreak: Thoughts on the Prejudices of Morality*, trans. R. J. Hollingdale (Cambridge: Cambridge University Press, 1982), 74–76. I owe this reference to David Hillman.

24. Parker, *Shakespeare from the Margins*, 124.

mode of competitive social practice. In this sense the term functions not just in Elam's terms as a "psychophysiological catch-all,"[25] but as a linguistic weapon, both offensive and defensive, against a world that Nym understands as conflictual at its core. In *Merry Wives*, as in *Henry V*, it is what Nym will not do that demonstrates a fixed belief in mutual resistance as the hallmark of his relations with the world. To deliver Falstaff's letter to Mistress Page becomes an unworthy act that Nym vows not to do: "I will run no base humor. Here, take the humor-letter; I will keep the havior of reputation" (1.3.77–78). Seeking to inform Page of Falstaff's adulterous intentions, Nym finds himself suddenly forced into the odd position of rhetor, moved reluctantly into the social intricacies of persuasion by the force of his passion (or appetite, or humor) for revenge against Falstaff's poor treatment of him. But Nym discovers that forwarding this revenge involves consecutive and deeply triangulated discourse, because he must convince a stranger who is his social superior of his veracity even though he can only point tautologically to the self-evidence of his humor—his inability to be other than he is—in order to do so: "And this is true; I like not the humor of lying. He hath wrong'd me in some humors. I should have borne the humor'd letter to her; but I have a sword, and it shall bite upon my necessity. He loves your wife: there's the short and the long. My name is Corporal Nym; I speak, and I avouch; 'tis true; my name is Nym, and Falstaff loves your wife. Adieu. I love not the humor of bread and cheese [and there's the humor of it]. Adieu" (2.1.128–37). The irony here is that Nym really *is* moved by a humor of revenge against Falstaff's negligence, but his overuse of the term and his inability to explain himself even as he endeavors mightily to do so cloud that emotional reality for his astonished listeners—whether or not the bracketed phrase from the quarto is included in his speech. The term "bread and cheese," according to most of the play's editors, signifies meager rations, a poor man's diet—hence metonymically the servile life Nym feels he has led in Falstaff's service. "The humor of bread and cheese" may be nonsensical—as Page's bemused response to this speech quoted below may indicate. But *to* humor bread and cheese, insofar it refers to an activity of mind upon the world, is Nym's way of rendering the object world phenomenological, making it an expressive part of his self-experience and consciousness (however we might wish to imagine the inner workings of that consciousness), putting himself into the object world. In this sense, all the humors named here—of bread and cheese, of lying, of letters needing to be delivered—seem to me at the heart of Nym's

25. Elam, *Shakespeare's Universe of Discourse*, 274.

labored efforts at sincerity, his attempts to have a communicable point of
view and to find a place for it in a phenomenologically resistant world.
Master Page's response cues us—superfluously, according to Elam[26]—to
marvel at Nym's inarticulateness and the odd discontinuity of his speech:
"'The humor of it,' quoth 'a! Here's a fellow frights English out of his wits"
(138–39). But, pace Elam, the phrase is wonderful, encompassing both
Nym's effect on language—frightening English out of its ability to mean
resourcefully—and the effect of Nym's language on Nym himself. In Nym's
eyes as self-declared humoral subject, the socially recognized autonomy of
the humors serves not only to excuse his boorishness but also to justify his
unwillingness to regulate, articulate, or reflect upon his words and actions
(on his words *as* actions)—or indeed upon the curious nature of his world.
In this respect, Nym's humors are both real and fictional insofar as the
word describes both the totality of his impulses and the core of his social
performance. The running of his bad humors against others, in that sense,
is his actions, the stream of impulsive behaviors and disconnected speech
that through their repetition constitute psychologically continuous self
(such as it is) in Nym. For my purposes here, Nym's importance is to
demonstrate how the humors, from being a physiological attribute or a
catch-all term in vogue—the two options offered earlier—may expand to
become the basis of a way of life, a way of being in the world. In Nym's
case, the way is maladaptive and inarticulate, identified by a prominent
impulsiveness and aggressiveness that he and others see in humoral terms.
He does not persuade Page of what he says, the letter does get delivered,
and the play's action moves on without him. "I never heard such a drawling,
affecting rogue," Page complains (2.1.140–41) on Nym's exit, marking in his
use of these pejorative adjectives the bold, or perhaps crudely unaware,
presumption involved in Nym's aggressively mannered, indolent self-
presentation before his social superiors. Thus, while Jonson would agree
with Nym in understanding the humors as part of the way things are, as a
given (like bread and cheese) in a world of elements, objects, and social
practices, he would disagree with Nym in finding the way things are to be
an adequate justification for the boorish self-acceptance that Nym, like so
many of Jonson's gulls, manifests.

A second case in point comes in Shylock's brilliant use of the term for
purposes of self-justification in a world he correctly believes is stacked
against him. His use of the term is a far more effective recognition
of humoralism's status as a discourse of nature to signify the materially

26. Ibid.

unanswerable and to promote an individual's social resistance. Before
Shylock enters the Venetian courtroom, the duke prejudges Shylock's obdu-
rateness in terms that radically qualify his claim to be a human being, calling him

> a stony adversary, an inhuman wretch,
> Uncapable of pity, void and empty
> From any dram of mercy.
>
> *(Merchant of Venice, 4.1.4–6)*

Such language of texture and moisture is implicitly humoral—the "dram" of
mercy anticipating Portia's famous description of mercy as heaven's gentle
rain. The concept of the natural humors is thus conveniently available to
Shylock when he rejects the duke's plea to accept repayment of Antonio's
debt in ducats rather than flesh or even to explain his refusal to do so. The
duke has framed the plea in terms of sympathy as the response properly
ordained by nature—the touch of "humane gentleness and love" (25)—to
the spectacle of extreme suffering, a response so natural that it is to be
found even among peoples whom the Elizabethans regarded as cultivating
ferocity. Even "stubborn Turks, and Tartars never train'd / To offices of tender courtesy" (32–33) would pity Antonio, the duke remarks, seeking perhaps to include the Jew in some part of Venetian corporate selfhood in
opposition to the barbaric Eastern Other. But the duke's rhetorical strategy
of calling on natural compassion not only to authorize Shylock's change of
heart but also to proclaim his city's confident expectation of it backfires.
Shylock initially bases his refusal to relent on the inviolability of his contract with Antonio—"if you deny it, let the danger light / Upon your charter
and your city's freedom" (38–39)—but he goes on to turn the duke's own
discourse of the natural body and its capacity for pity strongly against the
duke by invoking the equally natural status of his bodily "humor" and its
capacity for antipathy:

> You'll ask me why I rather choose to have
> A weight of carrion flesh than to receive
> Three thousand ducats. I'll not answer that;
> But say it is my humor, is it answer'd?
>
> . . . .
>
> Some men there are love not a gaping pig;
> Some that are mad if they behold a cat;
> And others, when the bagpipe sings i'th'nose,

Cannot contain their urine: for affection,
[Mistress] of passion, sways it to the mood
Of what it likes or loathes.

(40–52)

The brilliance of this reply lies precisely in Shylock's determination to broaden the scope of the natural to allow not only for the unpredictability of appetite's objects but for their evident predictability as well. His list includes those things most men actively like, such as roasted pig or bagpipe music, as well as those things they tolerate with indifference, such as the "harmless necessary cat" (55). In this account, as in Nym's, no object in the world is neutral or even self-same, because people will feel about it differently, will find it pleasing or not. It is important to note that Shylock's examples—the man who cannot hold his urine against the screech of the bagpipe or the man maddened by seeing a cat—not only indicate the involuntary power of the humors over the subjectified body but also, and once again, the early modern elision of the psychological and physiological. He thus reduces his animosity—animosity grounded complexly in personal history, wounded self-interest, and religious hatred—to an intense and by definition involuntary humoral incompatibility. He constructs his obduracy as a natural antipathy of the sort common in humans and animals both, indeed the sort of antipathy—as we have seen in chapter 3 among the wisely temperate animals in *La Circe* who eat what is good for them and avoid what is not—that keeps animate life safe from what would harm it. His strategy here is less to remind the duke of culture's strong effect on behavior (a Jew's allusion to the dietary prohibitions against roasted pig would accomplish that) than it is to ground behavioral difference in the undeniable variety and obduracy of the physical body's appetites and their resistance to reason. He uses bodily humors as an agreed-upon instance of what comes before cultural inscription, before religious and ethnic difference, before the history of Christians and Jews, even before will power. In this respect, the humors become a perfect instance of what Judith Butler sees as bodily materiality's uncontested status in Western discourse as sign of the irreducible (28). The effect is subversive: to point out how elites use the discourses of natural knowledge for their own ends and also—as Ulysses found out from his animal interlocutors—how those discourses may be used against them. Shylock, in support of his defiance of his Christian enemies and the Venetian state, can then invoke the doctrine of bodily humors himself as a determinative part of innermost bodily being that evades state manipulation and the subject's own articulation:

As there is no firm reason to be rend'red
Why he cannot abide a gaping pig;
Why he, a harmless necessary cat;
Why he, a woollen bagpipe, but of force
Must yield to such inevitable shame
As to offend, himself being offended;
So can I give no reason, nor I will not,
More than a lodg'd hate and a certain loathing
I bear Antonio.

(4.1.53–61)

The telling irony here lies in the multiple analogies among the several sorts of bodies affected by the humoral doctrine of mutual modulation between the early modern subject and its social and physical environment.[27] Shylock disingenuously constructs the duke's request that he explain himself as one involving a bilateral shame—the shame of the humoral body offended by an environment (here Venice) containing things that it cannot help but find disgusting (pig, cat, bagpipe, Antonio) and the reciprocal shame of that environment offended by the social consequences of its disgust. Shylock offers a mock apology, by describing, in the third person, the shame of the man who involuntarily offends against social codes, "himself being offended" (58). And he insinuates that Venice is also shamed when he is forced by the duke to remind everyone in the courtroom that someone so highly valued in Venice as Antonio could be found naturally disgusting by an abject lower Other such as Shylock.[28] Shylock thus relies here on his listeners' recognition not only that antipathies are natural and that the determinants of disgust vary among peoples or individuals but also, as William I. Miller notes, that disgust is a "(nearly) universal feature of human society"—a feature in which Jews *as human beings* can be understood to participate (15). What Shylock defines as the humoral body's inability to be other than it is—what we might call the Nym defense—becomes emblematized in the incontinent body of the man caught unaware by bagpipe music.[29] By means of such examples, Shylock claims to be physically unable to cease hating his enemy and to identify with him through

---

27. Sutton, *Philosophy and Memory Traces*, 39–41.

28. On the poetics of the low Other, see Stallybrass and White, 2–6.

29. The idea of an inability to hear bagpipe music without an involuntary physical reaction may be conventional; see young Knowell's question to Wellbred about whether Downright can "hold his water, at reading of a ballad" and Wellbred's response, "a rhyme to him is worse than cheese or a bagpipe" (*Every Man in His Humour*, 4.1.17–19).

pity instead. To the duke's unwillingness to accept him as fully human in Venice, Shylock responds by constructing Antonio as himself less than human to Shylock—like the gaping pig, the necessary cat, the intolerable bagpipe music. Bassanio immediately recognizes this implication of Shylock's argument, asking, "Do all men kill the things they do not love?" (4.1.66).

But the logic of Shylock's argument about Antonio extends further to encompass the political body of the state that suddenly finds itself legally unable either to regulate or to expel Shylock. In their embarrassment, all these humorally determined bodies point proleptically to Antonio, who, in terms responsive to Shylock's references to a phenomenal world full of more and less desirable or whole objects, objectifies himself as that "tainted wether of the flock . . . the weakest kind of fruit" (4.1.114–15). Perhaps equally important, at least for my purposes here, is the image that Bassanio employs in his outraged reaction to Shylock's refusal to show mercy:

> This is no answer, thou unfeeling man,
> To excuse the current of thy cruelty.
>
> (63–64)

Though Bassanio claims to be unpersuaded by Shylock's humoral logic, his reference to Shylock's cruelty as a current is itself humorally based, a localization of "psychological function by organ or system of organs."[30] Cruelty acts as a current in the blood because it is the effect of choler—the sharp humor produced by the gall bladder. Choler is what Hamlet famously accuses himself of lacking ("I am pigeon-liver'd, and lack gall / To make oppression bitter" [2.2.577–78]), but Shylock, for whom oppression is bitter indeed, does not lack for gall however we might wish to interpret it—as vengeful cruelty or as something more sympathetic, such as embattled courage, determination, or even self-defense.

It is key to recognize that all parties in this play's dispute, whatever else their disagreements, recognize the natural basis of the humors and the status of the passions they support and release as environmental determinants. By acknowledging Shylock's cruelty as a current in his blood, Bassanio in effect agrees to Shylock's brilliant naturalization of his hatred for Antonio as a form of material irreducibility. Antonio concedes much the same not only in the self-descriptions quoted above but earlier when he tells his friend despairingly that he may as well dispute with tide or wind as to

30. Park, "Organic Soul," 469.

seek to soften that—than which what's harder?—
His Jewish heart!

$$(4.1.79–80)$$

The anti-Semitism of such remarks distracts us from their contemporary logic: that the drying and hardening effects of choler, the bodily fluid produced by cruel or grasping behavior and reciprocally productive of it, would toughen the flesh of any heart and render it less receptive to entreaty. The same logic underlies Lear's anguished cry about his cruel daughters, "Is there any cause in nature that make these hard hearts?" (3.6.77–78).[31] And we have seen a similar logic of the hard heart in the wolf man Ferdinand's merciless behavior to his sister, the Duchess of Malfi. The dry-eyed Ferdinand, whose eyes dazzle, is like Shylock in this respect: he does not pity because he cannot cry, or cry because he cannot pity. This is their monstrousness. Indeed in his overpowering choler, which rhubarb cannot purge, Ferdinand can pity the Duchess less and less until she, as his choler's object and stimulant, is finally dead.

In *Merchant*, even Portia concedes the naturalness of Shylock's cruelty by figuring its opposite emotion, mercy or compassion, as a liquid belonging equally to the body and its environment—not as raging wind or mounting tide but as "gentle rain from heaven" dropping "upon the place beneath" (4.1.185–86). Whether or not the place beneath—in this case Shylock's heart—would soften as a result of such gentle (and here Gentile) moistening would thus depend, literally, on how hard it was in the first place; the change of heart will have to be a literal one. Again passions become ecological: this, at least in part, is why Portia assumes the natural too-hardness of Shylock's heart and turns instead to that product of culture, his written word, discovering release in a strict interpretation of the bond. She allows Shylock's excision of Antonio's flesh only on the condition that

> in the cutting it, if thou dost shed
> One drop of Christian blood, thy lands and goods
> Are by the laws of Venice confiscate.

$$(309–11)$$

In this stipulation, both nature and culture work on Portia's behalf: nature because Shylock cannot hope to cut flesh without spilling blood, culture because the legal distinction that she invokes between Christian and Jewish

31. Erickson, 14.

blood is located in a discursive register conveniently independent of the old fluid physiology. (The classical antecedents of humoralism, while recognizing geography as a form of innate difference in bodies, did not so recognize religion.)

Shylock and Portia manipulate different aspects of humoral discourse: Shylock its theoretically undeniable basis in nature, Portia its actual susceptibility to hegemonic redefinition or even displacement through the symbolic complexity of blood. It is in Shylock's interest—and perhaps a conventional element of Shylock's character as stage Jew—to portray the bodily humors as fixed and irreducible. More often in humoral discourse, however, the humors are represented as a part of the natural body that can and must be manipulated through various dietary regimes for the achievement of physical health and emotional stability.[32] But though in one sense all bodies were equally humoral since they were equally material—being composed of the same four humors—they were, as we have seen, humorally all different. For a traditional society like that of early modern England, as I suggested at the opening of this chapter, humoral difference guaranteed that the structure of humoralism would reflect hierarchical social values and could be used powerfully to naturalize them. Affect, that is to say, was expected to mirror the social hierarchy because both were built into the analogical order of things. Thus in *The Comedy of Errors*, part of the ethos of service in the Syracusan servant Dromio is subordinating his humor to that of his moody master Antipholus. "A trusty villain, sir," the wandering Antipholus tells a friendly merchant,

> that very oft,
> When I am dull with care and melancholy,
> Lightens my humor with his merry jests.
>
> (1.2.19–21)

Antipholus here invokes the neofeudal assumption that Dromio's service to him proceeds from the whole man, from body and mind, from interior and exterior, from his humorally saturated and socially subordinated flesh. The duty of the "villain"—the rascally low-born man—would thus include the subjection of his bodily substances to those of his master, here by directing his bodily humors into the production of jests in order to leaven his master's heaviness of mood. It does not matter whether we understand the jests

---

32. Schoenfeldt, 25.

to derive naturally and spontaneously from Dromio's humorality or to be produced by Dromio for purposes of entertainment. The social significance of jests in this context lies in their ability to temper the humors of a master and, not coincidentally, to express Dromio's own subordination. It is not surprising, then, that the Syracusan Antipholus reacts with outrage when the Ephesian Dromio fails to answer his question about the money entrusted to him:

> I am not in a sportive humor now:
> Tell me, and dally not.
>
> (58–59)

Dromio, expecting to receive what he calls a "dry" or choleric "basting" (2.2.63), becomes the object of his master's anger because it seems that he has neglected a fundamental discipline of service in hierarchical society— the humoral right of way and who gets to have it. This discipline, in his master's words, is to

> know my aspect,
> And fashion your demeanor to my looks.
>
> (2.2.32–33)

The play suggests that Dromio's inability to do so is in part a function of low-born men's unruly humoral propensities (to make ill-timed jokes or otherwise not know their place) and in part a function of the play's eerie duplication of masters, the confusing replication of Antipholuses to whom the bewildered servant-twins must respond. The play, that is, steers neatly between the poles of humoral determinism and environmental constructivism, finding a middle course in which the Dromios—being far less distinguishable from one another than the Antipholuses—both are and are not representatives of the humoral common man and the natural basis of servitude.[33]

Like the resistance mounted by Nym or Shylock, the subjection produced by the requirements of social deference has a humoral component and signifies a characteristic quality of flesh, spirits, and inner organs. The emotions associated with servitude would ostensibly be the cooler ones of timidity or even fearfulness, just as the emotions associated with resistance or mastery are hotter. The properly deferential servant—the servant who

---

33. On the distinguishability of the two Antipholuses, see Crane, 51–55.

feels the subjection required of his place—would in theory have a natural, bodily basis for matching his mood to that of his master, as the Syracusan Dromio used to do, balancing his master's heaviness with his own lightness. As a matter of bodily habitus, the servant should learn to incorporate his social inferiority into the quality of his substances and to limit the character of his moods. By the same token, the independent gentleman would claim possession of his own humor rather than seek subordination to those of others; this is why he would seek to "feed" his humor as part of his being in the world. The willingness of the sycophantic courtier to relinquish this emotional autonomy to a great man for the sake of social advancement prompts Jonson's contemptuous description of emotional vacuity in *Sejanus* and, significantly, of the unfirm flesh that goes with it, the

> soft and glutinous bodies, that can stick,
> Like snails, on painted walls.
>
> (1.8–9)

In this contemptuous model of abjection for the sake of advancement, clients have subjected themselves to complete body makeovers: "there be two," the Germanican Silius explains,

> whose close breasts,
> Were they ripped up to light, it would be found
> A poor and idle sin, to which their trunks
> Had not been made fit organs.
>
> (23–27)

Such malleability, contemptible in the body of an independent gentleman, is a signifier of humoral lack of worth and grotesque abjection. This is exactly what Dekker implies in the mock advice he offers in that piece of anticonduct literature *The Gull's Hornbook*, by describing "that true humorous gallant that desires to pour himself into all fashions, if his ambition be such to excel even compliment itself must as well practise to diminish his walks as to be various in his salads, curious in his tobacco, or ingenious in the trussing up of a new Scotch hose" (88). The multitude of fashionable behaviors that the humorous gallant aspires to adopt by pouring himself into them seems to involve a softening and remolding of the outer body—a diminishment of walks—even as it requires a complication of tastes within. As an example of such malleable adaptation of flesh to fashion and a reversal of the right order of things, Dekker recommends that the gallant "strive to fashion his legs to his silk stockings and his proud gait to his broad garters" (88). It is the natural resistance of solid flesh to the gull's desire for variousness and adaptability that, at least in part, inspires the horror of bodiliness that Barbara Correll finds animating Dekker's partly real, partly mock outrage here: "The horror of body, controlled by keeping the image of horror ever present, creates and maintains a repressive self-consciousness that renders one marketable or, as Dekker expresses it so well, allows one to publish one's suit: it is that investment in horror which is the necessary precondition in the urban world for the professional exchange relations that mark the mobile, negotiable, fluid economic urban environment."[34]

If, as Linda Charnes has argued, identity can be understood as a relatively fixed and objective feature of social (and/or textual) being and subjectivity as the moment-to-moment experience of that identity, then appropriate humoral subjectivity involves a temperate correspondence between one's humoral interior and the immediate environment, so to speak, of one's exterior social identity (75). Humoral inflection in the discourse of subjectivity is, as we have seen, a matter of qualities—of hot and cold, wet and dry. Thus in *Twelfth Night*, Fabian rebukes Sir Andrew Aguecheek for lacking the warmth proper both to his elite station as a knight and to the role of ardent suitor of Olivia. The latter's show of favor to Cesario, Fabian tells Sir Andrew disingenuously when the knight threatens to quit the household and give up publishing his suit, was intended "to put fire into your heart, and brimstone in your liver. You should then have accosted her, and with some excellent jests, fire-new from the mint, you should have bang'd the youth into dumbness" (3.2.20–23). Fabian tries to persuade the foolish knight that Olivia was hoping to heat him up and encourage the production not only of bold behaviors but of "excellent jests" as well. By wasting the opportunity, "you are now sail'd into the north of my lady's opinion, where you will hang like an icicle on a Dutchman's beard" (26–28).[35] Sir Andrew has returned to nature in this frighteningly comic image of castration, has become merely an elemental appendage to another, sturdier man's bearded masculinity.[36]

From a humoral point of view, it is easy to see that, by contrast with the thermally deficient Andrew, the steward Malvolio is almost literally too full

---

34. Barbara Correll, *The End of Conduct: "Grobianus" and the Renaissance Text of the Subject* (Ithaca, NY: Cornell University Press, 1996), 167.

35. Paster, "Nervous Tension," 122.

36. On the ubiquitous topos of castration in *Twelfth Night*, see Keir Elam, "The Fertile Eunuch: *Twelfth Night*, Early Modern Intercourse, and the Fruits of Castration," *Shakespeare Quarterly* 47 (1996): 1–36.

of himself, too full of radical heat and moisture and the prepossessing behaviors associated with them. It outrages Sir Toby and other members of the household that Malvolio should be found "yonder i' the sun practicing behavior to his own shadow" (2.5.16–17), mirroring himself to himself in a parodic imitation of gentlemen's conduct manuals, seeking out the natural light of autoscopic possibility, practicing self-advancement in its purest form as the psychophysiological looks for external reification.[37] At this moment, we recognize in Malvolio a form of humoral vanity and self-satisfaction that leads him to imagine Olivia's attraction to him straining against the linguistic constraints imposed by her maidenly modesty: "I have heard herself come thus near, that should she fancy, it should be one of my complexion" (24–26). Released here by his fantastic aspirations of marriage from the affective subjection required of social subordinates, Malvolio imagines himself as future determiner of affect in his little world, the weather-maker of his microclimate. He sees himself, newly ennobled and having sexually pacified Olivia with daytime dalliance that has left her sleeping on a daybed, as a man dictating mood, time, and place to others: "And then to have the humor of state; and after a demure travel of regard— telling them I know my place as I would they should do theirs—to ask for my kinsman Toby ... I extend my hand to him thus, quenching my familiar smile with an austere regard of control" (52–55, 65–66). In that imaginary quenching of the smile—the disciplinary cool wetness that dampens what Malvolio insinuates either as his own (hypothetical) tendency to brotherly warmth or the inappropriate warmth of boisterous Sir Toby—lies the humoral triumphalism of the new man on top.

What Malvolio finds in the forged letter—the letter that Fabian hopes will win Malvolio "liver and all" (2.5.95)—are not only specific requests for items of clothing and forms of behavior but an overall injunction to rise up humorally, to embolden his bodily substance, to remake his surface demeanor of "humble slough": "Thy Fates open their hands, let thy blood and spirits embrace them, and to inure thyself to what thou art like to be, cast thy humble slough and appear fresh" (146–49). The exhortation is to a new mode of self-presentation in Malvolio that, though it eventuates in bold smiles and yellow, cross-gartered stockings, begins as an elevation and expansion of bodily stuff.

In its focus upon the expressive production of bodily liquids, the letter's advice strongly resembles the encouragement that Sir Toby delivers to Sir Andrew: "My very walk should be a jig. I would not so much as make water

---

37. Whigham, *Ambition and Privilege*, 91–92.

but in a sink-a-pace" (1.3.129–31). Even more interesting, perhaps, it resembles that moment of erotic encounter in *Midsummer Night's Dream* when Titania, newly enthralled with Bottom, promises to etherealize him by means of a program of delicate sensual allurements produced by fairy attendants and designed to

> purge thy mortal grossness so
> That thou shalt like an aery spirit go.
>
> (3.1.160–61)

As I have argued elsewhere, the reformation through purge that Titania promises is both spiritual and physical in its aims and methods, since, along with the refinements in his environment, it involves a distinctly laxative diet of

> apricocks and dewberries,
> ... purple grapes, green figs, and mulberries.
>
> (166–67)

We are asked to imagine (if not necessarily to believe) that such a diet would have the effect of lightening his bodily substance and thus of refining the words and behaviors coming out of it.[38] As Thomas Walkington argues in *The Optick Glasse of Humors*, the right nutriment roused and lightened the spirits, which, in turn, lightened the flesh: "a mery pleasant man is more light then one that is sad, and a man that is deade is farre heavier than one aliue" (100–101).

The encouragement in all these cases presupposes the metonymic significance of fluids in the humoral body—blood and spirits standing here for bold behaviors, urination (as a still possible mode of male public display) standing in for ejaculation and the proof of expansive bodily capacities of all sorts. If the body is a container of the fluids—blood and spirits—that produce behaviors, then a bigger capacity for containment shows the bigger man. Like Sir Andrew, Malvolio is being invited not just to change his external demeanor—his "humble slough" of steward's clothing and deferential manner—but in effect to alter and expand the capacity of his internal substance or at least to perform the prepossessing behaviors that would signal (or, in the reciprocity of humoral logic, even produce) such an alteration and expansion. The advice, Maria tells Toby later, is

---

38. Paster, *Body Embarrassed*, 130–31.

specifically designed to offend Olivia in terms of humoral antipathy not unlike those that Shylock has offered the Duke of Venice—presenting her with a color she abhors, a fashion she detests, and a feigned mirth unsuitable for her mood as Maria reads it: "he will smile upon her, which will now be so unsuitable to her disposition, being addicted to a melancholy as she is" (2.5.200–202). And indeed, Olivia does exclaim right away to Malvolio about the inappropriateness of his affective display: "Smil'st thou? I sent for thee upon a sad occasion" (3.4.18–19). Like Dromio, Malvolio has offended against the humoral proprieties proper to his relation to Olivia as servant to mistress, even if the mistress herself is criticized as being "addicted to a melancholy" (2.5.202)—that is, to the by-products, both psychological and physiological, of her own complexion. He has been encouraged to become a humorous gallant, to pour himself into all fashions, but such changeability in this play is reserved for the wellborn—even the impoverished wellborn such as Viola and Sebastian.

The evident social fluidity, especially the fluidity of gender, that has so preoccupied recent criticism of *Twelfth Night* is—again as I have argued elsewhere—everywhere contained in the play by a more conservative biological discourse, which prescribes the blood and heat—hence the behavior—humorally proper to men and women, to the elite and their social inferiors.[39] Humoral impropriety in the case of the class-jumping Malvolio turns less upon gender than upon status, especially since his attentions are fixed on a woman who herself threatens the "natural" boundaries of gender by presuming to control male access to her person and fortune, to choose the object of her affections for herself, and to act vigorously in pursuit of those affections.[40] That both lady and steward threaten social norms in similar ways is clear in the exposure to which they are jointly subject in the famous dirty joke that emerges from Malvolio's attempts to decipher her handwriting: "By my life, this is my lady's hand. These be her very c's, her u's, and her t's, and thus makes she her great P's" (2.5.86–88). As critics have noted, Malvolio's spelling out of "c-u-t"—an Elizabethan slang word for vagina—enacts the misogynist reduction of all women to their genitalia, the metonymical displacement of the writing hand as the emblem of individuality by the vagina as emblem of female lowliness and lack of worth.[41] That reduction is itself aggravated in the satiric identification of Olivia, who

39. Paster, "Unbearable Coldness," 434–35.

40. Jean Howard, "Crossdressing, the Theater, and Gender Struggle in Early Modern England," *Shakespeare Quarterly* 39 (1988): 432–33.

41. Jonathan Goldberg, "Textual Properties," *Shakespeare Quarterly* 37 (1986): 213–17.

wants to be walled off and self-enclosed in her household, with her great "pees." It is an identification of the female body with incontinence and physical lack of control. For Malvolio to know Olivia's great pees, moreover, is to associate him with the lowly household task of waste removal, a job proper only to servants far below him in rank.[42] This image of excretion, coming so early in a scene where Malvolio thinks he is being enjoined to an elevation of bodily matter and social habitus thanks to the fates' recognition of his worthy blood and spirits, functions as a leveling reminder of the social limits of humoral transformation. For the behaviors that Maria's forged letter asks Malvolio to perform on command—the expenditure of spirit in incessant smiling, the cross-gartering that numbs and swells his legs—represent an extreme of humoral manipulation. "Sad, lady?" Malvolio exclaims when he first appears to Olivia in costume, "I could be sad. This does make some obstruction in the blood, this cross-gartering . . . Not black in my mind, though yellow in my legs" (3.4.20–21, 26–27). Here Malvolio's flesh and blood resist their appropriation by fashion, signal their resistance to melting. In humoral terms, Malvolio is punished physically for the excessive warmth of his aspirant blood and spirits by the imposition of "obstruction in the blood"—a mechanical obstruction that would slow and cool his blood. In this play, the steward "sick of self-love" who "tastes with a distemper'd appetite" (1.5.90–91) is not allowed to aspire romantically to the lady he serves. And he is also not allowed to enjoy the warmth and increase of blood and spirits such aspirations evidently produce; indeed he is humiliated because of them. The madness of which he is accused—"midsummer madness" (3.4.56) or the madness produced by the drying of the brain and spirits in hot weather—ironically acknowledges the great expenditure, again both physiological and psychological, that Malvolio's performance has required. In bodily terms, Malvolio has been trapped into committing a particularly egregious form of humoral insubordination—the failure to suit one's own humor and behaviors to those of one's social superiors—and is punished, spectacularly, with the symbolic social nullification and physical isolation reserved for those possessed by alien spirits. Even Sir Toby's punning allusion to Malvolio as being inhabited by scriptural devils—"if all the devils of hell be drawn in little, and Legion himself possess'd him" (85–86)—fosters the humoral context of Malvolio's entrapment: "Legion" was the name of an "unclean spirit" (Mark 5:8–9); here it is the domestic equivalent of the socially "unclean" spirit that the household revelers accuse Malvolio of becoming.

42. Paster, *Body Embarrassed,* 32–34.

But it is important to recognize how Malvolio's social offensiveness differs from the offenses committed by the gentlemanly aspirants of Jonsonian humors comedy. Indeed, while satire directed against a household steward did have some resonance for contemporary playgoers, insofar as Malvolio is seen sometimes as representing a new professional class, sometimes as representing unattractive Puritan behaviors, the codes of conduct mocked in *Twelfth Night* participate more in what Bryson calls modes of courtliness than in modes of urbanity. Olivia's narcissistic withdrawal from active management of her household has permitted a disturbance in its social hierarchy—the complementary forms of misrule manifested in Malvolio's aggressive interpretation of her wishes and in the out-of-season revelry by everyone else. That hierarchy is not restored by the gulling of Malvolio—which is just another manifestation of misrule—but by the arrival of Sebastian, a social aspirant undone by shipwreck who can legitimately claim to be birthright gentry and whose marriage to Olivia thus resolves a myriad of tensions generated by the combination of female rule, stewardly class-jumping, and the thermal inadequacies of the other men and near-men. Unlike the humorally deficient Sir Andrew and Viola, whose lack of a "little thing" signals her female coldness, Sebastian needs no encouragement to fight in response to Sir Andrew's attack—"Why, there's for thee, and there, and there. Are all the people mad?" (4.1.26–27)—or to draw first on Sir Toby: "If thou dar'st tempt me further, draw thy sword" (43). His spontaneous willingness to marry an overeager woman whom he does not know at all and whose sanity he doubts are also evidence that his blood and spirits willingly embrace what the Fates have handed him, with no need of a guileful letter to lead them on. He need not publish his suit, since his sister has already done so for him, and his behavior toward Olivia, Toby, and Sir Andrew demonstrates presence of the hot blood and spirits that Viola's physical timidity shows her to be lacking. In *Twelfth Night*, it is Sebastian who secures the humoral chain of being even as he resolves the crisis of sexual (non)difference that Cesario's imitation of him created.

Certainly by comparison to the urban world of Jonsonian comedy, the household hierarchy restored at the end of *Twelfth Night* is—in early modern terms—a belated and nostalgic one. Jonson's comedies—including the quarto version of *Every Man in His Humour* with its Italianate characters and setting—express Bryson's emergent codes of urbanity by constructing a society where more or less socially equal men of radically unequal talents, abilities, and means vie for recognition and approval mostly from one another rather than from some recognized source of social authority.[43] In these plays, the claim to possession of a humor is at the core of social performativity, the basis for any hope of preeminence, a mark of "individuality" achieved—paradoxically—through imitation. For London gallants at the end of the sixteenth century, as J. B. Bamborough has noted (103) and as we have seen in Dekker's *Gull's Hornbook*, having a humor came to mean having a whim or a caprice—as if the mind were suddenly flooded by the current of an impulse. What such a formulation occludes, however, is the social struggle for preeminence and individuation that the claim to having a humor represents. To be able to act boldly on one's whims, one's momentary passions, might well be thought of as the essence of what Bryson would call the codes of lordliness. In *Taming of the Shrew*, as I noted in chapter 2, it is the lord's whim to conduct an elaborate social experiment on the tinker Christopher Sly, whom he finds passed out from drink on an alehouse floor. It is the lord's humor to humor Sly, to endow Sly with humorality in the fashionable sense of the word, to manipulate the humoral chain of being in order to tease the base-born man with the humoral sensation of his own potential for lordliness. When Sly resists— "call me not honor nor lordship" (ind., 2.5–6)—the lord treats it as just another example of Sly's distemper and departure from the norms of his station in life: "Heaven cease this idle humor in your honor!" (13). But the play does suggest the limits of the lord's command over his servants when the page Bartholomew, dressed up as the "lord" Sly's wife, has to put off Sly's increasingly sharp demands for sexual gratification: "Servants, leave me and her alone. Madam, undress you, and come now to bed" (ind., 2.116–17). The page might be sexually available to the lord—though there is no textual evidence for this supposition—but he is apparently unwilling to be sexually available to a man so much his social inferior, since he begs his real master:

> Thrice-noble lord, let me entreat of you
> To pardon me yet for a night or two;
> Or if not so, until the sun be set.
>
> (ind., 2.118–20)

(Daytime dalliance—as Malvolio's daydream also suggests—was the prerogative of gentlemen who owned their own time. The page presumably hopes that nighttime will end his real lord's humorous experiment.)

43. P. K. Ayers says that Wellbred and Edward Knowell are "the first true gallants on the English Stage"; see "Dreams of the City: The Urban and the Urbane in Jonson's *Epicoene*," *Philological Quarterly* 66 (1987): 75.

But for the citizens and gentlemen in humors comedy with less power than Sly's lord, to announce a humor publicly is an attempt, rather like Nym's, to make their interiority have an effect within and upon a social and physical environment in full recognition of that environment's tendency to push back. Their need to be aggressive in their claims to individuality matches that of Nym, and many of Jonson's humoral characters share Nym's utter disregard for his own offensiveness. Indeed it is the mighty power of the social world's resistance to the claims of the humorous individual that gives action in Jonsonian comedy its tendency to devolve into quarrelsomeness—exemplified in the famous game of vapors in *Bartholomew Fair* in which *"every man"* is *"to oppose the last man that spoke, whether it concern'd him, or no"* (4.4.22 S.D.). Such occasions, as we shall see below, are the very antithesis of courtly subordination—a grotesque antithetical mirroring of courtly subjection by opposition for its own sake. For Jonson, as we shall see, quarrelsomeness, even more than capriciousness, is the primary form that humorality takes in urban characters. And quarrelsomeness is intimately related to what I referred to in chapter 1 as the "pneumatic character" of early modern life, with the swirling movements of passions among characters imitating the movements of wind and air in the atmosphere around them.

Air and passions, we need to remember, were among the six nonnaturals that helped to determine early modern well-being. In *The Optick Glasse of Humours*, Walkington suggests the importance of air to the character of the flesh and the soul housed within it: "Giue mee leaue to speake a little of the ayre: howe it is receiued into the body doth either greatly advantage or little availe the minde. It is certaine that the excellencie of the soule followes the purity of the heavens, the temperature of the aire" (26). If we think of air as a material presence rather than merely vacuity, it becomes a charged medium for all social exchange. Especially in the self-conscious and resonant atmosphere of the theater, air is what the playwright or his character says it is—"the air, look you, this brave o'erhanging firmament" (*Hamlet*, 2.2.300–301).[44] For Shakespeare and Jonson, in its human form as breath—sometimes with but also without speech—the pneumatic movements of air between characters become metonymic of their power relations, as characters strive for a dominance that they construe as an instrumentalization or a playing of one upon another. We have already noted this in chapter 1 in the terms of Hamlet's rebuke to Rosencrantz and Guildenstern: "Do you think I am easier to be play'd on than a pipe?" (3.2.369–70). We find it too

44. See Smith, 7–8.

in Maria's scornful account of Sir Andrew's quarrelsomeness: "He's a great quarreller; and but that he hath the gift of a coward to allay the gust he hath in quarreling, 'tis thought among the prudent he would quickly have the gift of a grave" (*Twelfth Night*, 1.3.30–33). Her pun on gust—as taste or appetite and as burst of air—establishes the connection between inside and outside worlds, suggests the link between movements of air and currents of emotion. In a pneumatic context, the claim to humorality is thus also, implicitly, a claim upon deference and a demand for social accommodation. Sometimes that demand is part of a claim to be accorded the rights of the gentleman, but in a variant case, it sometimes expresses a protodemocratic resistance to gentlemanly claims of privilege in the realm of affect, as when the lowly water-carrier Cob in *Every Man in His Humour* exclaims, "Nay, I have my rheum"—Cob's old-fashioned word for humor—"and I can be angry as well as another, sir" (3.4.12–13). Having the right to anger, having the right literally to give one's anger an *airing* that others must take in, and being able to feed one's humor—these become the watchwords for Jonson's male characters as they seek to promote their own interests and, as we shall see, for some of his more aggressive female ones as well.

But Jonson's representation of humorality is more complex—indeed more interesting—than his characters are inclined to make it seem in their repeated claims for what I am calling the humoral right of way. For Jonson makes use of both aspects of humoral discourse that I mentioned near the start of this chapter—one, the more or less Galenic biological discourse of the four qualities of heat, moisture, cold, and dryness that naturalizes even as it complicates the sources of human psychophysiological difference; the other, the social discourse of humorality through which individual charac-ters seek to advance themselves in individuated social existence against the panoply of social forces competing for emotional precedence. Jonson's char-acters claim their humorality in socially explicit terms—by declaring their need to feed their humors, their right to have a humor—even as they speak a figurative language that deeply embeds a physiological humorality that qualifies or even contradicts the individuating emphasis of their social claims. I want to follow this argument in several Jonson plays, concentrat-ing especially on *Every Man in His Humour* and *Bartholomew Fair*, in order to see how Jonson's humor characters respond to the built-in emotional pos-sibilities and constraints of the social order and how their hopes of advanc-ing their individuality fare in the fierce winds of social competition.

Every Man in His Humour suggests that Jonson understood the confus-ingly fluid relations of urban life to be themselves productive of emotional disorder between and within individual subjects. In his urban comedies, the social and emotional structure of deference and accommodation that I have called the humoral right of way seems ambiguous, in disrepair, or frighteningly open to radical renegotiation. Once Wellbred's dinner invitation to Edward Knowell has begun the movement from a paternal country household into the city, the action centers loosely around two households—those of Master Kitely and of Cob the water-carrier, where the presence of Wellbred and Bobadill as gentlemen lodgers has caused a disruption of order and authority leading to jealousy, anger, and periodic outbreaks of physical violence. Put otherwise, the evident confusions in the social hierarchy in the play's London breed confusions in the domestic and emotional hierarchies, too. When Cob declares that, even in his lowliness, he "can be angry as well as another, sir" (3.4.12–13), we can see how deeply into the social order the play's interest in the question of emotional autonomy or sway reaches. It is important to note that Cob's notion of affective privilege—having physiological "rheum" or humor—seems to reduce ultimately to a right to have and express anger as opposed to other, kindlier emotions. Anger maintains physical and psychological boundaries that other emotions might compromise. For Jonson, the overarching issues of civil life may thus reduce to the question of managing quarrelsomeness— which seems to be the characteristic temperature and endpoint of urban intercourse. This is not only because of the inevitability of anger, generally, but because of the incentives to aggression and impulsivity—both structural and psychophysiological—that exist when individuals have to negotiate their places in an unclear social order and are forced to share the same physical and symbolic spaces with equally anxious others.[45]

Jonson arranges the opening of *Every Man in His Humour* so as to emphasize the relation, in the display and management of anger, between the social and emotional hierarchies and between the two discourses of the humors. Stephen, the play's country gull, pays an early visit to the Knowell household in order to announce his sudden desire to learn the languages of hawking and hunting, because "he is for no gallant's company without 'em" (1.1.40). In old Knowell's long Polonian rebuke, a host of conservative ethical precepts, associated here with rural retirement, are naturalized by metaphors drawn from humoral biology.[46] Knowell counsels Stephen against spending money foolishly on "every foolish brain that humours you" (63) and thrusting himself boldly into company instead of waiting

45. Gil, 338–39.

46. On this speech, see Jonathan Haynes, *The Social Relations of Jonson's Theater* (Cambridge: Cambridge University Press, 1992), 37.

till men's affections, or your own desert,
Should worthily invite you to your rank.

(66–67)

His reproof, interestingly, includes a specific objection to having Stephen
look at him directly—"Nay, never look at me" (49). The moment is glossed
by Thomas Wright, who explains that it is not "good manners, that the infe-
riour should fixe his eyes vpon his superiours countenance . . . because it
were presumption for him to attempt the entrance or priuie passage into
his superiors minde" (29). Knowell's angry reaction suggests that Stephen's
eyes, attempting intersubjectivity without invitation, have claimed an
equality where it does not exist; he has broken a social rule of the hierarchized gaze especially at a time when eyebeams were thought to act upon
what they saw. More pointedly, Knowell adopts an elemental language of
the qualities to construe Stephen's bold attempts at gentlemanly display as
a shameful wasting of bodily stuff:

Nor would I you should melt away yourself
In flashing bravery, lest while you affect
To make a blaze of gentry to the world,
A little puff of scorn extinguish it,
And you be left, like an unsavoury snuff,
Whose property is only to offend.

(1.1.70–75)

Knowell's language returns us to the portrait of hyperresponsive flatterers
at the opening of *Sejanus*. He images what he regards as socially value-
less—including perhaps that human object called Stephen—as physically
malleable or insubstantial, an insignificant expenditure of heat in a larger
pneumatic world. Thus the "flashing" of Stephen's "bravery" does not refer
to a heat of estimable deeds proceeding from the inner worth but rather to
splendid clothes decking his outside (*OED, bravery*, 3b). The equation here
is between the expenditure of fortune and the expenditure of self. The contemptuous troping of Stephen's body as a tallow candle quickly burning
itself out with an extravagant little blaze of expensive, fashionable behaviors is thus both social and physiological, based on the early modern conception of physical life as sustained by the expenditure of radical heat and
moisture, ideally held in balance. In order to grasp the trope's inner logic—
even at the risk of grotesquely magnifying Stephen's importance—it should
be understood that moisture here is both bodily irrigation and fuel. As

Walkington explains, "Mans life saith *Aristotle*, is vpheld by two staffes: the one is . . . natiue heate, the other is, . . . radicall moisture" (64). He cites Aristotle's simile that "our heate is like the flame of a burning lampe; the moisture like the foieson or oyle of the lampe, wherewith it continues burning. As in the lampe, if there bee not a symmetrie and a just measure of the one with the other, they will in a short time, the one of them destroy the other" (64–65). In this comparison, blood is "the oyle of the lampe of our life" (111). Walkington uses the candle—here signifying soul or spirit—to describe the imbalance of a distempered soul: "a candle in the lanterne can yeeld but a glimmering light through an impure and darkesome horne" (23). An intemperate burning of bodily stuff—usually, as we have seen, by means of choler, and in Stephen choler expressed in modestly aggressive acts of social display such as a desire to learn hawking and hunting—leads to smoke, soot, and noxious vapors. Stephen's "blaze of gentry" threatens to extinguish Stephen's potentially worthy inner stuff—whether we construe that stuff as biological or social—just as Stephen's noxious behavioral display, imaged here as a smelly wick or an "unsavoury snuff," prompts another's scornful blowing out into social nullification. This is what it means to be subject to the pneumatic character of another's contempt, to the larger breath of the bigger man. Knowell's tropes of extinction and self-extinction furthermore stand in opposition to gentlemanliness as a measured maintenance of fortune and of bodily stuff—solidity contrasted to the evanescence of waxy, or fatty, bodiliness losing itself in melting and blazing. Knowell warns Stephen that gentility is merely

> an airy and mere borrowed thing,
> From dead men's dust and bones: and none of yours
> Except you make or hold it.

> (1.1.81–83)

This makes the contrast between substantial and insubstantial kinds of bodily being cognate with substantial and insubstantial forms of gentility.

My point in dwelling overlong on poor Stephen as a smelly, blown-out candle is that the overdetermined interplay between social and bodily formations here also runs throughout the play in the language that characters use to render sharp social judgments upon one another and to seek to invent or secure their places in a jostling urban world. An organic imagery—of environmental interactions of bodily mettle/metal with breath or air, water, and fire—attaches to characters in order that we may form judgments in material terms of their worth, their substantiality, their effect in the world, and their claims on our attention. The pun on *met-tle/metal* discussed in chapter 1 returns here with particular force in an early modern urban ecology of the passions—as a way of extending subject status to characters who claim to have humors but otherwise speak without benefit of interior complexity. Thus, clothes and behaviors—the expenditure of self in the world—become the surface ornamentations of metal on mettle, or they function in tropes of the tempered interactions of metals with air and fire. Young Knowell greets his cousin Stephen by mock-praising him as a man "so graced, gilded, or (to use a more fit metaphor) so tin-foiled by nature, as not ten housewives' pewter (again' a good time) shows more bright to the world than he" (1.3.91–93). The quarto text for the same speech adds, "Not that you have a leaden constitution, coz—although perhaps a little inclining to that temper and so the more apt to melt with pity when you fall into the fire of rage" (1.2.100–103). As in old Knowell's rebuke in the previous scene, Stephen is seen as still in danger of melting—this time not as a smelly candle but as a body thinly covered over with a protective or decorative layer of tin. As Miola points out in his edition of the 1601 quarto text for *Every Man in His Humour*, the trope systematically reduces Stephen from graced (with the air of gentility?) to gilded to covered with base metal. In both the 1601 quarto and the 1616 Folio texts of the play, Edward/Lorenzo junior's metaphor recognizes the use of lead to make tin and may also imply lead's softness and malleability and the dirty smoke involved in its smelting. Like tin, the trope implies, Stephen melts down messily at low temperatures; he will not last. The image of a gallant as a man covered in thin foil may also reflect the social distance and decline in early modern manhood from the sturdily carapaced figure of the armored knight. The same implied comparison between more and less worthy metals, we recall, lies behind Prince Hal's comparison of his future reformation to "bright metal on a sullen ground" (*1 Henry IV*, 1.2.212), which,

> glitt'ring o'er my fault,
> Shall show more goodly and attract more eyes
> Than that which hath no foil to set it off.

> (213–15)

And it returned in Middleton's *Chaste Maid in Cheapside*, as we saw in chapter 2, in Mrs. Yellowhammer's disparaging comments on her daughter's heaviness, as she tells Moll,

> You dance like a plumber's daughter and deserve
> Two thousand pound in lead to your marriage,
> And not in goldsmith's ware.
>
> (1.1.21–23)

Characters in this play turn repeatedly to a metal-based scale of values in offering judgments of fellow human beings—of their inner mettle. Old Knowell rebukes Brainworm, begging in disguise as a poor veteran, for being one of those men who do not care

> how the metal of your minds
> Is eaten with the rust of idleness.
>
> (2.5.104–5)

The play's urban gull Matthew reports to Bobadill that he and Downright have quarreled over a hanger, which Matthew valued "both for fashion and workmanship," as "most peremptory-beautiful and gentlemanlike" (1.5.72–73). Bobadill in reply mocks Downright as a man "born for the manger" who has "not so much as a good phrase in his belly, but all old iron and rusty proverbs! A good commodity for some smith to make hobnails of" (82–85). At these moments, self is imagined as a physical substance showing its innate properties—for remaining self-same or for becoming other—through its associations with a value-laden object world and with elemental interactions with the environment. Life in time is imagined as rusting in the air, or as melting with rage, or as being a man so old-fashioned that words rust in his belly before they are spoken.

A man's mettle is also signaled by the metal he wears on his person or attempts to purchase. Thus Stephen's unworthy—or perhaps merely middling—mettle is presumably to blame when he lacks the judgment to tell a good sword from a bad one, buying one of obviously poor quality on the disguised Brainworm's assurance that it is "a most pure Toledo" (2.4.72). The link between flesh and mettle comes in the quality of tempering, which is itself the heated interaction of qualities: the specially valued temper of Toledo swords, according to Miola, came "from some peculiar quality of the water [from the Tagus] in which the metal was plunged, while glowing from the forge."[47] In 1.5, the braggart soldier Bobadill, seeking to avoid any dangerous encounters at all, practices combat with a bed staff. And Justice Clement, surprised at Cob's temerity in speaking against taking tobacco,

---

47. See Miola's note to 2.1.78, in his edition of *Every Man in His Humour*.

scorns the water-carrier in metallic terms: "A slave that never drunk out of
better than pisspot metal in his life! And he to deprave and abuse the virtue
of an herb, so generally received in the courts of princes, the chambers of
nobles, the bowers of sweet ladies, the cabins of soldiers" (3.7.55–59). Cob,
drinking from a metal that his betters use only for chamber pots, becomes
in effect guilty of exchanging beer and urine, nutriment and excrement.
Base-born and base metal reveal their inner lack of worth in the eyes of
their betters.

The mechanism involved in all these metallic tropes is more than an
ethical judgment rendered by associating a character with an unworthy
substance; the force of analogical thinking or of embedded cosmological
epistemology requires us to think of the characters themselves either as
made of unworthy and insubstantial materials (Stephen as tin foil or smelly
tallow, Brainworm as rusting with inactivity, Cob as pisspot metal), as containing them or as being linked, analogically, to the properties of substances. In this logic, the old metal of scrap-iron words in irascible squire
Downright's belly leads to the rusty proverbs of his speech, much as
Andrew Aguecheek is encouraged to warm up his slow-cold wits for the
production of "excellent jests, fire-new from the mint" (*Twelfth Night*,
3.2.22). The structure of differences among men is thus materialized as
qualitative differences in the substance of their flesh, with flesh given properties analogous to objects in the world. This equation is not by itself novel:
we have already seen in chapter 1 how wrath hardens Pyrrhus in his rampage through Troy. We recognize the significance attributed to hardness
when Henry V exhorts his soldiers before Agincourt to

> stiffen the sinews, [conjure] up the blood,
> Disguise fair nature with hard-favor'd rage.
>
>   (3.1.7–8)

Or when Hamlet, raging against the men who would restrain him from pur-
suing the ghost, describes "each petty artere" in his body as "as hardy as the
Nemean lion's nerve" (1.4.82–83). The more particular question in humors
comedy involves what mettle/metal is proper to the complex interactions of
modern urban life, what are the proper psychophysiological mainsprings of
behaviors and conversation in such a confusing and ambiguous social
order.

That this is at least part of the question may underscore why Jonson
includes a braggart soldier and would-be fencing instructor such as Bobadill
in the populace of *Every Man in His Humour*'s London and why Brainworm

chooses a disguise as a turned-out veteran—that is, why he chooses a debased version of the archaic figure of the armed warrior in the heart of the city. But it also suggests the role of other elements in the determination of qualitatively proper flesh, in the reciprocal interactions that connect self and spirits to the environment. There is, for example, metaphorical reference to the quality of flesh implied in Wellbred's letter to young Knowell, which includes an invitation to meet a fellow poet, "a rhymer, sir, o' your own batch, your own leaven" (1.2.74–75). Poets are softer than warriors or even would-be gentlemen. The image of the body as tallow candle here yields to the yeastiness of flesh as dough—expansive, aerated, rising, an image that involves flesh with the elements of air and heat and moisture. Dough is metamorphic, its rising an absorbing of moisture and heat. Insofar as moisture and heat explain the activity of flesh and the spirits housed in a doughy body, the figure links flesh with the heated activity of spirits and the force of inspiration, the airy insubstantiality of poetic invention that old Knowell describes when he speaks of his son's aspirations to being a poet in humoral terms:

> Myself was once a student; and, indeed,
> Fed with the selfsame humour he is now,
> Dreaming on naught but idle poetry.

> (1.1.15–17)

Or, as the adjective "idle" suggests, doughy poets may be more phlegmatic than aerated. But the quality of their flesh and hence perhaps their minds—as the hint of disparagement here conveys—is bred of inactivity. This reflection on inactivity is presumably the force behind Wellbred's invitation to Edward to "come over to me quickly," to "make hither with an appetite" (1.2.72, 78) for a feast of gulls. (We shall contemplate the implications of eating gulls and feeding one's humor later.)

Characters here, as we have seen elsewhere, represent each other in terms of organic relationships to the elements, as if those relationships fixed them ethically and socially. We may wish to question or even dismiss specific judgments—Bobadill's judgment of Downright, for instance—even as we recognize the early modern habits of thought about self and the object world that such judgments represent. Of all the elements mentioned in the play, however, references to the air as the source of health, life, and power are particularly expressive. Characters more self-aware than Stephen understand and express their experience of this threatening penetrability and openness to others in their responses to the air. Thus when the

paranoically jealous Kitely confesses to having a headache, his wife replies
sweetly, "I pray thee, good sweetheart, come in; the air will do you harm, in
troth" (2.3.50–51). Kitely, presumably hearing "sweet hart," responds as if he
were an animal being hunted by its scent: "The air! She has me i'the wind!"
(53). In this grandiose paranoid fantasy, Dame Kitely is Diana and he is
Actaeon. The buried allusion is of course reminiscent of the opening of
Twelfth Night, where the lovesick Orsino imagines the beauty of his beloved
as having the power to purify the air:

> O, when mine eyes did see Olivia first,
> Methought she purg'd the air of pestilence!
> That instance was I turn'd into a hart.
>
> (1.1.18–20)[48]

Plague was thought to be airborne. The air Orsino breathed was pestilent
before he was in love, before Olivia was there to cleanse it. Kitely has the
opposite sensations: jealousy is a poisoning of his household air, the con-
tamination of one passion by another, the dampening of love's heat by
fear's cold, the erosion of love by fear. Jealousy

> May well be called poor mortals' plague:
> For, like a pestilence, it doth infect
> The houses of the brain. First it begins
> Solely to work upon the fantasy,
> Filling her seat with such pestiferous air,
> As soon corrupts the judgment; and from thence
> Sends like contagion to the memory:
> Still each to other giving the infection.
> Which, as a subtle vapour, spreads itself
> Confusedly through every sensive part,
> Till not a thought, or motion, in the mind,
> Be free from the black poison of suspect.
>
> (2.3.56–67)

This self-report depends on an analogy between domestic spaces and cognitive spaces, between the air occupying house and brain. We have seen

---

48. The allusion to hunting ("she has me in the wind") is missing in the quarto, so it is at least
possible that Jonson may indeed be thinking of *Twelfth Night* here; see *Every Man in His Humour*,
ed. Miola, 1.4.200–201.

Othello, too, express his sense of jealousy as living within an imprisoning miasma:

> I had rather be a toad
> And live upon the vapor of a dungeon
> Than keep a corner in the thing I love
> For others' uses.

$$(3.3.270–73)$$

Air takes on liquid properties in such figurations. Othello's later trope (in 4.2.61–62) of decayed love as a cistern poisoned by the presence of toads knotting and engendering within it also describes jealousy in terms of environmental pollution—the poisoning of a domestic landscape by emotional toxins. What citizen Kitely discovers is that having the gentlemanly Wellbred as a lodger is to have his domestic space invaded and turned into a "public receptacle / For giddy humour" (2.1.59–60)—a waste space for the expression of fashionable behaviors. But it is also to be penetrated psychophysiologically by the new distempered atmosphere that Wellbred and his followers create in his household. Jealousy reverses the cleansing effects of love; to be jealous is to live in a house of distemper, to be filled inside one's brain with a "black cloud" (2.3.71) of bad air. The action of this play, like other plays centered on jealousy, underscores the social contagion of which jealousy is both cause and effect. What Kitely articulates is like Othello's pain in his sense of being invaded by alien substances, but the imagery is etherealized and localized as one space in the brain infects the others.

If disease is the poisonous spread of bad air in one's internal spaces, then health is the balanced flow of bodily fluids, blood and air preeminent among them. In a firm and socially fixed body, it is the proportions of blood and air that express its particular ethical and moral weight. So when Kitely remembers Wellbred when he first was welcomed as gentleman lodger into his household, Kitely expresses Wellbred's attractiveness in terms of a balance of blood and aerated spirits:

> Methought he bare himself in such a fashion,
> So full of man, and sweetness in his carriage,
> And (what was chief) it showed not borrowed in him,
> But all he did, became him as his own,
> And seemed as perfect, proper, and possessed
> As breath, with life, or colour, with the blood.

$$(2.1.44–49)$$

Blood and breath, in this formulation, are metonymic of the behaviors they animate, so that Wellbred's initial self-possession is described as a proportion-ateness of lively breath and sanguine color. They produce what Kitely recog-nizes as authenticity, self-sameness—"all he did, became him as his own." Here, according to Walkington, lies the biological basis of Wellbred's gentle-manly preeminence: "if there were a monarch or prince to bee constituted over all temperatures, this purple sanguine complexion should, no doubts, aspire to that hie preheminence of bearing rule: for this is the ornament of the body, the pride of humors, the paragon of complexions, the prince of all tem-peratures, for blood is oyle of the lampe of our life" (110–11). What is impor-tant here is not to judge whether Kitely's praise of Wellbred is sincere or not (Kitely's jealousy makes this possibility doubtful) but to recognize his strategic desire to ground Wellbred's social preeminence and pleasing manner in human biology—even if, in the circularity of humoral logic, those material qualities of well-balanced breath and blood have to be inferred from the behaviors they are designed to explain. But this not-quite-metaphorical equa-tion of social preeminence with bodily health and solubility allows Kitely to describe the onset of urban gallantry in Wellbred as a communicable disorder that transforms Kitely's house and threatens its deferential order:

> He makes my house here common as a mart,
> A theatre, a public receptacle
> For giddy humour, and diseased riot;
> And here (as in a tavern, or a stews)
> He and his wild associates spend their hours,
> In repetition of lascivious jests,
> Swear, leap, drink, dance, and revel night by night,
> Control my servants: and indeed what not?
>
> (58–65)

Not surprisingly, Kitely goes on describe Wellbred's transformation as the heat-ing of his blood to diseased excess and an expansion of his breath into the air:

> if I should speak
> He would be ready from his heat of humour,
> And overflowing of the vapour in him,
> To blow the ears of his familiars
> With the false breath of telling what disgraces
> And low disparagements I had put upon him.
>
> (95–100)

Here Kitely establishes his sense of Wellbred's social preeminence by his dominance of the air, the "false breath" he blows into others' ears.

Like *Hamlet, Every Man in His Humour* is sensitive to the movements of breath and air between characters as signaling relations of power and preeminence—especially as breath is expended aggressively in laughter, anger, or scorn. In Hamlet, one key affective change took place when he moved from imagining himself passively as the object of another's scornful breath in the second soliloquy—who "plucks off my beard and blows it in my face, / Tweaks me by the nose, gives me the lie i'th'throat / As deep as to the lungs?" (2.2.573–75)—to rebuking Rosencrantz and Guildenstern for imagining him as their pipe to blow on. In the opening of *Every Man in His Humour*, after being scolded by his uncle, Stephen reverses the current of anger that he may not express and vents it onto a serving man— "Whoreson base fellow! A mechanical serving-man!" (1.2.24)—who accepts the unjustified tirade in deferential silence. Old Knowell, having threatened his nephew's pitiful blaze of gentility with the breath of social extinction, then rebukes Stephen for trying to inflate himself—or reinflate and reinflame himself—by expressing anger toward one who cannot reciprocate:

> You see, the honest man demeans himself
> Modestly toward you, giving no reply
> To your unseasoned, quarreling, rude fashion;
> And still you huff it, with a kind of carriage
> As void of wit as of humanity.
>
>   (28–32)

Stephen here inhales and exhales angrily—huffs it—at another's expense. The sequence of events—Knowell scolding Stephen, Stephen scolding the servant, the older man over the younger, the birthright gentleman over a serving man, his social inferior—offers a clear correspondence among the pneumatics of power, the humoral right of way, and the social hierarchy. But we soon see that the tin-foiled Stephen is himself merely instrumentation for the greater social powers of his cousin Edward and his friend Wellbred. Part of Edward's mock-praise of Stephen is as one who, with "every word" has left "the savour of a strong spirit" (1.3.90)—as if Stephen holds mastery over the field of air around him. (Since "savour" of a strong spirit suggests halitosis—and in performance could easily be made to do so through gesture—Edward's praise of Steven's strong words is even more equivocal.) But he and Wellbred regard all the gulls as "wind instruments"

(3.1.52) for them to play upon; Stephen is not only his cousin's drum, since "everyone may play upon him" (3.2.20–21), but also "a child's whistle" (22). Taken together, such tropes suggest not only Stephen's openness to the world but the internal emptiness or vacuity of a human shell who invites the aggressive breath of others. Far from being neutral, then, a vacant medium of social exchange in the play, the air is part of the social body vexed by the distempers of its quarreling members.

The social relations among Kitely, Wellbred, and Downright are particularly expressive of the mobility and fluidity of social relations in this play's London—since the half-brothers Wellbred and Downright are gentlemen but related to citizen Kitely by his marriage to their sister. We learn that some of Kitely's displeasure with Wellbred comes from the rancor of being mocked as a citizen: they

> Make their loose comments upon every word,
> Gesture, or look I use; mock me all over,
> From my flat cap unto my shining shoes.
>
> (2.1.102–4)

The emotional constraints imposed by class differences seem involved in Kitely's reluctance to express his anger to Wellbred directly. By using Downright as the agent of his disciplinary efforts, Kitely turns his attempts to dislodge or at least contain his gentleman lodger and his companions into a contest for gentlemanly preeminence between the brothers—the very relationship that Louis Montrose has identified as particularly prone to tension and hostility (28–54). The brothers are both disposed to a sudden anger that seems to express their sense of gentlemanly privilege and mark of superiority and which establishes the emotional character of their bitter competition. Downright sees himself as shamed by his brother's disorderly companions: "Let me not live, and I could not find in my heart to swinge the whole ging of 'em, one after another, and begin with him first" (2.2.27–29). Downright explodes to Kitely, "he mads me, I could eat my very spur-leathers for anger! But why are you so tame?" (2.1.78–79). But Wellbred himself is no less choleric in the face of his half-brother Downright's disapproval: "You are an ass, do you see," he tells Downright in a fury. "Touch any man here, and by this hand, I'll run my rapier to the hilts in you" (4.2.109–10). The point is not that Wellbred values most of his companions—we know that he does not—but that he regards public reproof from his brother as a point of dishonor. As Bridget tells Downright,

> you know
> My brother Wellbred's temper will not bear
> Any reproof, chiefly in such a presence,
> Where every slight disgrace he should receive
> Might wound him in opinion and respect.

> (4.3.17–21)

It might be fair to ask whose poor opinion and loss of respect Wellbred
fears, given the odd assortment of characters who follow in his wake; the
answer would have to come from that fantasy realm of the ideological—
where the illusion of visible social preeminence as a value in and of itself
would, Slavoj Žižek tells us, necessarily originate.[49] Certainly what Bridget's
remark points to is the competitive atmosphere established from the very
beginning of the play, when Wellbred invites young Knowell to visit him in
London and inspect the assortment of gulls he has assembled for their
mutual enjoyment as men of sense. Wellbred surrounds himself with
gulls—at least in part—to establish his social preeminence, but he can only
maintain that preeminence by inviting others to watch him enjoy it. This is
of course why he invites young Knowell to visit him in the city, but it is also
why he labels the poetaster Matthew and the braggart soldier Bobadill as a
"present" for Edward (1.2.73)—indeed as present of rarities more magnifi-
cent than the presentations made by the Levant Company to the Sultan of
Turkey. "I would ha' you make hither with an appetite," Wellbred tells
Edward in his letter. "If the worst of 'em be not worth your journey, draw
your bill of charges . . . and you shall be allowed your *viaticum*" (78–81). The
language here of gift-giving underscores the invitation as initiating a genial
competition in homosocial preeminence and explains the terms of reciprocal hospitality in Edward's response—to "furnish our feast with one gull
more toward the mess" and to equal Wellbred's "brace" by bringing his
cousin Stephen and finding one: "here's one, that's three: oh, for a fourth"
(1.3.56–57). This is why Edward seeks to encourage in Stephen the very
conduct his father has singled out for reproof and containment. "I will
be more proud," Stephen promises his cousin, "and melancholy, and
gentleman-like, than I have been" (104–5)—a pledge Edward takes as hope-
ful augury that "we may hap have a match with the city, and play him for
forty pound" (108–9).

The struggle between Edward and Wellbred for preeminence in the
matter of finding gulls and then feasting on them works to highlight the

---

49. Slavoj Žižek, *The Sublime Object of Ideology* (London: Verso, 1989), 45.

abundance and variety of urban humors generally, but the real point of the objectification of gulls is enhancing the subjectivity of the gentleman who finds, names, and masters them. The term for such enhanced subjectification is "feeding one's humor"—the process of enlarging the scope of one's ability to be socially capricious at the expense of others, to orchestrate men and dictate their manners as a form of social mastery. Here is where the humors as a social discourse find widest expression in Jonson's humors comedy—in the competitive claims to humorality by gulls who wish to claim individuality as a way of fixing their identities in the mobile, fluid exchanges of urban society and by young men such as Wellbred and Edward Knowell. They develop an appetite for the spectacle of others' affectations in order to enhance the quality of their self-experience. But in a setting in which the movement of air between characters is metonymic of power relations, in which men become wind instruments for others to blow upon, the experience of one's own humorality seems—like the process of garnering credentials as a gentleman—achievable only at others' expense. This is, of course, entirely predictable in societies like those in early modern comedy, where, as we have seen, the humoral hierarchy does indeed match—or is supposed to match—the social hierarchy. It should not be surprising, then, that emotional privilege can seem to be a commodity reserved only for the elite, or that lack of choice in one's social circumstances can seem synonymous with emotional enforcement.

The emotional constraints of the social hierarchy for everyone placed within it are especially clear in the humoral set-piece scene in 3.4 between Cob, the water-carrier, and Kitely's serving man Cash when Cash instructs Cob in the nuances of humorality—what it is and who is allowed to claim it. Cob enters complaining so bitterly of the disciplines of fasting days, when fish-eating was prescribed, that Cash wants to know "what moves thee to this choler?" (3.4.5). Cob seems to understand the question as an injunction to moderation: "Nay, I have my rheum, and I can be angry as well as another, sir" (11–12). He cites his possession of humor as proof that he exists, resents injury, and is moved by the self-love that moves everything else in early modern cosmology in general. If his answer sounds familiar, it is because it rests on exactly the same tautological premise as Shylock's refusal to answer the duke on the grounds of his natural antipathy for Antonio.[50] Here, however, social difference can only involve birth and rank, not ethnicity or religious difference, and Cash's superiority to Cob in the matter of humor reduces to a matter of linguistic currency: "Thy

50. Womack, 52.

rheum, Cob?" Cash asks, "Thy humour, thy humour?" (14), and he goes on to define humor in creatural terms as "a gentleman-like monster, bred in the special gallantry of our time by affectation; and fed by folly ... humor is nothing, if it be not fed ... It's a common phrase, 'Feed my humour'" (18–23). But possessing the humoral monster within is a luxury for the likes of water-carriers, as Cob instantly realizes.

Cob does not claim to have the social privilege or emotional autonomy of Wright's explosive aristocrat with the gunpowdered mind or even the emotional sway that Wellbred, Downright, and Justice Clement struggle to achieve throughout the play. He claims, as basic to his humanity, the right to be angry at externally imposed disciplines such as fasting. If such a right turns out to be monstrous and need special feeding such as might come in the form of quarreling, then Cob will try to forswear it: "humour, avaunt, I know you not, be gone. Let who will make hungry meals for your monster-ship, it shall not be I. Feed you, quoth he? 'Slid, I ha' much ado to feed myself; especially on these lean rascally days, too" (3.4.24–27). If gentlemen understand special feeding of their humors as a form of pleasure or self-enhancement, Cob understands it as a kind of work: "Let who will make hungry meals for your monstership, it shall not be I" (25–26). By insisting on the difference between necessary humors and gentleman-like humors, Cob recognizes the force of the social hierarchy as involving an emotional and behavioral hierarchy but also chooses his own degree of freedom from and within it: "I'll none on it" (24).

That Cob exercises this freedom querulously and unwisely—publicly fulminating against gentlemanly habits of smoking tobacco, beating his wife, finally incurring the wrath of Justice Clement—does not take away from the pointedness of Jonson's ethical distinction between the physiolog-ical humors, which one cannot choose not to have, and the social humors of caprice that one can freely renounce. If feeding social humors is supple-mentary to the elementary task of feeding physical humors, then humoral-ity itself becomes the prerogative of gentlemen—not the great equalizer defining the human. On this view, folly's feeding of gentlemanly humors becomes peripheral to, or even parasitic upon, the feeding essential to bio-logical life and perhaps essential as well to a social life understood in corpo-rate rather than individualistic terms. The point in noting the humoral language embedded in the quarrelsome exchanges in *Every Man in His Humour* is not only to suggest why geniality is so hard to come by in Jonsonian comedy but also to highlight how alert Jonson is to the ferocious social struggles that deploy humoral discourse in order to disguise affecta-tion as natural impulse. Jonson uses the periodic quarrels in *Every Man in*

His Humour to underscore how predictable it is in civil society for emotional unrestraint to be a function of relative social position, indeed for emotional unrestraint to be constitutively expressive of social privilege—as when Wellbred furiously defends his privilege to have whatever companions he pleases against his brother's equally vociferous disapproval. Even Stephen in his quest for recognition as a gallant seems to regard opposition for its own sake as gentlemanly prerogative, quarrelling with his cousin Edward Knowell over whether or not to buy the sword Brainworm wants to sell him by insisting, "but I will buy it now, because you say so . . . I have a mind to't" (2.4.77, 82). It is as if the emotional autonomy that Stephen equates with gentlemanliness reduces to irritability, quarrelsomeness, and opposition for its own sake. When a gentleman's assumption of emotional autonomy is married to social authority—as it is in the whimsical Justice Clement, for example—the results may include behavior notable even in a crowd of humorists. "He has a very strange presence, methinks," remarks Edward, "it shows as if he stood out of the rank from other men . . . They say, he will commit a man for taking the wall of his horse." Wellbred replies, "anything indeed, if it come in the way of his humour" (3.5.46–52). Perhaps this is the urban version of what Christopher Sly experiences in the induction to *The Taming of the Shrew,* for it is precisely his coming in the way of his lord's humor that leads to his amazing, if temporary, transformation. But since emotional unrestraint in *Every Man in His Humour* equates mostly to the dominant emotion of anger, the result, Jonson demonstrates, is structural encouragement to anger and opposition among men of equal station as a normal state of affairs.

What humors are to *Every Man in His Humour,* vapors are to *Bartholomew Fair*—*vapors* being a term that subsumes all forms of meaningful difference into its own endless metamorphoses, both grammatical and material. Jonson is forced into this verbal variation at least in part because, by 1614, the fashion of humoral affectation—of feeding one's humors in public—and the brief but substantial vogue of humors comedy had largely passed.[51] That Jonson wishes us to understand the two terms as nearly interchangeable is signaled by Jordan Knockem's Nym-like reliance on *vapors* as a personal verbal signature and catchall phrase for things as they are—especially emotionally driven things as they are: "Let's drink it out, good Urs, and no vapours" (1.2.3.22–23),

---

51. For a good overview of the phenomenon, see Miola's introduction in *Every Man in His Humour,* ed. Miola, 13–15.

Knockem tells Ursula on finding the irascible pig-woman again at the fair and hoping to enter into a comfortable business relationship with her. Yet it becomes clear in Knockem's endless playing with the word, as he wanders in and out of the action, that the vapors are conceptually even more useful than the humors were for expressing the deep reciprocity linking self to world in early modern cosmology. Knockem's tendency to use the term interchangeably as noun and verb makes us attend to *vapor*—both as word and as thing—as signifying agency of all kinds.

Humors and vapors are alike in being fluids: humors denote anything liquid but especially the living fluids of plant and animal bodies. Vapor is liquid involved with heat and air—matter in "the form of a steamy or imperceptible exhalation," an "emanation of imperceptible particles, usually due to the effect of heat upon moisture" (*OED*, 1 and 2a). Insofar as all life in Aristotelian biology involved the interactions of radical heat and moisture, a vapor was thus one of the basic physical activities of the humoral body and one way the human body expressed its likeness to elemental forms of atmospheric action. Vapors were part of the atmosphere within and without. Body and earth were alike in housing and producing vapors, good and bad, like the "vapor of a dungeon" that Othello would rather live upon

> than keep a corner in the thing I love
> For others' uses.

$$(3.3.271–73)$$

Many of the constituent elements of human bodies in the period are described as vapors: thus sleep was caused by vapors rising into the brain from the concoctions of the lower body; their release was fundamental to health. In *The Castel of Helth*, Elyot distinguishes among the consistencies of humors: "Of humors some are more grosse and colde, some are subtyle and hot, and are called vapours."[52] Here again we are reminded of the pneumatic character of early modern life in time, of the human body as a threshold for the passage of air, of human flesh as a sponge in the atmosphere. "For the matter of mans body," says Helkiah Crooke in 1615, "it is soft, pliable and temperate, readie to follow the Workeman in euery thing, and to euery purpose: for man is the moystest and most sanguine of all Creatures" (5). A 1623

---

52. Thomas Elyot, *The Castel of Helth* (London, 1541), 53r.

sermon of John Donne describes every man as "a spunge, and but a spunge filled with tears."[53]

Jonson's brilliance in *Bartholomew Fair* is first to establish the vapors as an idiosyncratic feature of one character's language—that is, as a part of verbal phenomenology, a word used to claim or prove individuality—and then to reify vapors theatrically in the redolent steam rising from the fair's central location, the booth where Ursula roasts her pigs and serves her ale. The transformation of pigs from animal to food to human self aligns with the fermentation of the ale to suggest the dynamism, causality, and endless transformability of the physical world and the human beings within it. In act 4 the vapors become the name of a word-and-drinking game structured around quarreling, created by an assortment of male characters including Wasp, the wrestler Puppy, Captain Whit, and Knockem's accomplice Val Cutting. (The latter is enjoined to keep the game going—we learn—in order to distract Wasp and eventually allow Edgworth to steal the marriage license that Wasp is guarding.) Language and stage properties come together to make vapors virtually a dramatic emblem—of physical appetite and reciprocity, of the metamorphosis of forms, of the human body as a threshold for the passage of air and other elements, and of language itself as an atmospheric social barometer.

I have written elsewhere of the conceptual force of the Bakhtinian grotesque body in *Bartholomew Fair*, especially as that grotesque body is exemplified in the play's leaky women, Win Littlewife and Mistress Overdo, who relieve themselves with an old bottle at the back of Ursula's booth.[54] Here I want to concentrate on the game of vapors as Jonson's emblematic representation, in this play, of male humorality in distilled form. As Jonson explains the game in a stage direction, the job of the game's players is "*to oppose the last man that spoke, whether it concern'd him or no*" (4.4.28 S.D.). The reason to call the game "vapors" has to do with Knockem's equation of humors and vapors—his reduction of vapors to moods (indeed to bad moods unless the word is otherwise modified). Thus when he asks Ursula for "a fresh bottle of ale, and a pipe of tobacco; and no vapours" (2.3.56–57), it is the power of her bad mood over himself and others that he fears. And it is to countervail her mood that he welcomes the arrival of Ezekiel Edgworth as bringing "a kind heart; and good vapours" (60–61). By act 4, when Jonson introduces the game of vapors, its most important player,

53. John Donne, *The Sermons of John Donne*, ed. George R. Potter and Evelyn M. Simpson, vol. 4 (Berkeley and Los Angeles: University of California Press, 1959), 337.

54. Paster, *Body Embarrassed*, 34–39.

Wasp, has been exhausted by a day spent wandering more or less aimlessly around the fair with Cokes's marriage license in a box. As Edgworth explains it to Quarlous and Winwife, "Yonder he is, your man with the box fall'n into the finest company, and so transported with vapours; they ha' got in a northern clothier, and one Puppy, a western man, that's come to wrestle before my Lord Mayor anon, and Captain Whit, and one Val Cutting, that helps Captain Jordan to roar, a circling boy: with whom your Numps is so taken, that you may strip him of his clothes, if you will. I'll undertake to geld him for you; if you had but a surgeon, ready, to sear him" (4.3.106–14). Wasp is transported by vapors—carried away by emotion—in several senses: he is transported by his own choleric vapors as one of the play's grumpiest characters, who, having spent the day looking for Cokes, is even grumpier than usual; and he is transported by the vaporish activity— human and gastronomic—that rises in the air around Ursula's booth. Finally, he is transported by the force of his new attraction to Val Cutting. It is the congregation of vapors—of physical steam, of quarreling language, of human moodiness—that reveals the production of emotion at the fair as a physical and social transaction between individuals rather than an experience within the body of the individual subject.[55] The fair itself, as an ephemeral occasion supported by its satisfaction of appetite and the release from the everyday that its customers seek, helps to underscore this definition of emotion. That is, both the fair's attention to appetite and its ephemerality align it with the humors and the passions that they breed. Here the humors and passions float free of their ordinary social contexts, especially in the game of vapors, where the participants have only just come together at the booth as strangers. Within that context, the game of vapors considers biological life functions to be both fundamentally pneumatic and fundamentally oppositional in nature, occurring in the public space of the air as the site and instrumentation of noise. The vapors are a language game structured around contradiction, produced through the warming stimulation of drink and the exhalation of air. As a symbol for embodied emotions, the game changes constantly yet predictably. Most important, perhaps, the nature of the vapors game goes unrecognized by all the participants. In order to participate in the game at all, each man must take turns, cooperate, and perhaps above all listen to one another; ordinary conversational deference and accommodation strategies may be stretched here almost beyond recognition, yet the structure of the game insists on

---

55. As M. L. Lyon and J. M. Barbalet point out, "emotion is not only embodied but also essentially social in character" (57).

contradiction as an intimately homosocial act, even among strangers. The result is a paradoxical set of speech acts—an improvised agreement to engage in contradiction—as the result:

> KNO. To what do you say nay, sir?
> WASP. To anything, whatsoever it is, so long as I do not like it.
> . . . .
> WHIT. Pardon me, little man, dou musht like it a little.
> CUT. No, he must not like it at all, sir; there you are i'the wrong.
>
> (4.4.28–32)

With its physical backdrop of the steam arising from Ursula's pig booth, which has its own fundamental concoctions of pig flesh, this occasion for playing a game of vapors shows emotionally embodied life as a difficult, fluid, but rule-bound form of play with opposition itself as its event, structure, and goal. It is also fundamentally an instrumentalization of air, with the thresholds of the players' bodies continually crossed and recrossed as characters take in the air (and sounds) of each other's contradictions, saying yea or nay in turn, and respond with their own. Yet the game holds its participants in social and emotional bonds as they negotiate the limits of their desire to disagree with one another as an expression of social form and improvisatory rule-making. As the one who declares the utter incommensurability of his appetites and his reasons, Wasp is probably the essential exponent of the game: "I have no reason, nor I will hear of no reason, nor I will look for no reason, and he is an ass that either knows any, or looks for't from me" (38–40). But in the metamorphic logic of the vapors, no position—even a confession such as "I have no sense" (45)—may long obtain. No sooner does Wasp relent on the question of whether or not he makes sense than the "vapor" of relenting is itself made the subject of debate— whether it is sufficient or not, sweet or stinking, and whether or not Wasp gives his vapor permission to stink. (Parsing nonsense is as risky as nonsense itself.) Wasp's final paradoxical position—a Cretan liar's declaration that he was "not i' the right, nor never was i' the right, nor never will be i' the right" (66–68)—is itself met by a paradoxical debate on whether or not anyone in the group is listening to what Wasp says.

The game's potential—the potential of language itself—to extend itself indefinitely as dialogic opposition is resolved by Quarlous and Winwife's desire to use Edgworth to steal the marriage license out of the box. But Quarlous's definition of the vapors as a "belching of quarrel" expresses the nature of vapors—and the humors they stand in for—exactly. As Quarlous seems almost to recognize in watching the spectacle of strangers listening intently to one another only for the purposes of contradiction, a quarrel belched is the physical product of drink and the social product of urban fair-going. It is an instrumentalization of air that is both humoral self-expression and physiological event, both language and sound, both mental intention and bodily eruption. It signals control and loss of control, aggression and release.

At such moments and in such phrases, Jonson invokes humorality, much as Shakespeare does, in order to represent the body and its products—even its affective products—as the endlessly renewable raw materials of social signification. Feeding one's humor, declaring one's humorality or lack of humorality, is, as we have seen, a complex social performance that relies upon the stern facts of bodily obduracy for its rhetorical persuasiveness and material power. But, as Shylock and others discover, humoral strategies do not always carry the day in a contest between bodily obduracy and the social hierarchy. To be in one's humor or out of it is not always in a man's power to decide.

EPILOGUE

The classical doctrine of the four humors gave playwrights—Shakespeare included—a theory of personality, behavior, status, gender, age, and ethnicity that had the distinct advantage of being rooted in what they believed to be indisputable facts about the human body and its relation to the natural world. At every moment in the course of a day, a month, a season, or a lifetime, these humors and the qualities residing in them were thought to calibrate a body's internal heat and moisture—what the Elizabethans called its temper or complexion. As one of the six Galenic nonnaturals that made up an individual subject's specific physical environment, the passions served as a powerful, if broad, focus for thinking about the relations between inside and outside, between bodily interiority and the phenomenal object world, between self and other even when the other is a servant, a woman, or a cat.

That we identify these emotions as identical to our own, though often expressed in an estranging discourse, speaks in part to the long dominance of psychological materialism and the historically specific bodily contents that it presupposed. Sutton, summarizing the consensus of medical historians on this point, argues: "only relatively recently medical theory's picture of the human body and its operations changed into that of a static, solid container, only rarely breached, in principle autonomous from culture and environment, tampered with only by diseases and experts."[1] Owsei Temkin

1. Sutton, *Philosophy and Memory Traces*, 41.

claims that the Galenic system with its six nonnaturals, animal spirits, and theory of temperaments, though subject to continuous adaptation and reinterpretation, "provided a medically useful classification of man, and a somatic theory of human behavior" that lasted into the nineteenth century (181). But the clear recognizability of the affects in early modern play texts speaks in part, as well, to the fact that certain basic emotions—love, hate, fear, anger, and sadness, for example—are broadly recognizable across wide distances of time and culture. This book has situated itself within the interstices between a historically specific early modern language of affect and theory of the body, on one hand, and a transhistorical register of emotional experience on the other. What I have advocated most strongly is that we recognize the literalism of early modern descriptions of the bodily events attendant upon emotional experience as a way of grasping or glimpsing early modern habits of bodily sensation and emotional experience. We do not believe in a somatic repertory composed of animal spirits, four humors, and temperaments measurable on axes of cold/hot, moist/dry. It is thus our tendency as modern readers, strongly influenced (as Taylor argues) by dualistic habits of thought, to read the discourse of psychophysiology as metaphorical. But modern discourses of the body continue to be pervaded by residues of the earlier psychophysiological lexicon—locutions such as high- or low-spiritedness, for example. "High" or "low" measured in relation to what bodily or affective center? we might ask. Spirits could be thought of as both quantifiable—produced in greater or lesser quantities by bodily concoction—and flocking in their numbers now to one part of the body and now to another. The register of high and low measured the numbers and kinds of bodily spirits as well as their location. And even subtler possibilities of measurement, as we saw, revolved around a social hierarchy of the spirits—with low spirits belonging properly to those lower down on the social scale.

I have argued generally for the importance of recognizing that Shakespeare's dramatic narratives of passion take place in an imagined physical and psychological environment epistemically prior to post-Enlightenment dualism. It is difficult for us to achieve such recognition, because we approach the plays, inevitably, with the mental and lexical habits that we have inherited from that dualism and are only now—thanks to the intellectual advent of cognitive science—beginning to discredit. To discard our deepest categories of thought almost as if they never were is especially difficult with the emotions because so much of the language of emotion from the early modern period has remained constant, even though what is imagined to happen in a body gripped by passion has radically changed over time as early modern versions of Galenism have been replaced by modern medicine and psychology. Because many important emotions are both transhistorical and transcultural, we can readily understand what characters mean to express even though the specifically bodily character of an early modern emotion—and the relation to the world an emotion is imagined to have—remains opaque and historically distant.[2] Furthermore, even though cognitive science and psychopharmacology are encouraging us to relinquish our belief in such dualisms as mind and body, reason and passion, our language of self-reference and of emotion is relentlessly dualistic. We remain locked in a puzzle of lexical self-contradiction about these fundamental issues, even if we do not experience this self-contradiction as anything but the ordinary workings of semantic variation and overlap, the ordinary excesses of the signifying chain.

I am not suggesting that Shakespeare and his contemporaries do not distinguish in their own terms between the brain and the mind or between physical and mental disease. Nor am I suggesting that dualistic habits of thought were unknown to the early moderns, preoccupied as they were with the relations of soul and body, reason and passion, spirit and flesh. But I am suggesting that much modern criticism—even criticism ostensibly founded on materialist premises—still tends to disembody human psychology thanks to what Elizabeth Hart and Mary Thomas Crane have called "foundational formalism" inherited from Saussure and Derrida.[3] And such forms of critical disembodiment entail a profound underestimation of the materialism so dominant in early modern discourses of soul and body and a misunderstanding of the bodily ecology of the passions of the soul in early modern thought.[4] The overriding consequence of such disembodiment is to flatten the emotional contours of early modern subjectivity for the sake of a self-same human subject that displaces the porous, penetrable, and above all labile subject of early modern humoralism. Such disembodiment removes the forcefulness of the humoral emotions—and the struggle for control over them—that are so powerfully recorded in the play texts that I have discussed in this book.

2. This is certainly the conclusion one derives from reading social anthropologists such as Anna Wierzbicka; see her book *Emotions across Languages and Cultures: Diversity and Universals* (Cambridge: Cambridge University Press, 1999), 273-307.

3. Crane, 4; see also F. Elizabeth Hart, "Matter, System, and Early Modern Studies: Outlines for a Materialist Linguistics," *Configurations* 6 (1998): 311-43.

4. See John Henry, "The Matter of Souls: Medical Theory and Theology in Seventeenth-Century England," in *The Medical Revolution of the Seventeenth Century*, ed. Roger French and Andrew Wear (Cambridge: Cambridge University Press, 1989), 87-113.

In the animated early modern cosmology, with its scale of ensoulment from sponges to people, it is entirely natural to read the constituent elements of the human body and the natural world as a divinely endowed set of mutually expressive signs.[5] The human body, though set apart by the existence of the rational soul, is nevertheless joined indissolubly to the rest of ensouled nature on the universal continuum and shares all of its passions with the animals stationed just below. Descartes succeeds in disturbing this continuum and beginning its slow demise when he denies the existence of the vegetable and sensitive souls in favor of a unitary soul and reduces the body's three kinds of spirits to only one—the animal spirits. At the same time, he begins the gradual epistemic process toward abstraction that overtakes early modern discourses of body and mind.[6] But as readers we must resist such abstraction because the vital continuum of ensoulment still exists for Shakespeare's characters and constrains us to think differently about how their passions are embodied and what embodiment means in a pre-Cartesian physical world.

5. See John Cottingham, "Cartesian Dualism: Theology, Metaphysics, and Science," in *The Cambridge Companion to Descartes*, ed. John Cottingham (Cambridge: Cambridge University Press, 1992), 238-39.

6. The result is what Cartesian scholars have called "interactionist dualism." For a persuasive account, see Theodore Brown, 1:47-49; and Gary Hatfield, "Descartes' Physiology and Its Relation to His Psychology," in *Cambridge Companion to Descartes*, 343-50.

BIBLIOGRAPHY

PRIMARY WORKS

Aristotle. *Historia animalium*. In *The Complete Works of Aristotle: The Revised Oxford Translation*, edited by Jonathan Barnes. Princeton, NJ: Princeton University Press, 1984.

Aubrey, John. *Aubrey's Brief Lives*. Edited by Oliver Lawson Dick. London: Secker and Warburg, 1949.

Bacon, Francis. *The Advancement of Learning and New Atlantis*. Edited by Arthur Johnston. Oxford: Clarendon Press, 1974.

———. "The Charge Touching Duelling." In *Francis Bacon: Selections*, edited by Brian Vickers. Oxford: Oxford University Press, 1996.

———. *Sylva Sylvarum; or, A Naturall Historie in Ten Centuries*. London, 1626.

———. *Works*. Edited by James Spedding, Robert Leslie Ellis, and Douglas Denon Heath. 7 vols. London: Longmans, 1857–74.

Bodin, Jean. *Universae naturae theatrum*. Frankfurt, 1597.

Bright, Timothy. *A Treatise of Melancholie*. London, 1586.

Burton, Robert. *The Anatomy of Melancholy*. Edited by Thomas C. Faulkner, Nicolas K. Kiessling, and Rhonda L. Blair. 6 vols. Oxford: Clarendon Press, 1989–2000.

Certain Sermons or Homilies (1547) and A Homily against Disobedience and Wilful Rebellion (1570): A Critical Edition. Edited by Ronald B. Bond. Toronto: University of Toronto Press, 1987.

Coeffeteau, Nicolas. *A Table of Humane Passions*. Translated by Edward Grimeston. London, 1621.

Congreve, William. *William Congreve: Letters and Documents*. Edited by John C. Hodges. New York: Harcourt, Brace, 1964.

Crooke, Helkiah. *Microcosmographia; or, A Description of the Body of Man*. London, 1615.

Dekker, Thomas. *The Gull's Hornbook*. In *Thomas Dekker*, edited by E. D. Pendry. Cambridge, MA: Harvard University Press, 1968.

———. *News from Graves-End*. London, 1604.

Descartes, René. "Treatise on Man." In *The Philosophical Writings of Descartes*, translated by John Cottingham, Robert Stoothoff, and Dugald Murdoch. Cambridge: Cambridge University Press, 1985.

A Dictionary of the Proverbs in England in the Sixteenth and Seventeenth Centuries. Edited by Morris Palmer Tilley. Ann Arbor: University of Michigan Press, 1950.

Donne, John. *The Sermons of John Donne*. Edited by George R. Potter and Evelyn M. Simpson. Vol. 4. Berkeley and Los Angeles: University of California Press, 1959.

du Bartas, Guillaume de Salluste. *The Divine Weeks and Works, translated by Joshua Sylvester.* Edited by Susan Snyder. Vol. 1. Oxford: Clarendon Press, 1979.

Elyot, Thomas. *The Castel of Helth*. London, 1541.

Ferrand, Jacques. *A Treatise on Lovesickness*. Translated by Donald A. Beecher and Massimo Ciavolella. Syracuse, NY: Syracuse University Press, 1990.

Ficino, Marsilio. *Three Books on Life*. Edited and translated by Carol V. Kaske and John R. Clark. Binghamton, NY: Medieval and Renaissance Text Society, 1989.

Galen. *On the Usefulness of the Parts of the Body*. Translated by Margaret Tallmadge May. 2 vols. Ithaca, NY: Cornell University Press, 1968.

Garzoni, Tommaso. *The Hospitall of Incurable Fooles*. London, 1600.

[Gelli, Giovan Battista]. *The Circe*. Translated by Thomas Brown (1702). Edited by Robert M. Adams. Rev. ed. Ithaca, NY: Cornell University Press, 1963.

———. *Circes of Iohn Baptista Gello*. Translated by Henry Iden. London, 1557.

[Gerardus]. *True Tryall and Examination of Mans Owne Selfe*. Translated by Thomas Newton. London, 1602.

Guazzo, Stefano. *The Civile Conversation of M. Steeven Guazzo*. Translated by George Pettie. London, 1581.

Hall, Joseph. *Meditations and Vows: Divine and Moral*. Edited by Charles Sayle. London: Grant Richards, 1901.

Harington, John. *A New Discourse of a Stale Subject, Called the Metamorphosis of Ajax*. Edited by Elizabeth Story Donno. New York: Columbia University Press, 1962.

Jest upon Jest: A Selection from the Jestbooks and Collections of Merry Tales Published from the Reign of Richard III to George III. Edited by Bruce R. Wardroper. London: Routledge and Kegan Paul, 1970.

Jonson, Ben. *The Alchemist*. Edited by F. H. Mares. The Revels Plays. Cambridge, MA: Harvard University Press, 1967.

———. *Bartholomew Fair*. Edited by E. A. Horsman. The Revels Plays. Manchester: Manchester University Press, 1960.

———. *Ben Jonson*. Edited by C. H. Herford and Percy Simpson. 12 vols. Oxford: Clarendon Press, 1925–52.

———. *Every Man in His Humour*. Edited by Robert S. Miola. The Revels Plays. Manchester: Manchester University Press, 2000.

———. *Every Man in His Humour*. In *The Complete Plays of Ben Jonson*, edited by G. A. Wilkes, vol. 1. Oxford: Clarendon Press, 1981.

———. *Every Man out of His Humour*. In *The Complete Plays of Ben Jonson*, edited by G. A. Wilkes, vol. 1. Oxford: Clarendon Press, 1981.

———. *Sejanus*. In *The Complete Plays of Ben Jonson*, edited by G. A. Wilkes, vol. 2. Oxford: Clarendon Press, 1981.

Lange, Johann. "Epistola XXI: De morbo virgineo." In *Medicinalium epistolarum miscellanea.* Basle: J. Operinus, 1554. Reprinted in *Classic Descriptions of Disease,* edited by Ralph H. Major. Springfield, IL: Charles C. Thomas, 1932.

———. *Epistolarum medicinalium.* Frankfurt: Andreas Wechel, 1589.

Lemnius, Levinus. *The Touchstone of Complexions.* London, 1581.

Lupton, Thomas. *A Thousand Notable Things.* London, 1579.

Madden, D. H. *The Diary of Master William Silence.* London: Longmans, Green, 1907.

Markham, Gervase. *Cavelarice; or, The English Horseman.* London, 1607.

Marlowe, Christopher. *The Jew of Malta.* Edited by N. W. Bawcutt. The Revels Plays. Manchester: Manchester University Press, 1978.

Middleton, Thomas. *A Chaste Maid in Cheapside.* Edited by R. B. Parker. The Revels Plays. London: Methuen, 1969.

Moffett, Thomas. *Health's Improvement.* London, 1655.

Montaigne, Michel de. *The Apology for Raymond Sebond.* In *The Complete Essays,* edited and translated by Donald M. Frame. Stanford, CA: Stanford University Press, 1958.

Nashe, Thomas. *The Unfortunate Traveller and Other Works,* edited by J. B. Steane. Harmondsworth, UK: Penguin Books, 1971.

———. *A Wonderfull . . . Prognostication.* In *The Complete Works of Thomas Nashe,* ed. Alexander B. Grosart, 2:143–52. London: Huth Library, 1883.

Oxford Dictionary of English Proverbs. Edited by F. P. Wilson. 3rd ed. Oxford: Clarendon Press, 1970.

Peacham, Henry. *Minerva Britanna.* London, 1612.

Plater, Felix, Abdiah Cole, and Nicholas Culpeper. *A Golden Practice of Physick.* London: Peter Cole, 1622.

Plutarch. "The Life of Marcus Antonius." In *Plutarch's Lives of the Noble Grecians and Romans,* translated by Thomas North (1579). Reprinted in *Narrative and Dramatic Sources of Shakespeare,* edited by Geoffrey Bullough, vol. 5. London: Routledge and Kegan Paul, 1964.

———. *The Philosophie, Commonlie Called the Morals . . . of Plutarch.* Translated by Philemon Holland. London, 1603.

The Problems of Aristotle. London, 1597.

Raleigh, Walter. *Skeptick, or Speculations.* London, 1651.

Reynolds, Edward. *A Treatise of the Passions and Faculties of the Soule of Man.* Edited by Margaret Lee Wiley. Gainesville, FL: Scholars' Facsimiles and Reprints, 1971.

Saviolo, Vincentio. *His Practice: In Two Books.* In *Three Elizabethan Fencing Manuals,* edited by James L. Jackson. London, 1595. Reprint, Delmar, NY: Scholars' Facsimiles and Reprints, 1972.

Selden, John. *Titles of Honor.* London, 1614.

"Selections from *Scogin's Jests.*" In *A Nest of Ninnies and Other English Jestbooks of the Seventeenth Century,* edited by P. M. Zall. Lincoln: University of Nebraska Press, 1970.

Shakespeare, William. *Hamlet.* Edited by G. R. Hibbard. Oxford: Clarendon Press, 1987.

———. *I Henry IV.* Edited by Judith Weil and Herbert Weil. New Cambridge. Cambridge: Cambridge University Press, 1997.

———. *Henry IV, Part I.* Edited by David Bevington. Oxford: Clarendon Press, 1987.

———. *Othello.* Edited by Norman Sanders. Cambridge: Cambridge University Press, 1984.

———. *The Riverside Shakespeare*. Edited by G. Blakemore Evans et al. 2nd ed. Boston: Houghton Mifflin, 1997.

Shepard, Thomas. *The Sincere Convert*. In vol. 1 of *The Works of Thomas Shepard*, 3 vols. Boston: Doctrinal and Tract Society, 1853. Reprint, New York: AMS, 1967.

Sidney, Philip. *The Countess of Pembroke's Arcadia (The Old Arcadia)*. Edited by Katherine Duncan-Jones. Oxford: Oxford University Press, 1985.

———. *The Defence of Poesy*. In *Sir Philip Sidney*, edited by Katherine Duncan-Jones. Oxford: Oxford University Press, 1989.

Spenser, Edmund. *The Faerie Queene*. Edited by Thomas P. Roche. New York: Penguin Books, 1978.

Stow, John. *The Survey of London*. With introduction and notes by Charles Lethbridge Kingsford. 2 vols. 1908. Reprint, Oxford: Clarendon Press, 1971.

Sydenham, Thomas. *The Entire Works of Dr. Thomas Sydenham*. Ed. John Swan. London, 1742.

Taylor, John. *Bull, Beare, and Horse*. In *Works of John Taylor, the Water Poet, Not Included in the Folio Volume of 1630. Third Collection*. London: Spenser Society, 1876. Reprint, New York: Burt Franklin, 1967.

Topsell, Edward. *The Historie of Foure-Footed Beastes*. London: William Jaggard, 1607.

———. *The Historie of Serpents*. London: Isaac Jaggard, 1608.

Vaughan, William. *Approved Directions for Health, Both Naturall and Artificiall*. London: T. S. for Roger Jackson, 1612.

Walkington, Thomas. *The Optick Glasse of Humors*. London, 1631. Reprint, edited by John A. Popplestone and Marion White McPherson, Delmar, NY: Scholars' Facsimiles and Reprints, 1981.

Webster, John. *The Duchess of Malfi*. Edited by John Russell Brown. The Revels Plays. Manchester: Manchester University Press, 1997.

Willis, Thomas. *Two Discourses concerning the Soul of Brutes*. Translated by S. Pordage. 1683. Reprint, with an introduction by Solomon Diamond, Gainesville, FL: Scholars' Facsimiles and Reprints, 1971.

Wilson, Thomas. *The Arte of Rhetorique*. Edited by Thomas J. Derrick. 1553. Reprint, New York: Garland, 1982.

Wright, Thomas. *The Passions of the Minde in Generall*. 1604. Reprint, edited and with an introduction by Thomas O. Sloan, Urbana: University of Illinois Press, 1971.

———. *The Passions of the Mind in General*. 1604. Reprint, edited by William Webster Newbold, New York: Garland, 1986.

SECONDARY WORKS

Adelman, Janet. "Making Defect Perfection: Shakespeare and the One-Sex Model." In *Enacting Gender on the English Renaissance Stage*, edited by Viviana Comensoli and Anne Russell. Urbana: University of Illinois Press, 1998.

———. *Suffocating Mothers: Fantasies of Maternal Origin in Shakespeare's Plays, "Hamlet" to "The Tempest."* London: Routledge, 1992.

Ashworth, William B. "Natural History and the Emblematic World-View." In *Reappraisals of the Scientific Revolution*, edited by David C. Lindberg and Robert S. Westman. Cambridge: Cambridge University Press, 1990.

Ayers, P. K. "Dreams of the City: The Urban and the Urbane in Jonson's *Epicoene*." *Philological Quarterly* 66 (1987): 73–86.

Babb, Lawrence. *The Elizabethan Malady: A Study of Melancholia in English Literature from 1580 to 1642*. East Lansing: Michigan State College Press, 1951.

Bamborough, J. B. *The Little World of Man*. London: Longmans, Green, 1952.

Barber, C. L. *Shakespeare's Festive Comedy: A Study in Dramatic Form and Its Relation to Social Custom*. Princeton, NJ: Princeton University Press, 1959.

Barkan, Leonard. *Nature's Work of Art: The Human Body as Image of the World*. New Haven, CT: Yale University Press, 1975.

Barthes, Roland. "Listening." In *The Responsibility of Forms*, translated by Richard Howard. Berkeley and Los Angeles: University of California Press, 1985.

Beier, Lucinda McCray. "In Sickness and in Health: A Seventeenth-Century Family's Experience." In *Patients and Practitioners: Lay Perceptions of Medicine in Pre-Industrial Society*, edited by Roy Porter. Cambridge: Cambridge University Press, 1985.

Berger, Harry, Jr. "Impertinent Trifling: Desdemona's Handkerchief." *Shakespeare Quarterly* 47 (1996): 235–50.

———. "The Prince's Dog: Falstaff and the Perils of Speech-Prefixity." *Shakespeare Quarterly* 49 (1998): 40–73.

Blair, Ann. *The Theater of Nature: Jean Bodin and Renaissance Science*. Princeton, NJ: Princeton University Press, 1997.

Boerher, Bruce. *Shakespeare among the Animals: Nature and Society in the Drama of Early Modern England*. London: Palgrave, 2002.

Bono, James J. *The Word of God and the Languages of Man: Interpreting Nature in Early Modern Science and Medicine*. Vol. 1, *Ficino to Descartes*. Madison: University of Wisconsin Press, 1995.

Boose, Lynda. "The Father's House and the Daughter in It: The Structure of Western Culture's Daughter-Father Relationship." In *Daughters and Fathers*, edited by Lynda E. Boose and Betty S. Flowers. Baltimore: Johns Hopkins University Press, 1989.

Breitenberg, Mark. *Anxious Masculinity in Early Modern England*. Cambridge: Cambridge University Press, 1996.

Brown, Roger, and Albert Gilman. "The Pronouns of Power and Solidarity." In *Style in Language*, edited by Thomas E. Sebeok. Cambridge, MA: MIT Press, 1960.

Brown, Theodore M. "Descartes, Dualism, and Psychosomatic Medicine." In *The Anatomy of Madness: Essays in the History of Psychiatry*, vol. 1, *People and Ideas*, edited by W. F. Bynum, R. Porter, and M. Shepherd. London: Tavistock, 1985.

Bruster, Douglas. *Drama and the Market in the Age of Shakespeare*. Cambridge: Cambridge University Press, 1992.

Bryson, Anna. *From Courtesy to Civility: Changing Codes of Conduct in Early Modern England*. Oxford: Clarendon Press, 1998.

Butler, Judith. *Bodies That Matter: On the Discursive Limits of Sex*. New York: Routledge, 1993.

Cefalu, Paul A. "'Damnèd Custom . . . Habits Devil': Shakespeare's *Hamlet*, Anti-Dualism, and the Early Modern Philosophy of Mind." *ELH* 67 (2000): 399–431.

Charnes, Linda. *Notorious Identity: Materializing the Subject in Shakespeare*. Cambridge, MA: Harvard University Press, 1993.

Chartier, Roger. "Social Figuration and Habitus: Reading Elias." In *Cultural History: Between Practices and Representations*, translated by Lydia G. Cochrane. Ithaca, NY: Cornell University Press, 1988.

Clark, Andy. *Being There: Putting Brain, Body, and World Together Again.* Cambridge, MA: MIT Press, 1997.

Clark, Stuart. *Thinking with Demons: The Idea of Witchcraft in Early Modern Europe.* Oxford: Clarendon Press, 1997.

Cohen, Jeffrey Jerome. *Medieval Identity Machines.* Minneapolis: University of Minnesota Press, 2003.

Corbin, Alain. *The Foul and the Fragrant: Odor and the French Social Imagination.* Cambridge, MA: Harvard University Press, 1986.

Correll, Barbara. *The End of Conduct: "Grobianus" and the Renaissance Text of the Subject.* Ithaca, NY: Cornell University Press, 1996.

Cottingham, John. "Cartesian Dualism: Theology, Metaphysics, and Science." In *The Cambridge Companion to Descartes,* edited by John Cottingham. Cambridge: Cambridge University Press, 1992.

Crane, Mary Thomas. *Shakespeare's Brain: Reading with Cognitive Theory.* Princeton, NJ: Princeton University Press, 2001.

Damasio, Antonio. *The Feeling of What Happens: Body and Emotion in the Making of Consciousness.* New York: Harcourt Brace, 1999.

Daston, Lorraine, and Katharine Park. *Wonders and the Order of Nature, 1150–1750.* New York: Zone Books, 1998.

de Grazia, Margreta. "The Scandal of Shakespeare's Sonnets." *Shakespeare Survey* 46 (1994): 35–49.

Deleuze, Gilles, and Félix Guattari. *A Thousand Plateaus: Capitalism and Schizophrenia.* Translated by Brian Massumi. Minneapolis: University of Minnesota Press, 1987.

Dessen, Alan C., and Leslie Thomson. *A Dictionary of Stage Directions in English Drama, 1580–1642.* Cambridge: Cambridge University Press, 1999.

Dickey, Stephen. "Shakespeare's Mastiff Comedy." *Shakespeare Quarterly* 42 (1991): 255–75.

DiGangi, Mario. "Queering the Shakespearean Family." *Shakespeare Quarterly* 47 (1996): 269–90.

Dixon, Laurinda. *Perilous Chastity: Women and Illness in Pre-Enlightenment Art and Medicine.* Ithaca, NY: Cornell University Press, 1995.

Doebler, John. "*Venus and Adonis*: Shakespeare's Horses." In *Images of Shakespeare: Proceedings of the Third Congress of the International Shakespeare Association, 1986,* edited by Werner Habicht, D. J. Palmer, and Roger Pringle. Newark: University of Delaware Press, 1988.

Dolan, Frances E., ed. *"The Taming of the Shrew": Texts and Contexts.* Boston: Bedford Books, 1996.

Douglas, Mary. *Purity and Danger: An Analysis of the Concepts of Pollution and Taboo.* 1966. Reprint, London: Ark, 1984.

Drakakis, John. "The Engendering of Toads: Patriarchy and the Problem of Subjectivity in Shakespeare's *Othello*." *Shakespeare-Jahrbuch* (Weimar) 124 (1988): 62–80.

Dunton-Downer, Leslie. "Wolf Man." In *Becoming Male in the Middle Ages,* edited by Jeffrey Jerome Cohen and Bonnie Wheeler. New York: Garland, 1997.

Ekman, Paul. "Biological and Cultural Contributions to Body and Facial Movement in the Expression of Emotions." In *Explaining Emotions,* edited by Amélie Oksenberg Rorty. Berkeley and Los Angeles: University of California Press, 1980.

Elam, Keir. "The Fertile Eunuch: *Twelfth Night,* Early Modern Intercourse, and the Fruits of Castration." *Shakespeare Quarterly* 47 (1996): 1–36.

———. *Shakespeare's Universe of Discourse: Language-Games in the Comedies.* Cambridge: Cambridge University Press, 1984.

Elias, Norbert. *The History of Manners.* Vol. 1 of *The Civilizing Process.* Translated by Edmund Jephcott. New York: Pantheon Books, 1978.

Enterline, Lynn. *The Tears of Narcissus: Melancholia and Masculinity in Early Modern Writing.* Stanford, CA: Stanford University Press, 1995.

Erickson, Robert A. *The Language of the Heart, 1600–1750.* Philadelphia: University of Pennsylvania Press, 1997.

Filipczak, Zirka Z. *Hot Dry Men Cold Wet Women: The Theory of Humors in Western European Art, 1575–1700.* New York: American Federation of Arts, 1997.

Fineman, Joel. "The Sound of *O* in *Othello*: The Real of the Tragedy of Desire." In *The Subjectivity Effect in Western Literary Tradition: Essays toward the Release of Shakespeare's Will.* Cambridge, MA: MIT Press, 1991.

Floyd-Wilson, Mary. *English Ethnicity and Race in Early Modern Drama.* Cambridge: Cambridge University Press, 2003.

Foucault, Michel. *The Order of Things: An Archaeology of the Human Sciences.* New York: Pantheon Books, 1971.

Fudge, Erica. *Perceiving Animals: Human and Beasts in Early Modern English Culture.* London: Macmillan; New York: St. Martin's, 2000.

Fumerton, Patricia. "Introduction: A New Historicism." In *Renaissance Culture and the Everyday,* edited by Patricia Fumerton and Simon Hunt. Philadelphia: University of Pennsylvania Press, 1999.

Gil, Daniel Juan. "At the Limits of the Social World: Fear and Pride in *Troilus and Cressida.*" *Shakespeare Quarterly* 52 (2001): 336–59.

Goldberg, Jonathan. "Textual Properties." *Shakespeare Quarterly* 37 (1986): 213–17.

Greenblatt, Stephen. "Fiction and Friction." In *Shakespearean Negotiations: The Circulation of Social Energy in Renaissance England.* Berkeley and Los Angeles: University of California Press, 1988.

———. "Invisible Bullets." In *Shakespearean Negotiations: The Circulation of Social Energy in Renaissance England.* Berkeley and Los Angeles: University of California Press, 1988.

Griffiths, Paul E. *What Emotions Really Are: The Problem of Psychological Categories.* Chicago: University of Chicago Press, 1997.

Grosz, Elizabeth. *Space, Time, and Perversion: Essays on the Politics of Bodies.* New York: Routledge, 1995.

Harris, Jonathan Gil. "This Is Not a Pipe: Water Supply, Incontinent Sources, and the Leaky Body Politic." In *Enclosure Acts: Sexuality, Property, and Culture in Early Modern England,* edited by Richard Burt and John Michael Archer. Ithaca, NY: Cornell University Press, 1994.

Hart, F. Elizabeth. "Matter, System, and Early Modern Studies: Outline for a Materialist Linguistics." *Configurations* 6 (1998): 311–43.

Hatfield, Gary. "Descartes' Physiology and Its Relation to His Psychology." In *The Cambridge Companion to Descartes,* edited by John Cottingham. Cambridge: Cambridge University Press, 1992.

Haynes, Jonathan. *The Social Relations of Jonson's Theater*. Cambridge: Cambridge University Press, 1992.

Henry, John. "The Matter of Souls: Medical Theory and Theology in Seventeenth-Century England." In *The Medical Revolution of the Seventeenth-Century*, edited by Roger French and Andrew Wear. Cambridge: Cambridge University Press, 1989.

Hillman, David. "Visceral Knowledge: Shakespeare, Skepticism, and the Interior of the Early Modern Body." In *The Body in Parts: Fantasies of Corporality in Early Modern Europe*, edited by David Hillman and Carla Mazzio. London: Routledge, 1997.

Howard, Jean. "Crossdressing, the Theater, and Gender Struggle in Early Modern England." *Shakespeare Quarterly* 39 (1988): 418–40.

———. "Scripts and/versus Playhouses: Ideological Production and the Renaissance Public Stage." *Renaissance Drama*, n.s., 20 (1989): 31–49.

Hutson, Lorna. "Civility and Virility in Ben Jonson." *Representations* 78 (2002): 1–27.

Ingold, Tim. Introduction to *What Is an Animal?* edited by Tim Ingold. London: Unwin Hyman, 1988.

Jackson, Stanley W. *Melancholia and Depression: From Hippocratic Times to Modern Times*. New Haven, CT: Yale University Press, 1986.

James, Heather. *Shakespeare's Troy: Drama, Politics, and the Translation of Empire*. Cambridge: Cambridge University Press, 1997.

James, Mervyn. *English Politics and the Concept of Honour, 1485–1642*. Oxford: Past and Present Society, 1978.

James, Susan. *Passion and Action: The Emotions in Seventeenth-Century Philosophy*. Cambridge: Cambridge University Press, 1997.

Jankowski, Theodora A. *Pure Resistance: Queer Virginity in Early Modern English Drama*. Philadelphia: University of Pennsylvania Press, 2000.

Keele, Kenneth D. "Physiology." In *Medicine in Seventeenth Century England*, edited by Allen G. Debus. Berkeley and Los Angeles: University of California Press, 1974.

King, Helen. *Hippocrates' Woman: Reading the Female Body in Ancient Greece*. London: Routledge, 1998.

King, Lester S. "The Transformation of Galenism." In *Medicine in Seventeenth Century England*, edited by Allen G. Debus. Berkeley and Los Angeles: University of California Press, 1974.

Klibansky, Raymond, Erwin Panofsky, and Fritz Saxl. *Saturn and Melancholy: Studies in the History of Natural Philosophy, Religion, and Art*. London: Thomas Nelson, 1964.

Korda, Natasha. *Shakespeare's Domestic Economies: Gender and Property in Early Modern England*. Philadelphia: University of Pennsylvania Press, 2002.

Kuriyama, Shigehisa. *The Expressiveness of the Body and the Divergence of Greek and Chinese Medicine*. New York: Zone, 1999.

Lanham, Richard. *Motives of Eloquence: Literary Rhetoric in the Renaissance*. New Haven, CT: Yale University Press, 1976.

Laqueur, Thomas. *Making Sex: Body and Gender from the Greeks to Freud*. Cambridge, MA: Harvard University Press, 1990.

LeDoux, Joseph. *The Emotional Brain: The Mysterious Underpinnings of Emotional Life*. New York: Simon and Schuster, 1996.

Lefebvre, Henri. *The Production of Space*. Translated by Donald Nicholson-Smith. Oxford: Blackwell, 1991.

Lloyd, G. E. R. *Science, Folklore, and Ideology: Studies in the Life Sciences in Ancient Greece.* Cambridge: Cambridge University Press, 1983.

Lukacher, Ned. *Daemonic Figures: Shakespeare and the Question of Conscience.* Ithaca, NY: Cornell University Press, 1994.

Lyon, M. L., and J. M. Barbalet. "Society's Body: Emotion and the 'Somatization' of Social Theory." In *Embodiment and Experience: The Existential Ground of Culture and Self,* edited by Thomas J. Csordas. Cambridge: Cambridge University Press, 1994.

Maclean, Ian. *Logic, Signs, and Nature in the Renaissance: The Case of Learned Medicine.* Cambridge: Cambridge University Press, 2002.

———. *Renaissance Nature of Women: A Study in the Fortunes of Scholasticism and Medical Science in European Intellectual Life.* Cambridge: Cambridge University Press, 1980.

Mallin, Eric. *Inscribing the Time: Shakespeare and the End of Elizabethan England.* Berkeley and Los Angeles: University of California Press, 1995.

Marshall, Cynthia. *The Shattering of the Self: Violence, Subjectivity, and Early Modern Texts.* Baltimore: Johns Hopkins University Press, 2002.

Masten, Jeffrey. *Textual Intercourse: Collaboration, Authorship, and Sexualities in Renaissance Drama.* Cambridge: Cambridge University Press, 1997.

Maus, Katharine Eisaman. *Inwardness and Theater in the English Renaissance.* Chicago: University of Chicago Press, 1995.

Mazzeo, Joseph A. "Universal Analogy and the Culture of the Renaissance." *Journal of the History of Ideas* 15 (1954): 299–304.

Mendelsohn, Everett. *Heat and Life: The Development of the Theory of Animal Heat.* Cambridge, MA: Harvard University Press, 1964.

Merleau-Ponty, Maurice. *The Phenomenology of Perception.* Translated by Colin Smith. London: Routledge, 1962.

Migiel, Marilyn. "The Dignity of Man: A Feminist Perspective." In *Refiguring Woman: Perspectives on Gender and the Italian Renaissance,* edited by Marilyn Migiel and Juliana Schiesari. Ithaca, NY: Cornell University Press, 1991.

Miller, William Ian. *The Anatomy of Disgust.* Cambridge, MA: Harvard University Press, 1997.

Miola, Robert S. "Aeneas and Hamlet." *Classical and Modern Literature* 8 (1988): 275–90.

Montrose, Louis Adrian. "'The Place of a Brother' in *As You Like It*: Social Process and Comic Form." *Shakespeare Quarterly* 32 (1981): 28–54.

———. *The Purpose of Playing: Shakespeare and the Cultural Politics of the Elizabethan Theatre.* Chicago: University of Chicago Press, 1996.

Mullaney, Steven. "Mourning and Misogyny: *Hamlet, The Revenger's Tragedy,* and the Final Progress of Elizabeth I: 1600–1607." *Shakespeare Quarterly* 45 (1996): 139–62.

Neely, Carol Thomas. *Broken Nuptials in Shakespeare's Plays.* New Haven, CT: Yale University Press, 1985.

———. "Documents in Madness: Reading Madness in Shakespeare's Tragedies and Early Modern Culture." *Shakespeare Quarterly* 42 (1991): 315–38.

Neill, Michael. "'Unproper Beds': Race, Adultery, and the Hideous in *Othello.*" *Shakespeare Quarterly* 40 (1989): 383–412.

Nietzsche, Friedrich. *Daybreak: Thoughts on the Prejudices of Morality.* Translated by R. J. Hollingdale. Cambridge: Cambridge University Press, 1982.

Oates, Caroline. "Metamorphosis and Lycanthropy in Franche-Comté, 1521–1643." In *Fragments for a History of the Human Body, Part One*, edited by Michel Feher. New York: Zone Books, 1989.

Onians, Richard Broxton. *The Origins of European Thought about the Body, the Mind, the Soul, the World, Time, and Fate*. Cambridge: Cambridge University Press, 1951.

Padel, Ruth. *In and out of the Mind: Greek Images of the Tragic Self*. Princeton, NJ: Princeton University Press, 1992.

Park, Katharine. "The Concept of Psychology." In *The Cambridge History of Renaissance Philosophy*, edited by Charles B. Schmitt et al. Cambridge: Cambridge University Press, 1988.

———. "The Organic Soul." In *The Cambridge History of Renaissance Philosophy*, edited by Charles B. Schmitt et al. Cambridge: Cambridge University Press, 1988.

Parker, Patricia. "Gender Ideology, Gender Change: The Case of Marie Germain." *Critical Inquiry* 19 (1993): 337–64.

———. "Murder in Guyana." *Shakespeare Studies* 28 (2000): 169–74.

———. *Shakespeare from the Margins: Language, Culture, Context*. Chicago: University of Chicago Press, 1996.

Paster, Gail Kern. *The Body Embarrassed: Drama and the Disciplines of Shame in Early Modern England*. Ithaca, NY: Cornell University Press, 1993.

———. "The Humor of It: Bodies, Fluids, and Social Discipline in Shakespearean Comedy." In *A Companion to Shakespeare's Works*, edited by Jean E. Howard and Richard Dutton, vol. 3, *The Comedies*. Malden, MA: Blackwell, 2003.

———. "Nervous Tension." In *The Body in Parts: Fantasies of Corporeality in Early Modern Europe*, edited by David Hillman and Carla Mazzio. London: Routledge, 1997.

———. "Pulse, Muscle, Blood, Breath, and Colour." Review of *The Expressiveness of the Body in Ancient Greek and Chinese Medicine*, by Shigehisa Kuriyama. *Metascience* 10 (2001): 329–33.

———. "Purgation as the Allure of Mastery." In *Material London Circa 1600*, edited by Lena Cowen Orlin. Philadelphia: University of Pennsylvania Press, 2000.

———. "The Unbearable Coldness of Female Being: Women's Imperfection in the Humoral Economy." *English Literary Renaissance* 28 (1998): 416–40.

Paster, Gail Kern, Katherine Rowe, and Mary Floyd-Wilson. Introduction to *Reading the Early Modern Passions: Essays in the Cultural History of Emotion*, edited by Gail Kern Paster, Katherine Rowe, and Mary Floyd-Wilson. Philadelphia: University of Pennsylvania Press, 2004.

Patterson, Annabel M. *Fables of Power: Aesopian Writing and Political History*. Durham, NC: Duke University Press, 1991.

Pope, Maurice. "Shakespeare's Medical Imagination." *Shakespeare Survey* 38 (1985): 175–86.

Pouchelle, Marie-Christine. *The Body and Surgery in the Middle Ages*. Translated by Rosemary Morris. New Brunswick, NJ: Rutgers University Press, 1990.

Rambuss, Richard. *Closet Devotions*. Durham, NC: Duke University Press, 1998.

Reed, Edward S. "The Affordances of an Animate Environment: Social Science from the Ecological Point of View." In *What Is an Animal?* edited by Tim Ingold. London: Unwin Hyman, 1988.

Robbins, Mary E. "The Truculent Toad in the Middle Ages." In *Animals in the Middle Ages: A Book of Essays*, edited by Nona C. Flores. New York: Garland, 1996.

Roberts, Jeanne Addison. *The Shakespearean Wild: Geography, Genus, and Gender.* Lincoln: University of Nebraska Press, 1991.

Roper, Lyndal. *Oedipus and the Devil: Witchcraft, Sexuality, and Religion in Early Modern Europe.* London: Routledge, 1994.

Rorty, Amélie Oksenberg. Introduction to *Explaining Emotions,* edited by Amélie Oksenberg Rorty. Berkeley and Los Angeles: University of California Press, 1980.

Russell, James A. "Is There Universal Recognition of Emotion from Facial Expression? A Review of Cross-Cultural Studies." *Psychological Bulletin* 115 (1994): 102–41.

Salingar, Leo. *Shakespeare and the Traditions of Comedy.* Cambridge: Cambridge University Press, 1974.

Schiebinger, Londa. *The Mind Has No Sex? Women in the Origins of Modern Science.* Cambridge, MA: Harvard University Press, 1989.

Schiesari, Juliana. *The Gendering of Melancholia: Feminism, Psychoanalysis, and the Symbolics of Loss in Renaissance Literature.* Ithaca, NY: Cornell University Press, 1992.

Schoenfeldt, Michael C. *Bodies and Selves in Early Modern England: Physiology and Inwardness in Spenser, Shakespeare, Herbert, and Milton.* Cambridge: Cambridge University Press, 1999.

Scott-Warren, Jason. "When Theaters Were Bear-Gardens; or, What's at Stake in the Comedy of Humors." *Shakespeare Quarterly* 54 (2003): 63–82.

Shapin, Steven. *A Social History of Truth: Civility and Science in Seventeenth-Century England.* Chicago: University of Chicago Press, 1994.

Siraisi, Nancy G. *Medieval and Early Renaissance Medicine: An Introduction to Knowledge and Practice.* Chicago: University of Chicago Press, 1990.

Smith, Bruce. *The Acoustic World of Early Modern England: Attending to the O-Factor.* Chicago: University of Chicago Press, 1999.

Snow, Edward A. "Sexual Anxiety and the Male Order of Things in *Othello.*" *English Literary Renaissance* 10 (1980): 384–412.

Snyder, Susan. *The Comic Matrix of Shakespeare's Tragedies: "Romeo and Juliet," "Hamlet," "Othello," and "King Lear."* Princeton, NJ: Princeton University Press, 1979.

Solomon, Julie R. "From Species to Speculation: Naming the Animals with Calvin and Bacon." In *Women and Reason,* edited by Elizabeth D. Harvey and Kathleen Okruhlik. Ann Arbor: University of Michigan Press, 1992.

Stallybrass, Peter. "Patriarchal Territories: The Body Enclosed." In *Rewriting the Renaissance: The Discourses of Sexual Difference in Early Modern Europe,* edited by Margaret W. Ferguson, Maureen Quilligan, and Nancy Vickers. Chicago: University of Chicago Press, 1986.

Stallybrass, Peter, and Allon White. *The Politics and Poetics of Transgression.* Ithaca, NY: Cornell University Press, 1986.

Streip, Katharine. "'Just a Cérébrale': Jean Rhys, Women's Humor, and Ressentiment." *Representations* 45 (Winter 1994): 117–44.

Strier, Richard. "Against the Rule of Reason: Praise of Passion from Petrarch to Luther to Shakespeare to Herbert." In *Reading the Early Modern Passions: Essays in the Cultural History of Emotions,* edited by Gail Kern Paster, Katherine Rowe, and Mary Floyd-Wilson. Philadelphia: University of Pennsylvania Press, 2004.

Sugden, Edward H. *A Topographical Dictionary to the Works of Shakespeare and His Fellow Dramatists.* Manchester: Manchester University Press, 1925.

Sutton, John. "Body, Mind, and Order: Local Memory and the Control of Mental Representations in Medieval and Renaissance Sciences of Self." In *1543 and All That: Image and
Word, Change and Continuity in the Proto-Scientific Revolution*, edited by Guy Freeland
and Anthony Corones. Dordrecht: Kluwer Academic, 2000.

———. *Philosophy and Memory Traces: Descartes to Connectionism*. Cambridge: Cambridge
University Press, 1998.

———. "Porous Memory and the Cognitive Life of Things." In *Prefiguring Cyberculture: An
Intellectual History*, edited by Darren Tofts, Annemarie Jonson, and Alessio Cavallaro.
Cambridge, MA: MIT Press, 2003.

Tapper, Richard. "Animality, Humanity, Morality, Society." In *What Is an Animal?* edited by
Tim Ingold. London: Unwin Hyman, 1988.

Taylor, Charles. *Sources of the Self: Making of the Modern Identity*. Cambridge, MA: Harvard
University Press, 1989.

Temkin, Owsei. *Galenism: Rise and Decline of a Medical Philosophy*. Ithaca, NY: Cornell
University Press, 1973.

Thomas, Keith. *Man and the Natural World: A History of the Modern Sensibility*. New York:
Pantheon Books, 1983.

Tomlinson, Gary. *Metaphysical Song: An Essay on Opera*. Princeton, NJ: Princeton University
Press, 1999.

Traub, Valerie. "The (In)significance of 'Lesbian' Desire in Early Modern England." In *Erotic
Politics: Desire on the Renaissance Stage*, edited by Susan Zimmerman. London:
Routledge, 1992.

———. "Jewels, Statues, and Corpses: Containment of Female Erotic Power in Shakespeare's
Plays." *Shakespeare Studies* 20 (1988): 215–38.

———. *The Renaissance of Lesbianism in Early Modern England*. Cambridge: Cambridge
University Press, 2002.

Walker, D. P. "Francis Bacon and *Spiritus*." In *Science, Medicine, and Society in the
Renaissance: Essays to Honor Walter Pagel*, edited by Allen G. Debus, vol. 2. New York:
Science History Publications, 1972.

———. "Medical Spirits in Philosophy and Theology from Ficino to Newton." In *Music, Spirit,
and Language in the Renaissance*, edited by Penelope Gouk. London: Variorum Reprints,
1985.

Wallace, Karl R. *Francis Bacon and the Nature of Man: The Faculties of Man's Soul:
Understanding, Reason, Imagination, Memory, Will, and Appetite*. Urbana: University of
Illinois Press, 1967.

Whigham, Frank. *Ambition and Privilege: The Social Tropes of Elizabethan Courtesy Theory*.
Berkeley and Los Angeles: University of California Press, 1984.

———. *Seizures of the Will in Early Modern English Drama*. Cambridge: Cambridge
University Press, 1996.

———. "Sexual and Social Mobility in *The Duchess of Malfi*." *PMLA* 100 (1985): 167–86.

Wierzbicka, Anna. *Emotions across Languages and Cultures: Diversity and Universals*.
Cambridge: Cambridge University Press, 1999.

———. "Human Emotions: Universal or Culture-Specific?" *American Anthropologist* 88
(1986): 584–94.

Wiles, David. *Shakespeare's Clown: Actor and Text in the Elizabethan Playhouse*. Cambridge:
Cambridge University Press, 1987.

Wilson, Elizabeth A. "Melancholic Biology: Prozac, Freud, and Neurological Determinism."
    Configurations 7 (1999): 403–19.

Womack, Peter. *Ben Jonson*. Oxford: Basil Blackwell, 1986.

Woodbridge, Linda. *The Scythe of Saturn: Shakespeare and Magical Thinking*. Urbana:
    University of Illinois Press, 1994.

Wright, George T. "Hendiadys and *Hamlet*." *PMLA* 96 (1981): 168–93.

Žižek, Slavoj. *The Sublime Object of Ideology*. London: Verso, 1989.

Note: Italicized page numbers indicate figures.